Case is an introduction for students of linguistics to the ways relations between words in sentences are marked in languages. It describes the systems of suffixes familiar from languages like Latin and also the roles of prepositions, postpositions and the use of the pronominal elements on verbs. One of the most interesting features of case is the recurrence of apparently idiosyncratic patterns and devices in otherwise unrelated languages. This book picks out these recurring strategies and explores their significance. It provides the background against which the case marking of particular languages can be best understood. *Case* contains in addition a useful discussion of the theoretical problems in identifying cases and the basis for distinguishing case relations from cases. A final chapter looks at the origins and development of case-marking devices.

CAMBRIDGE TEXTBOOKS IN LINGUISTICS

General Editors: J. BRESNAN, B. COMRIE, W. DRESSLER,
R. HUDDLESTON, R. LASS, D. LIGHTFOOT, J. LYONS,
P. H. MATTHEWS, R. POSNER, S. ROMAINE, N. V. SMITH,
N. VINCENT

CASE

CASE

BARRY J. BLAKE

PROFESSOR OF LINGUISTICS
LA TROBE UNIVERSITY

CAMBRIDGE
UNIVERSITY PRESS

Published by the Press Syndicate of the University of Cambridge
The Pitt Building, Trumpington Street, Cambridge CB2 1RP
40 West 20th Street, New York, NY 10011–4211, USA
10 Stamford Road, Oakleigh, Melbourne 3166, Australia

First published 1994

Printed in Great Britain at the University Press, Cambridge

A catalogue record for this book is available from the British Library

Library of Congress cataloguing in publication data

Blake, Barry J.
Case / Barry J. Blake.
   p.   cm. – (Cambridge textbooks in linguistics)
Includes bibliographical references and indexes.
ISBN 0-521-44114-5 (hardback). – ISBN 0-521-44661-9 (paperback)
1. Grammar, Comparative and general – Case.   I. Title.   II. Series.
P240.6.B57   1994
415 – dc20   93-19796 CIP

ISBN 0 521 44114 5 hardback
ISBN 0 521 44661 9 paperback

CONTENTS

FIGURES

TABLES

PREFACE

I can remember my first encounter with case quite clearly. It was in 1949. The language was Latin and the book was *Latin for today*. The first sentence was *Discipulī, pictūram spectāte* and it came with a translation 'Pupils, look at the illustration'. I cannot say that I quickly became enamoured of case. There was not much pleasure to be had in memorising paradigms, but eventually there were rewards: the rolling hexameters of Virgil, the cleverly contrived odes of Horace and the epigrammatic prose of Tacitus, all exploiting the genius of a highly inflected language, a language where grammatical functions were expressed in the most highly condensed fashion, a single short suffix on a noun expressing case, number and sometimes gender, a single suffix on a verb expressing tense, aspect, mood, voice and the person and number of the subject.

There were other minor encounters with the language of Beowulf and the language of Njal, but my next significant encounter with case came in 1966. In that year I took up a fellowship to study Australian Aboriginal languages and I was sent to western Queensland to record Kalkatungu, or Kalkadoon in the more familiar spelling, a language which at that time had no more than a dozen fluent speakers. Like most Australian languages Kalkatungu had a well-developed case system. For Kalkatungu there was no available grammar and therefore no paradigms to learn. The paradigms had to be built up by a mixture of elicitation and recording of discourse.

These experiences are reflected in the present book. A concentration on Latin is entirely proper in a book on case, since our traditional notions of case and grammatical relations were developed with reference to Ancient Greek and Latin. If we set out to label cases in a previously undescribed language, it behoves us to apply the labels as far as possible in a way that is consistent with the traditional description of Latin. The strain of Australian Aboriginal examples that runs through the book is fortuitous, but not, I think, unfortunate. Though it reflects the background the author happens to have, it is not inappropriate, given that Australia provides, or at least did provide, the richest large-scale concentration of inflectional case languages anywhere in the world. These languages obviously developed without any influence from Indo-European and they provide an independent perspective from which to view the case languages of our western tradition.

This book is aimed at two types of reader. Firstly it is written for senior students and academics in linguistics. Secondly it is written for senior students and academics whose field is a particular language or group of languages, students of the classical languages, for instance, or scholars of Slavonic. For all readers the book will provide a global perspective against which particular case manifestations can be judged, and for those not already versed in the literature of cross-language comparison it will reveal fascinating regularities.

Case has aesthetic properties. To the student of literature this is probably most evident in text, where an author successfully exploits the succinct means of relating words that an inflectional case system provides and the freedom of word order usually attendant on the presence of case. But there is also beauty in the system. This is nowhere more apparent than in Kalkatungu. I like to tell my students that it was a language 'more perfect than the Greek, more copious than the Latin'. Not only did it have a system of nine cases, it had a number of valency-changing derivations that allowed different alignments of semantic role and grammatical relation. Moreover, it had a separate system of clitic pronouns, a referent-tracking system based on alternating the transitivity of the verb, and a word order maximally sensitive to the demands of discourse. Whether there were poets and orators who availed themselves of this marvellous instrument I do not know. 'Full many a flower is born to blush unseen and waste its sweetness on the desert air.'

A book cannot be written without contributions from many sources. I would like to thank first of all the following who supplied me with information: Keith Allan, Ketut Artawa, Peter Austin, Greg Bailey, Joan Barclay-Lloyd, Robert Bauer, Edith Bavin, Byron Bender, David Bradley, Kate Burridge, Mehmet Celik, Wally Chafe, Hilary Chappell, Bernard Comrie, Grev Corbett, Bob Dixon, Mark Durie, Nick Evans, Caspar de Groot, Nurcan Hacioglu, Luise Hercus, Greg Horsley, Edrinnie Kayambazinthu, Miriam Meyerhof, Marianne Mithun, Isabel Moutinho, Johanna Nichols, William O'Grady, John Painter, Jan Rijkhoff, Graham Scott, Anna Siewierska, Jae Jung Song, Stan Starosta, Sandy Thompson and Nigel Vincent. I would also like to thank Julie Reid, who read the manuscript from the point of view of my potential readership, and I would particularly like to thank Rodney Huddleston, who oversaw the writing on behalf of the publisher and made numerous helpful suggestions.

Others who facilitated the work include Judith Ayling, who was always available on the e-mail to help with queries, and the staff of the Borchardt Library at La Trobe, particularly the inter-library loan staff. My biggest debt is to the secretaries of the Department of Linguistics, Dothea Haynes and Barbara Upton, particularly Barbara who did the final formatting. '... hands worked busily a day, and there she stands. Will't please you sit and look ... ?'

ABBREVIATIONS

A	The agent argument of a transitive verb or any argument that is treated in the same way grammatically.
ab	abessive
abl	ablative
abs	absolutive
acc	accusative
agt	agent
all	allative
ap	antipassive
aux	auxiliary
ben	beneficiary, benefactive
caus	causative
com	comitative
COR	correspondent
dat	dative
decl	declension
DO	direct object
ds	different subject
du	dual
el	elative
erg	ergative
evid	evidential
exp	experiencer
f	feminine
fa	future actor
fem	feminine
fin	finite
fut	future
gen	genitive
ger	gerundive

ia	instrumental advancement
ill	illative
imp	imperative
impf	(a) imperfect
	(b) imperfective
in	inessive
inc	inclusive
inch	inchoative
inf	infinitive
inst	instrumental
int	interrogative
IO	indirect object
loc	locative
m	masculine
mabl	modal ablative
masc	masculine
neut	neuter
nm	nominaliser
nom	nominative
NP	noun phrase
npst	non-past
O	object
obj	object
obl	oblique
obv	obviative
P	The patient argument of a transitive verb or any argument that is treated in the same way grammatically.
par	partitive
part	participle
pass	passive
pat	patient
perf	(a) perfect
	(b) perfective
pl	plural
plur	plural
poss	possessor
ppart	past participle
pperf	pluperfect
pres	present tense
prop	proprietive

prpart	present participle
purp	purpose, purposive
recip	recipient
refl	reflexive
rel	(a) relative
	(b) relative case
S	(a) the single argument of a one-place verb
	(b) subject (as in SOV subject-object-verb)
	(c) sentence (as in S → NP VP)
sg	singular
sing	singular
ss	same subject
subj	subject
trans	translative
V	verb (as in SVO subject-verb-object)
voc	vocative
VP	verb phrase
1	(a) first person
	(b) subject (in Relational Grammar)
2	(a) second person
	(b) direct object (in Relational Grammar)
3	(a) third person
	(b) indirect object (in Relational Grammar)
-	separates morphs and the corresponding glosses: Spanish *virtud-es* (virtue-PL) 'virtues'
.	separates multiple glosses of a single morph or wordform: German *trank* (drink.PAST) 'drank'
=	separates a clitic from its host

1
Overview

1.1 Inflectional case

  Case is a system of marking dependent nouns for the type of relationship they bear to their heads. Traditionally the term refers to inflectional marking, and, typically, case marks the relationship of a noun to a verb at the clause level or of a noun to a preposition, postposition or another noun at the phrase level. Consider the following Turkish sentence,

(1)   *Mehmet adam-a elma-lar-ı ver-di*
     Mehmet.NOM man-DAT apple-PL-ACC give-PAST.3SG
     'Mehmet gave the apples to the man.'

In this sentence *-ı* indicates that *elmalar* is the direct object of the verb *vermek* 'to give'. The suffix *-ı* is said to be an accusative (or objective) case marker and the word form *elmaları* is said to be in the accusative case.[1] The suffix *-ı* also indicates that *elmalar* is specific, since in Turkish only specific direct objects are marked as accusative. *Adam* is marked by the suffix *-a* which indicates that it is the indirect object. *Adama* is in the dative case. *Mehmet* contrasts with *elmaları* and *adama* in that it bears no overt suffix. It is said to be in the nominative case, which in this sentence indicates the subject.[2]

  The term **case** is also used for the phenomenon of having a case system and a language with such a system is sometimes referred to as a **case language**.

  Our definition of case refers to marking dependent nouns for the type of relationship they bear to their heads. This definition obviously embodies certain assumptions about what is a head and what is a dependent or modifier. The verb is taken to be the head of the clause, since it largely determines what dependents may be present. *Vermek* 'to give', for instance, is a three-place verb that takes three arguments: a giver (expressed in (1) by the subject in the nominative case), a gift (expressed in (1) by the direct object in the accusative case) and a recipient (expressed by the indirect object in the dative case). A verb may also have other dependents expressing, for instance, time or location, which, though not licensed by a particular verb, are nevertheless modifiers of the verb.

Turkish has a system of six cases as in Table 1.1. The locative marks location as in *Istanbul-da* 'in Istanbul', and the ablative indicates 'from' or 'out of' as in *Ankara-dan* 'from Ankara'. The genitive is used in phrases like *adam-ın ev-i* 'the man's house' where *ın* corresponds to 's in English. There is a complication. Note that *ev* 'house' bears a suffix *-i* which is a third person possessive form translatable as 'his', 'her' or 'its'. In Turkish 'the man's house' is literally 'the man's, his house'. The genitive meets the definition of case on the assumption that *ev* is the head of a noun phrase and *adam* a dependent.

In (1) the cases are determined or governed by the verb. *Vermek* 'to give' requires a subject in the nominative, an indirect object in the dative and a direct object in the accusative (if specific) or nominative (if non-specific). Cases can also be governed by prepositions or postpositions. Turkish has postpositions which govern the ablative like *dolayı* 'because of': *toplantı-dan dolayı* 'because of the meeting', and *sonra* 'after': *tiyatro-dan sonra* 'after the theatre'.[3]

The word forms displayed in Table 1.1 make up a **paradigm**, i.e. they constitute the set of case forms in which the lexeme *adam* can appear.[4] In Turkish one could say that there is only one paradigm in that a constant set of endings is found for all nouns. It is true that noun stems of different shapes take different inflectional suffixes, but all these differences are phonologically conditioned by principles of vowel harmony and the like. The locative, for instance, has the form *-da* following stems with back vowels and *-de* following stems with front vowels. The *d* of this suffix devoices to *t* following a stem-final voiceless consonant: *kitap-ta* 'on (the) book'.[5] One could refer to *-da*, *-de*, *-ta* and *-te* as case markers or one could consider that at a more abstract level there was only one locative case marker. We need to make a distinction between **cases** (of which there are six in a system of oppositions), and the **case markers** or **case forms** through which the cases are realised. A case marker is an affix and a case form is a complete word. In Turkish the case affixes can be separated from the stem, so it is possible to talk about case markers. In some languages, however, it is not possible to isolate a case suffix, so it is necessary to talk in terms of the various word forms that express the cases of the stem. These are case forms. (See also Seidel 1988: 36.)

It is also necessary to make a further distinction between the cases and the **case relations** or **grammatical relations** they express. These terms refer to purely syntactic relations such as subject, direct object and indirect object, each of which encompasses more than one semantic role, and they also refer directly to semantic roles such as source and location, where these are not subsumed by a syntactic relation and where these are separable according to some formal criteria. Of the two competing terms, case relations and grammatical relations, the latter will be

Table 1.1 *Turkish case system*

nominative	*adam*
accusative	*adamı*
genitive	*adamın*
dative	*adama*
locative	*adamda*
ablative	*adamdan*

adopted in the present text as the term for the set of widely accepted relations that includes subject, object and indirect object and the term case relations will be confined to the theory-particular relations posited in certain frameworks such as Localist Case Grammar (section 3.4.4) and Lexicase (section 3.4.5).

Grammatical relations need not be in a one-for-one correspondence with cases. In Turkish the nominative expresses the subject, but not all noun phrases in the nominative are subject, since, as noted above, the nominative also marks a non-specific direct object of a transitive verb (see (1) in chapter 5).

There is a widely held view, explicit, for instance, in Relational Grammar (section 3.4.3), that all dependents can be allotted to a particular grammatical relation whether purely syntactic or semantic. However, in practice it is often unclear how certain dependents are to be classified. For this reason I will refer, for the most part, to cases as having functions or meanings. These terms are traditional and they can be taken to be theory-neutral or perhaps pre-theoretical. The term **function** will range over well-defined grammatical relations such as direct object and other relations such as 'agent of the passive verb' where different theories might ascribe the function to different relations. The term **meaning** will cover not only semantic roles that are demarcated by case marking or some other formal means, but also semantic roles that are distinguished only on intuitive grounds, roles whose status remains unclear in the absence of some argumentation.

Turkish is a convenient language to use to illustrate case since it is an agglutinative language, i.e. one in which there are affixes that are easily separable from the stem and from one another. With nouns, the stem, the number marking and the case marking are all separable (except for some phonological assimilations). This can be seen in *elma-lar-ı* in (1) where *-lar* is the plural marker and *ı* the accusative case marker. However, the traditional notion of case was developed on the basis of Ancient Greek and Latin where there are several complicating factors. In Latin, for instance, it is not possible to separate number marking from case marking. The two categories have fused representation throughout the system or **cumulative exponence** as Matthews calls it (Matthews 1974/1991). This means separate paradigms for the two number categories, singular and plural. Moreover, there are different case/number markers for different stem classes. Traditionally five such classes are recognised, and there are also variations within the classes. The five classes, or declensions as they are usually referred to, are illustrated in Table 1.2: the first declension (*ā*-stems), second declension (*o*-stems), third declension (consonant stems and *i*-stems), the fourth (*u*-stems) and fifth (*ē*-stems). The designations *ā*-stems, *o*-stems, etc. are not synchronically transparent and reflect the product of historical reconstruction. For practical purposes there are five arbitrary declensions, though the term *i*-stem has some relevance for those members of the third declension that have -*i* in the ablative singular, accusative plural and genitive plural.

In Latin there is also a three-way gender distinction: masculine, feminine and neuter. With a few exceptions male creatures are masculine and females feminine, but inanimates are scattered over all three genders (though almost all neuter nouns are inanimate). There is a partial association of form and gender in that *ā*-stems are almost all feminine and *o*-stems mostly masculine (except for a sub-class of neuters represented by *bellum* in Table 1.2). This means that there can be fusion of gender, number and case. The point is illustrated in Table 1.2 where we have *domina* 'mistress (of a household)' illustrating feminine *ā*-stems and *dominus* 'master (of a household)', which is based on the same root, representing masculine *o*-stems. As can be seen from Table 1.2 the word form *domina* simultaneously represents nominative case, feminine gender and singular number, *dominum* represents accusative case, masculine gender and singular number, and similarly with other word forms.

In Latin there is concord between a noun and an attributive or predicative adjective. This concord is sensitive to case and number, and those adjectives that belong to the first and second declension are sensitive to gender so we find *domina bona* 'good mistress' and *nauta bonus* 'good sailor' where *nauta* is one of the few nouns of masculine gender in the first declension. With adjectives of the first and second declensions the inflections simultaneously represent case, number and gender without exception.

As can be seen six cases are recognised: nominative, vocative, accusative, genitive, dative and ablative; however, no paradigm exhibits six different forms. In the traditional descriptions a case is established wherever there is a distinction for any single class of nominals. The vocative, the case used in forms of address, has a distinctive form only in the singular of the second declension. Elsewhere there is a common form for the nominative and vocative; however, distinct nominative and vocative cases are recognised for all paradigms.

Each case has a number of functions, which can be summarised as follows. The nominative encodes the subject and nouns that stand in a predicative relation to the subject as in *Dominus est cōnsul* 'The master is consul.' The accusative encodes

Table 1.2 *Latin case paradigms*

	1 *ā*-stems feminine *domina* 'mistress'	2 *o*-stems masculine *dominus* 'master'	neuter *bellum* 'war'	3a cons. stems *cōnsul* 'consul'	3b *i*-stems *cīvis* 'citizen'
			singular		
Nominative	*domina*	*dominus*	*bellum*	*cōnsul*	*cīvis*
Vocative	*domina*	*domine*	*bellum*	*cōnsul*	*cīvis*
Accusative	*dominam*	*dominum*	*bellum*	*cōnsulem*	*cīvem*
Genitive	*dominae*	*dominī*	*bellī*	*cōnsulis*	*cīvis*
Dative	*dominae*	*dominō*	*bellō*	*cōnsulī*	*cīvī*
Ablative	*dominā*	*dominō*	*bellō*	*cōnsule*	*cīvī, cīve*
			plural		
Nominative	*dominae*	*dominī*	*bella*	*cōnsulēs*	*cīvēs*
Vocative	*dominae*	*dominī*	*bella*	*cōnsulēs*	*cīvēs*
Accusative	*dominās*	*dominōs*	*bella*	*cōnsulēs*	*cīvīs, cīvēs*
Genitive	*dominārum*	*dominōrum*	*bellōrum*	*cōnsulum*	*cīvium*
Dative	*dominīs*	*dominīs*	*bellīs*	*cōnsulibus*	*cīvibus*
Ablative	*dominīs*	*dominīs*	*bellīs*	*cōnsulibus*	*cīvibus*

	4 *u*-stems *manus* 'hand'	5 *ē*-stems *diēs* 'day'
		singular
Nominative	*manus*	*diēs*
Vocative	*manus*	*diēs*
Accusative	*manum*	*diem*
Genitive	*manūs*	*diēī*
Dative	*manuī*	*diēī*
Ablative	*manū*	*diē*
		plural
Nominative	*manūs*	*diēs*
Vocative	*manūs*	*diēs*
Accusative	*manūs*	*diēs*
Genitive	*manuum*	*diērum*
Dative	*manibus*	*diēbus*
Ablative	*manibus*	*diēbus*

the direct object and nouns that stand in a predicative relation to the object as in *Fēcerunt dominum cōnsulem* 'They made the master consul.' It also expresses destination as in *Vādō Rōmam* 'I am going to Rome' and extent as in the following,

(2)   *Rēgnāvit   is   paucōs   mensīs*
        rule.PERF.3SG   he.NOM   few.PL.ACC   month.PL.ACC
        'He ruled for a few months.'

A number of prepositions govern the accusative including all those that indicate 'motion towards' or 'extent'. In fact a construction like *Vādō Rōmam* where the accusative expresses destination without being governed by a preposition is mainly confined to the names of towns and small islands; compare *Vādō ad urbem* 'I am going to the city' and *Vādō in urbem* 'I am going into the city.'

The genitive is mainly used to mark noun phrases as dependents of nouns, i.e. it is primarily an adnominal case. Among its adnominal functions is the encoding of possessor: *cōnsulis equus* 'the consul's horse'. The genitive is also used to mark the complements of certain verbs. For example, with some verbs of remembering and forgetting it marks the entity remembered or forgotten (3); with some verbs of reminding the person reminded is encoded as an accusative-marked direct object and the entity to be remembered is put in the genitive (4), and with verbs of accusing, condemning or acquitting the accused is expressed as a direct object in the accusative with the fault or crime in the genitive (5):

(3)   *Diēī   meminerit   cōnsul*
        day.GEN   remember.FUT.PERF.3SG   consul.NOM
        'The consul will remember the day.'

(4)   *Cōnsulem   amicitiae   commonefēcit*
        consul.ACC   friendship.GEN   remind.PERF.3SG
        'He reminded the consul of friendship.'

(5)   *Parricīdiī   cōnsulem   incūsat*
        parricide.GEN   consul.ACC   accuse.3SG
        'He accuses the consul of parricide.'

The main function of the dative is to mark the indirect object. A few three-place verbs like *dāre* 'to give' take a direct object in the accusative and an indirect object in the dative (6). A few score of two-place verbs take only one object, an indirect object in the dative. These include *crēdere* 'to believe', *nocēre* 'to be harmful to' and *subvenīre* 'to help' as in (7):

(6)   *Dominus*   *equum*   *cōnsulī*   *dedit*
      master.NOM   horse.ACC   consul.DAT   give.PERF.3SG
      'The master gave the horse to the consul.'

(7)   *Mihi*   *subvēnistī*
      me.DAT   help.PERF.2SG
      'You have helped me.'

The ablative in Latin represents the syncretism or merger of three once-distinct cases: the ablative, the locative and the instrumental. It is not surprising then to find that it expresses source, location and instrument. It is also described as having a number of other functions including expressing the 'agent of the passive', i.e. the demoted subject of the corresponding active as in *vīsus ā cōnsule* 'seen by the consul'.

Although the ablative alone can express a variety of relations to the verb of the clause, in most functions it is usually governed by a preposition. Prepositions governing the ablative include *ex* 'out of' (*ex Italiā* 'from Italy'), *in* 'in' (*in Italiā* 'in Italy') and *cum* 'with' (*cum amīcīs* 'with friends'). One function where it is normally used without any preposition is the instrumental as in *manū* 'by hand'. A handful of verbs take a complement in the ablative case. These include *ūtī* 'to use' and *vescī* 'to feed on'.

1.2   Other manifestations

The definition of case given in section 1.1 above can be regarded as a central definition. There are also manifestations of case that do not mark the relationship of dependent nouns to their heads, and others that do not form a system for marking nouns, at least not in an obvious sense, inasmuch as the exponents are prepositions or postpositions.

1.2.1   *Concordial case*

In some languages, including Indo-European case languages like Latin and Ancient Greek, case marking appears not only on nouns but on certain dependents of the noun such as adjectives and determiners. The following example is from Plato. *Bios* is a nominative singular form of a second declension (*o*-stem) masculine noun, the nominative indicating that *bios* is the subject of the predicate. The definite article and the adjective are in the nominative singular masculine form, their **concord** in case, number and gender indicating that they are dependents of *bios*,[6]

(8)   *Ho*   *anexetastos*   *bios*   *ou*
        the.NOM.SG   unexamined.NOM.SG   life.NOM.SG   not
        biōtos   *anthrōpō*
        livable.NOM.SG   man.DAT.SG
        'The unexamined life is not livable for man.'

This example also illustrates concord between a predicative adjective (*biōtos*) and the subject (*bios*). See also section 4.2.

Although the use of the nominative on *ho* and *anexetastos* would appear to meet the definition of case in that it marks these words as dependents of *bios*, it does not mark the type of dependency. We could compare an adnominal genitive construction such as *ho anthropou bios* (the.NOM.SG man.GEN.SG life.NOM.SG) 'the life of man' where the genitive signals a type of dependency and meets the terms of the central definition offered in section 1.1.

1.2.2   Case on non-nouns

Although case is typically a property of nouns, case marking is often found on certain classes of word that are not obviously nouns by independent criteria. In the previous sub-section it was mentioned that case could extend via concord to determiners and adjectives. Adjectives in Ancient Greek and Latin decline like nouns and can appear as the head of a noun phrase as in Greek *hoi polloi* (the.NOM.PL many.NOM.PL) 'the many' and *to meson* (the.NOM.SG middle.NOM.SG) 'the middle'. Adjectives in these languages are analysable as a sub-class of noun, and the Greek grammarians referred to them as the 'noun adjective' as opposed to the 'noun substantive', a usage that remained current until recent times. The definite article in Ancient Greek, however (illustrated by *ho* in (8) above), could not stand as the head of a noun phrase and must therefore be ascribed to a different part of speech. Dionysius Thrax called it *arthron* (article). As shown in (8) the article took case (and number and gender) by concord.

Adverbs of place, time and manner play a role analogous to case-marked nouns. For instance, Latin *Unde fugit* 'Whence flees he?' can be answered by an ablative-marked noun expressing source: *Corinthō fugit* 'From Corinth he flees.' *Unde* the interrogative adverb and a noun in the ablative seem to bear the same relation or function. Adverbs of place, time and manner may bear no case marking, fossilised case marking, or case marking parallel with that of corresponding nouns. In Latin, examples of fossilised case marking are common, but there are also examples like *quā* 'by what way?' and *eā* 'by that way' where the *-ā* would appear to be parallel with the ablative *-ā* of the first declension singular. The presence or absence of identifiable case marking would appear to be of little importance; what is significant is the parallelism of function between adverbs and case-marked nouns. If grammatical relations are to be ascribed to nouns, it would seem logical to ascribe such relations to adverbs of place, time and manner. One can then specify that a complement of a particular verb must be in, say, the locative grammatical relation. This requirement can be fulfilled in a language like Latin by a noun in the ablative case (usually with an appropriate preposition) or by a locative adverb. See also section 1.3.3 and Table 2.3.

1.2.3 Vocatives

In the traditional description of Ancient Greek and Latin a **vocative** case appears (Table 1.2). The vocative is used as a form of address. In Latin, for instance, *domine* is the form used to address one's master as in *Quō vādis, domine?* (whither go.2SG lord.VOC) 'Where are you going, master?'. Vocatives do not appear as dependents in constructions, but rather they stand outside constructions or are inserted parenthetically (see (9) in chapter 4).[7] They are unlike other cases in that they do not mark the relation of dependents to heads. For these reasons vocatives have not always been considered cases (Hjelmslev 1935: 4). In Ancient Greek and Latin the vocative's claim to being a case is structural. The vocative is a word-final suffix like the recognised case suffixes. However, modified forms of nouns used as forms of address also occur in languages that do not have case inflection. In Yapese (Austronesian), for instance, there is no morphological case marking on nouns, but personal names have special forms used for address. There is no reason to consider that these modifications of names constitute a vocative case (Jensen 1991: 229f).[8]

1.2.4 Ungoverned case

In case languages one sometimes encounters phrases in an oblique case used as interjections, i.e. apart from sentence constructions. Mel'čuk (1986: 46) gives a Russian example *Aristokratov na fonar*! 'Aristocrats on the street-lamps!' where *Aristokratov* is accusative. One would guess that some expressions of this type have developed from governed expressions, but that the governor has been lost. A standard Latin example is *mē miserum* (1SG.ACC miserable.ACC) 'Oh, unhappy me.' As the translation illustrates, English uses the oblique form of pronouns in exclamations, and outside constructions generally.

1.2.5 Analytic case markers

In most languages adpositions (prepositions or postpositions) play at least some part in marking the relations of dependent nouns to their heads. In Japanese, for instance, postpositions perform this function to the exclusion of case affixes. In the following Japanese example *ga* marks the subject, *ni* marks the indirect object and *o* marks the direct object,

(9)   *Sensei   ga   Tasaku   ni   hon   o   yat-ta*
        teacher   SUBJ   Tasaku   IO   book   DO   give-PAST
        'The teacher gave Tasaku a book.'

Adpositions can be considered to be analytic case markers as opposed to synthetic case markers like the suffixes of Turkish or Latin. The main difference in case marking between a language like Japanese and a language like Latin is that in the former there are no case suffixes, just the postpositions, whereas in the latter there are case suffixes as well as adpositions. In Latin, which is fairly typical of languages having analytic as well as synthetic case markers, prepositions are like verbs in that they govern cases, and combinations of preposition and case suffix can serve to mark the relations of nouns to the verb. In the following examples we have a transitive verb governing the accusative (10a), a preposition *in* governing the accusative (10b), an intransitive verb governing the ablative (10c) and a preposition *in* governing the ablative (10d),

(10)   accusative
        a. *Mīlitēs vident urbem*   'The troops see the city.'
        b. *Mīlitēs vādunt in urbem*   'The troops go into the city.'

            ablative
        c. *Mīlitēs potiuntur urbe*   'The troops are in control of the city.'
        d. *Mīlitēs manent in urbe*   'The troops stay in the city.'

In (10d) the ablative indicates location (in the context of *manēre* 'to remain' and *urbs* 'city') and *in* specifies 'inside' as opposed to *super* 'above', *sub* 'under', etc. Together the preposition and the case suffix indicate the relationship of *urbs* to the verb. Note that *in* can also govern the accusative as in (10b) where the combination of *in* + accusative signals 'into'. Most prepositions in Latin govern one particular case, but some like *in* can govern the accusative or the ablative. In some languages all adpositions require the same case, e.g. in Indo-Aryan languages postpositions with few exceptions require the 'oblique' case (see (11) below) and in English all prepositions govern the accusative (*with me, from her*, etc.). In situations like these it has been argued that the case suffix is redundant and the adposition bears the sole burden of marking the relation of dependent nouns to their heads as in Japanese.

In Hindi-Urdu, as in a number of other Indo-Aryan languages, there are three layers of case-marking elements: inflectional case, primary postpositions and secondary postpositions. Leaving aside the vocative, the inflectional case system distinguishes two cases, nominative and oblique. The nominative covers both subject and object and is generally referred to in Indo-Aryan linguistics as the direct case.

The oblique case is used with the primary postpositions such as *se* instrumental/ablative, *mē* locative, *ke* genitive and *ko* dative/accusative (it is used with indirect objects and specific, animate direct objects). There is also a third set of local postpositions that follow *ke* genitive,

(11)   a. *ləṛka* (nominative, alternatively direct)
             'boy'
         b. *ləṛke* (oblique)
         c. *ləṛke ko* (oblique + dative postposition)
             'to the boy'
         d. *ləṛke ke sath* (oblique + genitive postposition + *sath* 'with')
             'with the boy'

Where inflectional case and adpositions co-occur in a language, the adpositional system normally exhibits finer distinctions than the inflectional system. This is nowhere better illustrated than in languages like English and Hindi where the case system is near-minimal. In Hindi the secondary postpositions, which mostly express local notions such as 'between', 'in front of' and 'behind', make more distinctions than the primary postpositions.[9]

Although one can easily separate different layers of case marking in a particular language, as in Hindi for instance, it can be difficult to determine whether a single layer of case marking in a particular language is affixial or adpositional. Where the markers in question figure in concord, they are clearly affixes, but where they occur only once in a phrase, usually at the end, there can be some doubt about whether they are inflections or free forms.

There are two kinds of evidence that can be sought, phonological and distributional. If the case marker in question displays a number of variants determined by the nature of the word or stem to which it is adjacent (excluding the effect of some kind of pervasive, phonetically motivated rule), then it is an affix. In Korean, for instance, the subject-marking form (which corresponds to Japanese *ga* as in (9)) has the shape *-ka* after stems ending in a vowel and *-i* after stems ending in a consonant. This would seem to indicate that the subject marker is a suffix. The *-ka/-i* alternation is phonologically conditioned and has some phonological motivation insofar as a consonant-initial suffix follows vowels and a vowel-initial suffix follows consonants, but it is not part of a pervasive rule (like syllable-final devoicing of obstruents in German).

In English there is clear distributional evidence to show that prepositions are words rather than prefixes, since they can stand on their own as in *Who did she give it to?* Evidence of this type is not forthcoming for most languages. Co-ordination of nouns would appear to provide a criterion. One might expect that case markers would have to appear on every co-ordinated noun whereas a preposition or postposition could appear only before or after the sequence of co-ordinated nouns. It turns out, however, that markers which are integrated into a stem, i.e. markers that would appear to be affixes on phonological grounds, are often restricted to one occurrence in phrase-final position with co-ordinated nouns. In Korean, for instance, the nominative or subject marker, *-ka/-i*, referred to above, cannot be used within a phrase co-ordinated with *kwa* (O'Grady 1991: 7),[10]

(12)　　a. *Joe-kwa　Mary-ka　　yenay-lul　hanta*
　　　　　　Joe-AND　Mary-NOM　love-ACC　do
　　　　　　'Joe and Mary are in love.'
　　　　b. **Joe-ka-kwa　Mary-ka　yenay-lul　hanta*

A piece of distributional evidence that might be thought relevant is whether the case-marking form always appears adjacent to the head. In Japanese and Korean the order within noun phrases is determined by a modifier-head principle so that a noun is always in phrase-final position. In the Australian language, Diyari, however, the order is generally determiner-noun-adjective and the case marking is phrase-final. However, there is no chance of taking this marking to be postpositional on the grounds that it can be separated from the head noun by a dependent adjective, since the markers in question are very much integrated into the final word of the phrase whether it be a noun or an adjective. The ergative suffix, for instance, has phonologically and morphologically determined allomorphs such as *-ndu* with female personal names and *-yali* with singular common nouns of two, four or five syllables whose final vowel is *i* or *u* (Austin 1981a: 48–9). Interestingly this integrated marking need be used only on the last of a series of co-ordinated nouns. Clearly an affix can have a scope beyond the word of which it forms part.

There is one further complication. There are forms that are analysable as separate elements from the point of view of syntax (i.e. they are words), but which are pronounced as part of an adjacent word. Such forms are called **clitics**. If they are pronounced as part of the following word, they are **proclitics**. If they are pronounced as part of the preceding word, they are **enclitics.** The two varieties can be illustrated from French where the subject pronouns are normally proclitic, but can be enclitic in certain circumstances, in interrogatives, for instance, in those varieties that use subject-verb inversion,

(13)　　*Où descends-tu?*
　　　　'Where do you get off?'

　　　　A l'arrêt de la rue de Rivoli, je vais faire des emplettes
　　　　'At the Rue de Rivoli stop, I'm going to do some shopping.'

The forms *tu* and *je* are enclitic and proclitic respectively in these examples. They cannot be stressed or pronounced as words separate from the adjacent verb. If stress is required, special non-clitic forms *toi* and *moi* must be used in addition.

Some prepositions and postpositions may be analysable as proclitics and enclitics respectively. In Turkish, for instance, there is a form *-ile/-ila* which can express instrument or accompaniment. In phrases such as *tren-le* 'by train' and *kız-lar-la* 'with the girls' it appears in reduced form and exhibits vowel harmony. It looks like a case suffix. However, it can be pronounced as a separate word and, like a number of other postposition-like forms, it governs the genitive with singular pronouns. This would indicate that it is a postposition that can be cliticised, i.e. that can be treated as a clitic. The form *-ile/-ila* is different from the French pronouns in that the latter are always clitics, whereas *-ile/-ila* may or may not be used as a clitic.

The view adopted in this work is that phonological integration into a host is the best guide to the affixial status of a case marker, but the fact remains that there are many phrase-final, non-integrated case markers to be found in languages, and grammars often describe them as suffixes, postpositions or particles without any discussion of the basis for the decision.[11]

1.3 Competing mechanisms

Case in its most central manifestation is a system of marking dependent nouns for the type of relationship they bear to their head. However, it is not the only grammatical mechanism for marking head-modifier relations. One important type of alternative is the principle of marking the head rather than the dependent (cf. Nichols 1986). Another common option is to use word order rather than head or dependent marking. Other means include the use of relator nouns and possessive adjectives. One could take the view that all these means of expressing grammatical relations are forms of case marking. The point is discussed briefly in section 3.3.

1.3.1 Head marking

In many languages, in the majority in fact, there is some kind of pronominal representation of certain core grammatical relations quite apart from their representation via noun phrases. This representation is almost always on the predicate, often on a grammatical (auxiliary) verb. In a few languages it is enclitic to the first constituent of the clause (e.g. in some Pama-Nyungan and in some Uto-Aztecan languages). In the following Swahili example the third person singular subject is represented by the first order prefix on the verb (*a-*) and the third person singular object by the third order prefix (*-m-*) (Hinnebusch 1979: 219). In Swahili, as in other Bantu languages, nouns fall into gender classes. Each class is marked by a prefix, which also appears via concord on adjectives and determiners. Nouns for humans take the prefix *m-* in the singular. This can be seen in the phrase *mwanamke mrembo*,

(14) *Ali   a-na-m-penda   m-wanamke   m-rembo*
      Ali   3SG-PRES-3SG-love   M-woman   M-beautiful
      'Ali loves a beautiful woman.'

The grammatical relation most frequently represented in this way is the subject; however, some languages, including Swahili, also represent the direct object or other complements in this way. Traditionally the marking on the verb is referred to as subject agreement, object agreement, etc., but this term is also used for the type of subject-verb agreement found in French and the Germanic languages as in English *She runs* versus *They run*. There is an important difference. In French and the Germanic languages the subject noun phrase cannot normally be omitted with a finite, non-imperative verb, but in the majority type, illustrated by Swahili, the noun phrases corresponding to the relations represented on the verb can be omitted. In Swahili one can say *anampenda*, which means 'S/he loves him/her.' The term **cross-referencing agreement** is sometimes used for the Swahili type as opposed to the Germanic type (Bloomfield 1933: 193ff).

There is a further complication. It has been claimed that in languages with cross-referencing agreement the pronominal representation on the verb sometimes is interpretable as a mere agreement marker with the cross-referenced noun phrase bearing the appropriate grammatical relation, while in other instances the pronominal marker is the sole exponent of the relevant relation and the cross-referenced noun phrase a mere adjunct in a kind of apposition with the pronominal element.[12] It is not appropriate to go into this question here. Suffice it to say that the cross-referencing pronominal elements serve as an alternative to case in signalling grammatical relations. Where there is more than one set of cross-referencing elements, the sets may be distinguished by order or by form or both. In Swahili the subject and object forms are always distinguished by their position and in a majority of instances by differences of form as in (14) above.

Where differences of form are involved these differences are likely to reflect earlier differences of case in the free forms from which they are derived. In many of the Northern languages of Australia the bound pronoun for first person singular subject is *nga* and the object form is *ngan*. The *-n* clearly signals the object relation, and probably derives from an accusative, but it is a moot point whether one should refer to marking on pronominal elements in the verb as case marking.[13]

Another type of marking on the verb that could be considered head marking is marking to indicate change of valency. The presence of a passive marker on the verb, for instance, is a form of head marking that determines how dependent marking is to be interpreted. In Latin *Gallī vincunt* is 'The Gauls conquer', but the addition of the passive marker *-ur* to the verb yields *Gallī vincuntur* 'The Gauls are (being) conquered.'[14]

In some languages the person and number of a dependent possessor noun is cross-referenced on the head-possessed noun as in Hungarian *az ember haz-a* (the man house-3SG), literally, 'the man his house', i.e. 'the man's house'. An example of marking both the head and the dependent in a possessive construction was given from Turkish in section 1.1.

Another type of head marking in noun phrases indicates the presence of a dependent. In Semitic languages a noun with a noun dependent is in what is called the construct state. In Arabic, for instance, 'the book of the king' is *kitābu lmaliki* where *kitābu* 'book' is in the construct state (a nominative form lacking both the definite article and the *-n* that marks indefiniteness) and *lmaliki* is genitive (Kaye 1987: 678). In Persian a noun with dependent is suffixed with *-e: ketằb-e mán* 'book of me, my book' (Windfuhr 1987: 532).

1.3.2 *Word order*

Fairly obviously word order is an alternative to case marking in distinguishing subject from object in languages like English, Thai, Vietnamese and Indonesian, all of which use the order subject-verb-object as their unmarked option. In English the word order also distinguishes the patient object from the recipient or beneficiary object in double object constructions where the patient object always follows the other object: *She gave me good marks*, *She cut me a bunch of dahlias*.

It has frequently been observed that there is a correlation between the presence of case marking on noun phrases for the subject-object distinction and flexible word order and this would appear to hold true. From the work of Greenberg it would also appear that there is a tendency for languages that mark the subject-object distinction on noun phrases to have a basic order of subject-object-verb (SOV), and conversely a tendency for languages lacking such a distinction to have the order subject-verb-object (SVO) (Greenberg 1963). The following figures are based on a sample of 100 languages. They show the relationship between case and marking for the 85 languages in the sample that exhibit one of the more commonly attested basic word orders. The notation [+ case] in this context means having some kind of marking, including adpositions, on noun phrases to mark the subject-object distinction (Mallinson and Blake 1981: 179).

(15)　　　 VSO [+ case]　3　　 SVO [+ case]　9　　 SOV [+ case]　34
　　　　　　　　 [– case]　6　　　　　 [– case]　26　　　　　　 [– case]　7

The SVO 'caseless' languages are concentrated in western Europe (e.g. English), southern Africa (e.g. Swahili) and east and southeast Asia (e.g. Chinese and Vietnamese).

1.3.3 *Adverbs and relator nouns*

It is common in Australian languages to use 'location words' in conjunction with the locative case. The locative signals location or proximity in general and the location word indicates the specific orientation of the located entity with reference to the location. The following example is from Pitta-Pitta,

(16) *Nhangka-ya   thithi   kunti-ina   kuku-ina*
       sit-PRES   old.bro   house-LOC   back-LOC
       'Elder brother is sitting at the back of the house.'

Kuku-ina can be identified with *kuku* '(anatomical) back', but it is not an ordinary noun here; it cannot be qualified. In any case the full range of words that can be used to signal relative orientation cannot be analysed in terms of stems identifiable with nouns and suffixes identifiable with case markers. Words like *kukuina* in (16) are used as dependents of the verb in parallel with locative-marked nouns. Their position relative to the locative-marked noun is not fixed and the two need not be contiguous. A good literal translation of (16) would be 'Elder brother is sitting by the house, at the back.'

In (16) the adverb-like word is parallel with the locative-marked word. Another possibility is for the relative orientation to be specified by a word that is in series between the head and the location. This is the situation with words like *top* as in *It stands on top of the cupboard* and *front* as in *She is sitting in front of the house*. *Top* and *front* are nouns in that they stand at the head of noun phrases, but they are different from the common nouns *top* and *front* in that they cannot be modified by an indefinite article nor by adjectives. They belong to a small sub-class of nouns that are sometimes referred to as **relator nouns**.[15] Location words used in parallel with locative-marked nouns, i.e. words like *kukuina* in (16) could also be taken to be relator nouns rather than as adverbs.

Relator nouns are a feature of Chinese. In the following example *qiántou* 'front' is the head of a noun phrase just as 'front' is in the translation. It is the complement of *zhàn-zai* and it has *de* as its dependent which in turn has *dà-mén* as its dependent (Starosta 1988: 203),

(17) *Tā   zhàn-zai   dà-mén   de   qiántou*
       s/he   stand-at   big-gate   of   front
       'S/he is standing in front of the main door.'

Chinese also employs combinations of nouns and locational noun roots. The locational forms do not occur as separate lexical items and in some descriptions they are treated effectively as postpositions or 'locative particles' (Li and Thompson 1981: 25, 390ff). Since combinations of noun plus locational form can be governed by prepositions, a better analysis might be to take the combinations to be pseudocompounds ('pseudo-' since the second element does not occur as a free form). Such an analysis is adopted in Starosta (1988: 206). In the following example *mén qián* is a pseudocompound,

(18)   *Tā   zhàn-zai   dà   mén   qián*
            s/he   stand-at   big   gate   front
            'S/he is standing at the main door front.'

Under this interpretation the locative relationship is treated derivationally. In various varieties of colloquial English such compounding occurs to produce locative adverbs: *He went States-side. She went sundown-way* (i.e. west). Location is also treated derivationally in formations such as *homewards*, *skywards* or Keats' *Lethe-wards*. In Bantu languages locative marking on nouns is derivational. As noted in connection with the Swahili example given above (14), nouns in Bantu languages fall into a number of classes. Each class is marked by a prefix. The classes are associated with humans, plants and so on, and there are separate classes for the plurals of the various classes. To express location a noun is derived into one of several locative classes. In Swahili, for instance, there is a *pa-* class for specific location, a *ku-* class for 'to', 'from' and nonspecific location, and a *m(u)-* class to express inside. The word for 'house' is *nyumba*. It is normally in the *n-* class. To express 'in the house' *nyumba* is suffixed with *-ni* and put in the *m(u)-* class. The *n-* and *m(u)-* prefixes do not appear directly with *nyumba*, but they do appear on dependents via concord and on the verb via cross-referencing agreement. Compare the following examples,

(19)   *Nyumba   i-na   mi-lango   mi-wili*
            house   N-has   MI-door   MI-two
            'The house has two doors.'

(20)   *Nyumba-ni   m-na   wa-tu*
            house-LOC   MU-has   WA-person
            'In-the-house has people.'

In (19) *nyumba* is in the *n-* class which takes *i-* as its cross-referencing agreement marker for subject. In (20) *nyumba* is suffixed with *-ni* , which looks like an inflectional locative case suffix, but *nyumba* is now in the *mu-* 'inside' class as indicated by the subject marker on the verb. The fact that *nyumbani* is cross-referenced by a subject marker indicates that it is a subject. *Nyumbani* is not an inflected form of *nyumba*, but a form derived into another class. Normally a noun inflected for locative or marked by a locative adposition could not function as subject or object. The Bantu languages have incorporated both number (singular versus plural) and location into a noun class or gender system.

1.3.4 Possessive adjectives

A pronominal dependent of a noun can be expressed in the genitive case, but in some languages possessive adjectives perform a similar function. In Old English *mīn* is the genitive case form of the first person pronoun; *mīn bāt* is 'my boat'. However, genitive forms like *mīn* were reinterpreted as stems and used as possessive adjectives. Thus 'He saw my boat' was expressed as *Hē seah mīnne bāt* where *mīn* takes the masculine, accusative, singular inflection in concord with *bāt*.

In Latin genitive forms of pronouns were generally used as objective genitives and possessive adjectives were used in a 'subjective' role. For instance, *tua memoria mei* (your memory me.GEN) means 'Your recollection of me' where *tua*, the possessive adjective, corresponds to the subject of the corresponding verb and *mei*, the possessive pronoun, to its object or genitive complement.

2
Problems in describing case systems

2.1 The traditional analysis

The western tradition of describing case systems can be traced back to the Greeks. Ancient Greek, like the other 'older' Indo-European languages, was a fusional inflecting language in which case marking could not be separated from number marking, where there was also some fusion of the stem and inflection, and where gender correlated closely with declensional type in the first (feminine) and second (masculine) declension. In other words Greek was structurally parallel with Latin as illustrated in section 1.1. Given this kind of structure it is not surprising that the Greek descriptions of case were based on the word rather than on stems and suffixes. The modern concept of the morpheme (the smallest meaningful, or better, smallest grammatical segment) is not very useful in languages where the expression of several grammatical categories has fused representation across the whole language, i.e. what Matthews calls cumulative exponence or cumulation (Matthews 1974/1991).

Cases were described in terms of what are called here case forms, where a case form is an inflected form of a noun. Since the inflection of case and number is fused, it would be more accurate to talk of case/number forms. The term case is from Latin *cāsus*, which is in turn a translation of the Greek *ptōsis* 'fall'. The term originally referred to verbs as well as nouns and the idea seems to have been of falling away from an assumed standard form, a notion also reflected in the term 'declension' used with reference to inflectional classes. It is from *dēclīnātiō*, literally a 'bending down or aside'. With nouns the nominative was taken to be basic, with verbs the first person singular of the present indicative. For Aristotle the notion of *ptōsis* extended to adverbial derivations as well as inflections, e.g. *dikaiōs* 'justly' from the adjective *dikaios* 'just'. With the Stoics (third century, BC) the term became confined to nominal inflection (Sittig 1931: 3, Calboli 1972: 87).

The nominative was referred to as the *orthē* 'straight', 'upright' or *eutheia* 'straight', 'direct' form and then as the *ptōsis orthē*, *ptōsis eutheia* or later *ptōsis onomastikē* 'nominative case'. Here *ptōsis* takes on the meaning of case as we know it, not just of a falling away from a standard. In other words it came to cover all cases not just the non-nominative cases, which in Ancient Greek were called collectively *ptōseis plagiai* 'slanting' or 'oblique cases' and for the early Greek grammarians comprised *genikē* 'genitive', *dotikē* 'dative' and *aitiatikē* 'accusative'. The vocative, which also occurred in Ancient Greek, was not recognised until Dionysius Thrax (c. 100 BC) admitted it, which is understandable in light of the fact that it does not mark the relation of a nominal dependent to a head (see section 1.2.3, cf. Hjelmslev 1935: 4, Calboli 1972: 102). The received case labels are the Latin translations of the Greek ones with the addition of ablative, a case found in Latin but not Greek. The naming of this case has been attributed to Julius Caesar (Sittig 1931: 1). The label accusative is a mistranslation of the Greek *aitiatikē ptōsis* which refers to the patient of an action caused to happen (*aitia* 'cause'). Varro (116 BC–27?BC) is responsible for the term and he appears to have been influenced by the other meaning of *aitia*, namely 'accusation' (Robins 1967: 35, Calboli 1972: 100).

Case systems of the type represented by Latin and Ancient Greek present two major problems for description. One is the problem of distinguishing the cases; the other is the problem of describing their meaning and function. Distinguishing the cases is a problem, since different classes of stem exhibit a different range of distinctions, i.e. the paradigms are not isomorphic (see Table 1.2). The traditional solution is to identify cases across stem classes on the basis of the functions they have in common. Describing the meaning and function of the cases traditionally involved finding a principal meaning, which is reflected in the label, as well as listing a range of separate meanings or functions. Theories of how cases are to be distinguished and of how their meanings and functions are to be described are discussed in the remainder of this chapter.

2.2   Distinguishing cases

2.2.1   *The distributional approach*

As noted in section 1.1, cases are traditionally recognised on the basis of a distinction of case form for any one group of nouns. There is no requirement that the distinction be made for all classes of noun. In Latin (see Table 1.2), as in other Indo-European case languages, the nominative and accusative have distinct case forms for masculine and feminine nouns, but there is neutralisation, or **syncretism** as it is often called, of the distinction with neuter nouns. There is also neutralisation of nominative and accusative with plural nouns of the fourth and fifth declensions and third declension consonant stems. Nevertheless, we recognise the distinction as applying to all nouns, since it allows us to make exceptionless generalisations about the forms used for various functions in various syntactic contexts.

Essentially the traditional method involves aligning paradigms on the basis of functions and then referring to the rows of the sets of paradigms (as in Table 1.2) in relating expression and function. In Latin, for instance, we want to be able to make statements like the following:

(i)   the accusative is used to express the direct object
(ii) the accusative is used to express the object of certain prepositions
(iii) the accusative is used to express duration: *xxvii annos* 'for 27 years'.

It does not matter, for the purposes of this rule, that the accusative is realised by a form identical to the nominative in some paradigms.

This is not the only way of dealing with the neutralised distinctions. We could recognise only the formally distinct forms in each paradigm and relate these directly to the functions. For the first declension singular there would be a nominative-vocative, an accusative, a genitive-dative and an ablative. For the second declension singular non-neuter there would be a nominative, vocative, accusative, genitive and dative-ablative, and so on. Rules for encoding syntactic functions would have to refer to these case forms. For example, rule (i) above, which states that the direct object is expressed in the accusative case, would have to be amended as follows:

(iv) The direct object is expressed thus:
      With masculine and feminine singular nouns of any declension the accusative is used.
      With plural nouns of the first and second declensions the accusative is used.
      With plural nouns of the third, fourth and fifth declensions and with all neuters the nominative-vocative-accusative is used.

In the traditional descriptions the indirect object is described as being in the dative. If we were to describe the case forms in which it appears, the rule would read something like this:

(v)   The indirect object is expressed thus:
      With nouns of the first and fifth declensions singular the genitive-dative is used.
      With nouns of the third and fourth declensions singular the dative is used.
      With nouns of the second declension singular and with all plurals the dative-ablative is used.

The list of case forms given in (iv) for the direct object would have to be repeated for all the functions of the traditional accusative, of which there are about four. Similarly the list of case forms given in (v) for indirect object would have to be repeated for all the functions of the traditional dative, of which there are six or so.

This shows that an attempt to link the case forms directly to functions in Latin is unwieldy. A consideration of concord shows it is unworkable.

In Latin, attributive adjectives agree with their head noun in case, number and gender. Adjectives belong either to the first and second declensions (e.g. *bonus* (masc.) *bona* (fem.) *bonum* (neuter)) or to the third (e.g. *tristis* (masc. and fem.) *triste* (neuter)). Where an adjective makes more distinctions than the noun it modifies, an insuperable problem arises for a description based directly on distinct case forms. The word form *dominae*, for instance, can be genitive or dative. If it is modified by a third declension adjective like *tristis* (which declines like *cīvis* in Table 1.2), there is no way of determining whether the adjective should be genitive *tristis* or dative *tristī*, yet only one of these will be appropriate to the syntactic context. On the other hand, if the traditional method is used, no difficulty arises. One has a simple rule to the effect that an adjective shows concord in case, number and gender with the noun it modifies. Where there is syncretism as with *dominae* which realises genitive and dative singular (as well as nominative and vocative plural), two homophonous case forms are recognised. *Dominae* (genitive) takes *tristis* to yield *dominae tristis* 'of the sad mistress' and *dominae* (dative) takes *tristī* to yield *dominae tristī* 'to the sad mistress'.

Where a distinctive case form is very restricted in its distribution, it might seem tempting not to establish a case that applies across the spectrum. In Latin the vocative is distinct from the nominative only with non-neuter nouns of the second declension singular (cf. *domine* and *dominus* in Table 1.2). One might be tempted to subcategorise only non-neuter nouns that were of the second declension as [± vocative]. Under this interpretation, a first declension noun like *Maria* as in *Ave, Maria* 'Hail, Mary!' would be nominative not vocative though used as a term of address. However, this interpretation is hardly workable where a masculine noun of the third, fourth or fifth declension singular is modified by an adjective of the first/second declension as in *O sol laudande* 'Oh sun, worthy of praise' where *sol* is third declension. Here the distinctive vocative case form appears on the modifier but not the head. To operate the concord rule consistently it is necessary to recognise a vocative case for nouns in general.

However, there is one point overlooked in the traditional description and that is the pattern of syncretisms. In a language like Latin these may seem rather random at first, but two syncretisms predominate. These are the syncretism of nominative and accusative in all neuters and many plurals, and the syncretism of dative and ablative in all plurals plus the singular of the second declension and the singular of the *i*-stems in the third declension. If we exclude the vocative on the grounds that it is not strictly a case and if we note that the genitive is almost exclusively an adnominal case, we are left with four adverbal cases which the pattern of syncretisms divides into two groups: nominative plus accusative, and dative plus ablative. This grouping can be shown to be significant on other grounds. The nominative and accusative, for instance, typically encode the complements of the vast majority of verbs whereas the dative encodes the indirect object of only a small number of verbs and the ablative encodes the complement of only a handful.[1] The ablative and the dative, to a great extent, encode adjuncts (see section 2.3.2). Generalisations across cases, including syncretisms, can be captured in feature notation. This is taken up in section 2.3.4 below.

2.2.2 Non-autonomous case

In some languages a particular function or meaning is recognised in the case system not by any distinctive case forms at all but rather by different syncretisms in different paradigms. In Russian, for instance, the partitive sense, as with complements of *nemnogo* 'a little', is expressed by using genitive forms. However, with some masculine singular nouns a form coinciding with the dative is an option. Table 2.1 presents some case forms of *syr* 'cheese' and *xleb* 'bread'. With *syr*, one can say *nemnogo syra* or *nemnogo syru* 'a little cheese'. With *xleb* one can say only *nemnogo xleba* not **nemnogo xlebu*. There is no case form peculiar to the partitive function, but the function is treated differently from both the genitive functions (possessor, etc.) and dative functions (recipient, etc.), as a comparison of paradigms reveals. Mel'čuk calls a case which does not have a case form or case marker peculiar to itself a **non-autonomous case** (1986: 66).

A similar situation occurs in Latin where location is normally expressed by the ablative usually governed by the preposition *in*. However, with towns and small islands, where no preposition is used, location is expressed by case forms identical to the genitive for names belonging to the first or second declension singular: *Rōmae* 'at Rome', *Mīlētī* 'at Miletus'. There are a few third declension singular names with forms the same as the dative: *Karthāginī* 'in Carthage' (although the ablative *Karthāgine* is an alternative). There is also *rūrī* (third declension) 'in the country' and *domī* 'at home'. *Domus* 'home' has a mixture of second and fourth declension forms. The genitive is *domūs* or *domī*.

Since the expression of location involves different patterns of syncretism with different declensions, the locative function is distinguished and we could recognise a locative case as in Table 2.2. However, if we try to claim that all forms expressing location are in the locative case, a problem arises. Take the noun *urbs* 'city'. 'In the city' is expressed by *urbe* as in the following example where *urbe* is in apposition with the locative *Antiochae*.

Table 2.1 *The Russian partitive*

	'cheese'	'bread'
nominative	*syr*	*xleb*
accusative	*syr*	*xleb*
genitive	*syra*	*xleba*
partitive	*syra, syru*	*xleba*
dative	*syru*	*xlebu*

Table 2.2 *Latin locative forms*

	Rome 1st decl.	Miletus 2nd decl.	Carthage 3rd decl.
genitive	*Rōmae*	*Mīlētī*	*Karthāginis*
locative	*Rōmae*	*Mīlētī*	*Karthāginī*
dative	*Romae*	*Mīlētō*	*Karthāginī*
ablative	*Rōmā*	*Mīlētō*	*Karthāgine*

(1)   *Archias   poeta   Antiochiae   natus   est,   celebrī*
Archias   poet   Antioch.LOC   born   is.3SG   thronging.ABL
quondam   urbe   et   copiosā
once   city.ABL   and   wealthy.ABL
'The poet Archias was born in the once populous and wealthy city of Antioch.'

Cicero, pro Archia poeta 4:53

This might at first appear to confirm the idea that *urbe* and all ablative forms expressing location are locative forms homophonous with the ablative; after all, apposition is normally considered to involve case concord. But note the adjective *copiosā* which agrees with *urbe*. If a locative noun like *Antiochae* were to control concord, it would require *copiosae*.[2] Clearly there is a paradigmatic opposition between forms in -*ae* (locative) and forms in -*ā* (ablative). We can make the opposition clearer by considering the apposition of phrases expressing 'at my home' and 'at my villa', namely *domī meae*, *villā meā*. The case form *domī* is traditionally called locative (it is homophonous with the genitive). The case form *villā* is ablative. If we claim that it is a locative homophonous with the ablative, we are confronted with having to explain an opposition between *meae*, which is required by *domī*, and *meā*, which is required by *villā*, both these forms belonging to the same paradigm, namely first declension singular. The conclusion must be that there is a locative case, but that it is confined to certain nouns such as *domus* and to

Table 2.3 *Latin adverbs*

	'to'		'at'		'from'
quō	'whither'	*ubi*	'where'	*unde*	'whence'
hūc	'hither'	*hīc*	'here'	*hinc*	'hence'
illūc	'thither'	*ibi, illīc*	'there'	*illinc*	'thence'

adjectives in concord with them. One would also have to allow that in the situation illustrated in (1), and perhaps more generally, apposition operates on the basis of a function or relation rather than case, in this instance on the basis of the locative grammatical relation.

Quite apart from these locative forms there are locative adverbs. In fact Latin makes a three-way distinction between 'to', 'at' and 'from' forms (Table 2.3). The occurrence of a set of distinct forms expressing location adds to the evidence afforded by the vestigial locative case that there is a locative grammatical relation.

2.2.3   The formal approach

In section 2.2.1 it was argued that it would be unwieldy to link case forms directly with functions and impossible where there was concord involving a modifier that belonged to a paradigm more differentiated than the paradigm of the head (recall the distinction between *dominae tristis* 'of the sad mistress' and *dominae tristī* 'to the sad mistress'). Nevertheless, there are descriptions of case that deal either wholly or at least partly in case forms or case markers rather than traditional cases, although such descriptions do not involve the worst case scenario outlined with reference to Latin in section 2.2.1.

Direct reference to case markers and case forms is common practice among Australianists describing the core case system of Pama-Nyungan languages. Among these languages it is common to find the case-marking schema shown in Table 2.4.

At this point the pre-theoretical syntactic functions S, A and P will be introduced. S is the single argument of an intransitive predicate; A is the agent argument of a transitive verb, and P is the patient argument of a two-place transitive verb. The terms A and P extend beyond agent and patient to other roles that are treated grammatically in the same way as agent and patient respectively, so not only would *Martha hit Ruben* be described in terms of A and P, but so would *Martha saw Ruben*. The definition 'A is the agent argument of a transitive verb' is meant to exclude the agent adjunct of the passive, since this agent is not treated the same way grammatically as the agent argument of a transitive verb.[3]

As can be seen from Table 2.4, nouns in Pama-Nyungan languages have case marking for A function opposed to an absence of case marking for S and P func-

Table 2.4 *Core case marking in Pama-Nyungan*

function	noun	pronoun
P	-Ø	-nya or -nha
S	-Ø	-Ø
A	-lu, -ngku, -Tu	-Ø
Instrumental	-lu, -ngku, -Tu	-

T stands for an alveolar stop which may assimilate to match a dental, retroflex or palatal stem-final consonant.

tions. The marking for A function is generally known as ergative case marking and a system of case marking that makes an SP-versus-A distinction is referred to as an **ergative system**, an ergative-nominative system or an ergative-absolutive system. The term absolutive is used in some circles for a case or case form covering S + P functions.[4] Normally such forms are unmarked. With pronouns, or at least with first and second person pronouns, most Pama-Nyungan languages have case marking for P, i.e. accusative case marking, opposed to a common marking for S + A, which is usually zero, at least for non-singular pronouns. A system that makes an SA-versus-P distinction is called an **accusative system**.

If one were to recognise cases on the basis of distinctive marking in any one paradigm or distinctive treatment across paradigms as in the classical tradition, then one would need to recognise a nominative for S function, an accusative for P function and an ergative for A function. These cases would not be exclusive to S, P and A since they encode nominals in a predicative relation to S and to P (*Mick is a man*, *They made him a man*), both objects in double object constructions (*She gave the man bread*) and nominals in apposition to S, P and A. Also, in a majority of Pama-Nyungan languages the ergative expresses the instrumental function as well as A. In a traditional-type analysis the accusative would be said to be expressed by -*nha* (or in some languages -*nya*) with pronouns and by -Ø with nouns. The ergative would be described as being expressed by case markers such as -*lu*, -*ngku*, etc. with nouns and Ø with pronouns. However, in Australianist practice nouns are said to operate in an ergative-absolutive paradigm and pronouns in a nominative-accusative paradigm. A noun marked by -*lu* or -*ngku* etc. is said to be in the ergative case, but an unmarked pronoun in A function is described as being in the nominative case. Conversely a pronoun marked by -*nha* or -*nya* is said to be in the accusative case, but an unmarked noun in P function is said to be in the absolutive case.

Since one of the paradigms involved is a noun paradigm and the other a pronoun paradigm, problems of concord do not loom large, but they do occur.[5]

Consider the following sentence from Pitjantjatjara (Bowe 1990: 49),

(2)   *Paluru=rni   tjitji   tjukutjuku-ngku   nya-ngu*
        3SG.ERG=1SG.O   child   small-ERG   see-PAST
        'He saw me when he was a small child.'

Paluru is a pronoun in A function. The form is the same as would be used for
S function; there is no specifically ergative marking, and the ergative gloss given
here is in accordance with the traditional interpretation of case. The bound
pronoun *-rni*, which is enclitic to the first constituent encodes the direct object
(glossed as O). The phrase *tjitji tjukutjuku-ngku* bears the ergative case marker
indicating that it is to be construed with *paluru* rather than *-rni*. The simplest
way to account for this ergative marking is via a general rule for predicative
nominals to the effect that they agree in case with their controller, but such a rule
cannot be stated if it is dependent on whether the controller bears particular case
marking.

Another problem arises with whole-part constructions where, as in Australian
languages generally, the whole and the part appear in parallel with the case appropriate to their function in the clause. In Pitjantjatjara a pronoun whole and a noun
part encoding the patient of a transitive verb will not match in case marking, since
the pronoun will have accusative marking but not the noun (Bowe 1990: 54),[6]

(3)   *Tjilka-ngku   ngayu-nya   tjina   waka-rnu*
        prickle-ERG   1SG-ACC   foot.ACC   pierce-PAST
        'A prickle pierced my foot.'

If we adopt the traditional approach (as anticipated in the glossing), then an example like this will simply fall under the general rule of case matching and will not
require specification of case marking for nouns in P function as opposed to pronouns in P function.[7]

Another circumstance where a noun and pronoun are likely to be used in parallel
is where a noun is used to fill in the reference of a non-singular pronoun. For
instance, 'the white man and I' is typically something like *ngali walpala* (we.two
white.fella) in Pama-Nyungan languages. If such a phrase is used to encode the
patient of a transitive verb, there would be accusative marking for the pronoun but
not the noun, and therefore another exception, under Australianist practice, to an
otherwise general principle of concord.

The use of case forms rather than cases in the syntax would have been impossible for a language like Latin or Ancient Greek for the reasons given earlier.
However, the practice manages to survive in Australia for a number of reasons:

(a) The case-marking asymmetry is largely confined to the core cases, i.e. those expressing S, A and P (see section 2.3.2)

(b) The number of separate paradigms involved is fewer

(c) The fact that the differences are between a noun paradigm and a pronoun paradigm reduces the concord problem

(d) The distribution of the morphologically unmarked forms is probably seen as significant. In a traditional analysis of case in terms of distribution, this would be obscured. However, if cases are described in terms of distinctive features, shared characteristics can be captured. This is discussed in section 2.3.4.

In Lak, a Daghestan language of the Caucasus, the A of a transitive verb is expressed in the genitive except with first and second person pronouns where it appears in the unmarked nominative form (Table 2.5). This distribution raises the possibility of recognising a non-autonomous ergative case that is homophonous with the genitive in the noun paradigm and with the nominative in the first and second person pronoun paradigms. Mel'čuk (1986: 67–8), however, argues against establishing a non-autonomous ergative on the grounds that no particular lexical items need be referred to.

The partitive in Russian is also non-autonomous (see section 2.2.2) in that it always coincides with the genitive or dative. However, it is peculiar to certain lexical items, and Mel'čuk suggests that it would be more complex to specify that one should use the dative in certain contexts if the noun concerned were x, y, z, etc., than to specify that the partitive should be used. Using the partitive enables us to state the expression of dependents in three or so contexts in an exceptionless way, and the specification of the words that take the dative-type form need be given only in the lexicon.[8]

In grammars of Turkish one finds reference to two cases occurring in one syntactic environment (see, for instance, Lewis 1967). A number of postpositions are said to govern the genitive of singular pronouns and the nominative of other nominals. One such postposition is *için* 'for'.[9]

(4)   a. *siz-in için*   (you-GEN for)   'for you' (sing.)

          b. *siz-ler için*   (you-PL.NOM for)   'for you' (plur.)

          c. *bu adam için* (this man.NOM for) 'for this man'

In Turkish there is no concord and one of the stem classes involved is pronominal anyway. There would be no advantage in establishing a non-autonomous case just for the object of one group of prepositions.

A similar situation occurs in Hindi. The ergative postposition *ne*, like other post-

Table 2.5 *Lak case-marking schema*

	noun	pronoun
function		
P, S	nom	nom
A	gen	nom
Genitive	gen	gen

positions governs the oblique case.[10] However, with first and second person pronouns, it governs the nominative. There would be no advantage in establishing a third case which coincided with the nominative for first and second person pronouns and the oblique elsewhere, particularly as such a non-autonomous case would be peculiar to a single syntactic environment, namely complement of *ne*.

One final point. In a majority of Pama-Nyungan languages the same case markers express the A of a transitive verb and the instrumental. The two functions can be distinguished on syntactic grounds (see section 3.2.1), but there is no reason to recognise two cases. Typically there is a different distribution of case markers with respect to these two functions since the instrumental does not normally occur with pronouns. Instrumentals are virtually always inanimate and inanimates tend not to be represented by pronouns in Australian languages. In a few languages, however, the instrumental expresses the indirect cause ('because of') or aversive function ('what is to be avoided'). This is the situation in Margany, for instance (Breen 1981: 303–8). In such a language the instrumental occurs with pronouns and there is an opposition in the pronoun paradigm between -*Ø* case marking for A function and instrumental markers like -*tu* for instrumental function. In this situation two separate cases need to be recognised, ergative and instrumental as displayed in Table 2.6.

2.2.4 *Summary*

The traditional model for describing case systems is based on Ancient Greek and Latin where three factors are prominent:

(a) There are numerous paradigms (when number is taken into account) with different patterns of syncretism (i.e. the paradigms are not isomorphic).

(b) For each case there are a number of functions.

(c) There is concord between the head of a noun phrase and its dependents.

Given these factors it is difficult to see how one could arrive at a simpler analysis than the traditional one. The only disadvantage is that there is no reference in a

Table 2.6 *Margany case system (partial)*

		noun	pronoun
function	case		
P	accusative	-Ø	-nha
S	nominative	-Ø	-Ø
A	ergative	-ngku, -tu	-Ø
Inst	instrumental	-ngku, -tu	-tu

traditional description to the pattern of syncretisms in particular paradigms. All such syncretism is treated as non-significant.

Where there is only a small number of paradigms, say two; where the number of functions is small, and where there is little or no concord, it is not impossible to deal in case forms (or case markers). This is the current practice among Australianists where nouns have ergative marking for A function and zero for S and P while pronouns have accusative marking for P and zero for S and A. Such a model of description picks out the pattern of what are, from the traditional point of view, syncretisms.

Where a function or functions can be expressed by one case form with some nouns and another case form with others, it is possible to establish a non-autonomous case with no forms peculiar to itself. This is worthwhile in some instances as with the Russian partitive where the syncretisms are irregular (lexical) and there are a number of functions involved. Where a single function or syntactic environment is concerned and where the case form alternation is simple as in Turkish where certain prepositions govern the genitive of singular pronouns and the nominative otherwise, it is simpler to treat the alternation as an alternation in case.

2.3   Meanings and functions

Traditionally cases are described as having a number of functions or meanings. The accusative in Ancient Greek, for instance, is described as denoting the direct object and the two objects in a double object construction.

(5)   *Edidaxan   ton   paida   tēn   mousikēn*
        taught.3PL   the.ACC   boy.ACC   the.ACC   music.ACC
        'They taught the boy music.'

There is also an accusative of respect or reference which typically marks the complement of adjectives and indicates in respect of which field the adjectival property holds (Smith 1888: 150).

(6)   *Oudeis   anthrōpos   autos   panta   sophos*
     no   man.NOM   self.NOM   all.ACC   wise.NOM
     'No man is himself wise in everything.'

Lastly there is the adverbial accusative which expresses extent in distance or time.

(7)   *Treis   mēnas   emeinen*
     three.ACC   months.ACC   stayed.3SG
     'He stayed three months.'

Typically the rationale for separating meanings or functions is not made explicit. Some distinctions appear to have a syntactic basis, but others are semantically based and in the absence of explicit criteria there is the possibility that the distinctions are based on the intuition of the grammarian. In fact this is more than a possibility given that different writers come up with different classifications of the meanings and functions of a particular system. However, with the examples of the Greek accusative quoted above, there would appear to be a sound syntactic basis for the distinctions. Objects are governed by a specific set of verbs, namely transitive verbs; the accusative of respect is a complement of adjectives and participles, and adverbial accusatives are adjuncts that can be modifiers of any predicate and can co-occur with objects and respect complements.

In the description of case meanings and functions a number of general distinctions emerge. The first is between the nominative and the other cases; the second is between the grammatical and the semantic cases, and the third is between complements and adjuncts. These distinctions are described in the following subsections.

2.3.1 *Nominative versus oblique*

One of the distinctions that goes back to the Greeks is that between the nominative and the other cases, collectively the oblique cases (cf. section 2.1). In some languages there is a formal distinction between the nominative and the oblique cases inasmuch as there is a special stem for the obliques. This is the situation in many Dravidian and Daghestan languages, for instance (see examples in section 4.4.2). The term nominative (Greek *onomastikē*, Latin *nōminatīvus*) means 'naming'; the nominative is the case used outside constructions, the case used in isolation, the case used in naming. In most languages the nominative bears no marking, but consists of the bare stem; it owes its status as nominative to the existence of marked cases. Indo-European case languages are unusual in having a marked nominative in most paradigms. In chapter 2 of *Peri hermeneias* Aristotle declared that only the nominative is a noun, the other forms being cases of nouns. The distinguishing feature of the nominative for the Greeks was that it was the only form that could encode the subject of an existential predicate. One modern view is that the nominative represents the noun as a 'concept pure and simple' (Juret 1926: 16), that the nominative form is the case of pure reference (de Groot 1956: 189).[11] Hjelmslev repudiated the nominative-oblique distinction, but described the nominative as a form that could only be defined negatively (Hjelmslev 1935: 2, 96). Behind all these views lies the notion that the nominative simply denotes an entity not a relation between an entity and a predicate.

Jakobson saw the leading role of the nominative to be the expression of the topic, another notion that goes back to the Greeks and the division of the clause into *onoma* and *rhēma*. *Onoma*, originally 'name', later 'noun', is effectively subject when applied to the structure of the clause. *Rhēma*, 'saying', 'proverb', later 'verb', is effectively predicate phrase (cf. Robins 1967: 26–7, Calboli 1972: 89). The nominative is compatible with carrying the topic function, since the nominative has no clear relational content. People frequently want to talk about entities designated by nouns, but not so often about relations to entities. For this reason, locatives, ablatives, etc. are not normally topics. In fact the locative subjects of Bantu languages, which can be topics (see (20) in chapter 1), are unusual.

As noted above, the nominative is generally thought of as the case used outside syntax, the case used in naming, the case used in talking about a lexeme, but Rubio argues that in Latin the accusative as well as the nominative is used in isolation and metalinguistically. He sees both of them as cases of pure denotation (1966: 95–7). We are reminded of the use of the oblique forms of pronouns in English: *Who wants it? Me. Me, I'll get it.* de Carvalho also notes that the accusative in Latin is used out of context (1982: 257ff, 1985). He sees the nominative in more positive terms as the case in which one expresses the protagonist (1982: 248, 263).

A curious fact about the nominative is its neglect in grammars of the classical languages. It is true that it has fewer functions and is used in a smaller range of syntactic contexts than any of the oblique cases, but it tends to be dismissed cursorily. Woodcock 1959, in a fairly detailed treatment of the Latin case system, omits it altogether.

In sum, the nominative is the case used in isolation and is usually morphologically unmarked. It is the case in which the subject is normally encoded (though not in ergative languages; see section 3.2) and since the subject is characteristically associated with the topic of a sentence, there is an association of nominative and topic.

2.3.2 *Grammatical and semantic cases*

Another distinction that is often made is between grammatical (or syntactic) cases and semantic (or concrete) cases. The grammatical cases are traditionally taken to include the nominative and accusative and often the genitive

(Kuryłowicz, for instance, includes the genitive (1949, 1964: 188)), and should include the dative and the ergative. The basis for the distinction is often not made clear, but if the criterion for classifying a case as grammatical or syntactic is that it expresses a purely syntactic as opposed to semantic relation, then the dative and ergative should certainly be included since the dative encodes the indirect object and the ergative encodes A or what is often referred to as 'transitive subject'. In this text the 'transitive subject' will be referred to as the ergative relation. The distinction between A and the ergative relation is that A is a pre-theoretical term of universal applicability, whereas the term ergative relation should only apply where A is demarcated by some formal means such as ergative case marking.

If the distinction between grammatical and semantic cases were to be clearcut, the grammatical cases would encode only purely syntactic relations and the semantic cases would encode only homogeneous semantic relations such as location or source. However, it is common for a syntactic case to encode a semantic relation or role that lies outside of whatever syntactic relation it expresses. In Latin, for instance, the accusative not only expresses the direct object it also expresses the semantic role of destination, which can be shown not to be subsumed under direct object. On the other hand there are situations where the so-called semantic cases encode a purely syntactic relation. This commonly occurs with the passive where the demoted subject is often expressed via a semantic case. In Latin the 'agent' of the passive is normally expressed in the ablative governed by *ā/ab*. This 'agent' is not a semantic agent, but may cover a range of roles that can be expressed as subject including true agents (*occīsus ā cōnsule* 'killed by the consul'), experiencers (*amāta ā cōnsule* 'loved by the consul' and perceivers (*vīsus a cōnsule* 'seen by the consul').

The Latin ablative clouds the distinction between the grammatical and semantic cases in another way inasmuch as the ablative is semantically diffuse. As pointed out in section 1.1, the ablative expresses the semantic roles of source, location and instrument. Latin has no semantic case where there is a one-for-one relationship betweeen case and semantic role, but in languages with larger case systems there are frequently cases that at least approximate to being semantically homogeneous (cf. Agud 1980: 454).

Perhaps one could argue that a case is syntactic if its primary function is to encode a purely syntactic relation. Kuryłowicz (1964: 181–3) argues that expressing the direct object is the primary function of the accusative since all the adverbial functions are determined by context, in particular by the choice of verb or the choice of accusative noun. An accusative of destination is found only with verbs of motion (Latin: *īre Rōmam* 'to go to Rome') and an accusative of extent is used only with nouns referring to measures of distance or periods of time (Latin: *rēgnāre septem annōs* 'to reign seven years', *ambulāre mīlia tria* 'to walk three miles').

It is also convenient for the purposes of making certain generalisations (see, for instance, section 5.2) to distinguish the cases that encode the complements of typical one-place and two-place transitive verbs. These comprise nominative, ergative and accusative. I shall refer to these as the **core** cases and to the others as **peripheral** cases. There is another set of terms in use, namely direct and oblique. But this use of oblique is confusing, since the nominative-oblique distinction is better established.

In some treatments the term **local cases** is used to cover cases designating notions of place such as location, source, destination or path.

These distinctions are summarised in Table 2.7.

2.3.3 Complements and adjuncts

A number of writers including Kuryłowicz (1949, 1964) and Touratier (1978) distinguish between instances where cases are governed by verbs or prepositions and instances where they express adjuncts. What they appear to have in mind is the redundancy involved in marking a dependent whose role is already implicit in the choice of verb or preposition. In Latin most two-place verbs take an accusative complement, but, as illustrated in section 1.1, some take complements in the genitive, dative or ablative. *Ūtī* 'to use', for example, governs the ablative as in *gladiō ūtor* 'I am using a sword.' We might compare the use of the ablative to express an adjunct with instrumental function as in *gladiō ferīre* 'to wound with a sword'. Kuryłowicz takes governed, peripheral case marking with verbs (as in *gladiō ūtor*) to be 'voided of its semantic contents' and to have become 'an allomorph of the ending of the accusative (of direct object), a simple sign of syntactical subordination' (1964: 193). In similar vein Nichols considers that in Russian there is no difference in syntactic relations between the accusative complement of *ljubit'* 'to love', the instrumental complement of *interesovat'sja* 'to be interested in', the dative complement of *udivljat'sja* 'to be surprised at' and the prepositional complement of *serdit'sja* 'to get angry with', which takes a preposition *na* 'on(to)', which in turn governs the accusative. She describes all of these as the 'first object' (Nichols 1983: 171).

However, there are problems with these views. Complements with indirect or peripheral case marking can usually be shown to be syntactically distinct from accusative-marked direct objects in that while direct objects match the subject of a corresponding passive, for two-place verbs with a peripheral-marked complement there is no corresponding passive. Semantically there are problems too. If one takes the governed ablative of a Latin verb like *ūtī* 'to use' to be 'voided of its semantic contents', this implies, as Touratier points out, that the ablative in an adjunct phrase as in *gladiō ferīre* 'to wound with a sword' realises a different morpheme (Touratier 1978: 102). However, the choice of governed case is relatable

Table 2.7 *Types of case*

grammatical	core	nominative accusative ergative
		genitive dative
semantic	local*	locative ablative allative perlative
		instrumental comitative etc.

* Other local cases are possible, but they all involve the combining of location, source, destination and path with other notions.

here and elsewhere to the use of cases in adjunct functions. The ablative in Latin is the case used to express the instrumental function and this would appear to be appropriate for *ūtī* 'to use'. Worse still for the view that governed cases are not significant is the fact that some alternations occur and these tend to be meaningful. In Latin *moderarī* 'to govern' takes the dative or the accusative. The dative tends to be used with reference to governing one's tongue *moderarī linguae* or one's anger *moderarī īrae*, i.e. to exercising self-restraint, whereas the accusative tends to be used for governing or controlling something external whether it be horses or territory.[12] It is true that case marking is partly arbitrary, but it is not random (cf. Nichols 1983: 190). One broad generalisation that holds across languages is that verbs taking peripheral complements are not activity verbs involving impingement on a patient, though this is not to imply that all verbs with accusative-marked direct objects are such verbs.

Writers like Kuryłowicz and Touratier are right to point out the redundancies in case use. A clear instance can be found in English where verbs and prepositions always govern the accusative, which therefore contributes practically nothing to the meaning. However, where verbs and prepositions can govern various cases, the choice is likely to be significant. Even where a case makes no independent contribution to the meaning because the role is determined by the verb or adposition, the case can still have a meaning, even if there is redundancy (as with the Latin verb *ūtī* 'to use' governing the instrumental ablative). Moreover, the choice of case may have syntactic significance, e.g. marking a direct object as opposed to a peripheral complement, which in turn can have discourse-pragmatic significance.[13]

2.3.4   Case features

As noted in section 2.3 cases are traditionally described as having a number of functions. A typical Latin grammar will list the principal functions of the ablative as separation, instrumental and locative. Within 'separation' there will be subtypes such as separation or source (*Athēnīs redeō* 'I return from Athens'), origin (*optimīs parentibus nātus* 'born of excellent parentage') and comparison (*lūce clārior* 'clearer than daylight'). In using a single expression unit such as the ablative case to express a number of different functions, the language is exploiting the notion of complementary distribution. The functions can usually be distinguished by the choice of governor or the choice of lexical item bearing the case. In the phrase *Athēnīs redeō* 'I return from Athens' the separation or source sense is deducible from the meaning of *redīre* 'to return'; in *Athēnīs habitō* 'I live in Athens' the locative sense is deducible from the meaning of *habitāre* 'to live in'; in the sentence *Totā Italiā erat bellum* (all.ABL Italy.ABL was war) 'There was war throughout Italy' the locative sense is deducible from the fact that *Italia* refers to a place (cf. Rubio 1966: 155–87). This complementarity raises the possibility of arriving at a single generalised meaning of which the particular meanings are predictable variants. The notion of a generalised meaning, for which the German term **Gesamtbedeutung** (whole/aggregate meaning) is sometimes used, can also be arrived at via a different path. Instead of considering the particular meanings or functions of a case, one can look at cases solely from the point of view of their position in the system of cases, in the system of oppositions. One can then allot them a characterisation that is sufficient only to distinguish each case from the others in the same system.

The origin of the generalised meaning goes back to the classical period, but it becomes prominent in the thirteenth century, both in the work of the Byzantine grammarian Maximus Planudes (1260-c.1310) and in the work of the scholastic grammarians (Hjelmslev 1935: 11f, Serbat 1981a: 24–6), where generalised characterisations were exploited in presenting case inventories as systems. Simon of Dacia (=Denmark), for instance, characterised the Latin genitive and ablative as expressing origin as opposed to the dative and accusative which express what I will call destination. A cross-cutting distinction is made between relations of substance to substance, i.e. adnominal relations, and relations of substance to action, i.e. adverbal relations (Serbat 1981a: 24–6). These binary distinctions can be presented in terms of distinctive features as shown in Table 2.8.

The notion of markedness was not a feature of pre-twentieth-century linguistics. Obviously there is some redundancy in having ± values for both substance-to-substance and for substance-to-action. Simon includes a further distinction between intransitive cases (nominative and vocative) and transitive ones. Nominative is characterised as expressing the *suppositum actuale* and the vocative as expressing

Table 2.8 *Latin case system (Simon of Dacia)*

	nom	acc	gen	dat	abl
origin	-	-	+	-	+
destination	-	+	-	+	-
substance-to-substance	-	-	+	+	-
substance-to-action	-	+	-	-	+

the *suppositum virtuale*. The *suppositum* is what is presupposed or given and the *suppositum actuale* relates to the discourse function of the subject. Communication presupposes a speaker (or writer or signer) and an addressee. The addressee is the *suppositum virtuale*. Simon's treatment of the nominative/vocative opposition does not bring out clearly the unmarked character of the nominative vis-à-vis the vocative, although *actuale* as opposed to *virtuale* could be interpreted as indicating this. Establishing these generalised characterisations can involve overlooking or minimising part of the evidence. Simon takes the dative to express the relations of substance-to-substance (adnominal), but the dative has adverbal as well as adnominal functions.

A contemporary, Martin of Dacia, produced a system which recognised that the dative and ablative cases had both adnominal and adverbal functions, though he seems to have overlooked the fact that the genitive in Latin has some limited adverbal functions. As noted in section 1.1, a few verbs such *oblivisci* 'to forget' and *misererī* 'to pity' take genitive complements. His system has the virtue of picking out the cases that can be adnominal (genitive, dative, ablative) from those that cannot (see (10) below). A notable feature of Martin's system is that it is localist. In a localist theory not only are the local cases characterised by local notions such as source and destination, but the other cases are also interpreted as more abstract instantiations of these notions. In Martin's system the nominative is seen as a case of origin since the action typically proceeds from the subject, and the vocative is characterised in terms of the feature 'towards' since communication is directed towards an addressee (Serbat 1981a: 26–7). A point about this system that may seem curious is that Martin characterises the dative as a 'to' case and the accusative as a 'towards' case. Even those unsympathetic to abstract characterisations of cases would probably be happy to see a common feature such as 'to' used to capture the notion of destination common to the accusative and dative. Martin may have been motivated to find a way of distinguishing the [+ terminus] cases without resorting to the adnominal/adverbal distinction. His system is displayed in terms of features in Table 2.9.

The interpretation of the case system of Ancient Greek developed by the Byzantine scholar Maximus Planudes, as presented in Hjelmslev (1935: 13–15), is

Table 2.9 *Latin case system (Martin of Dacia)*

	nom	acc	gen	dat	abl	voc
origin	+	-	+	-	-	-
terminus	-	+	-	+	+	-
substance-to-substance	-	-	+	+	+	-
substance-to-action	+	+	-	+	+	-
to		-		+	-	-
from		-		-	+	-
towards		+		-	-	+

displayed in Table 2.10. In Greek there were five cases: nominative, accusative, genitive, dative and vocative (though the vocative is excluded in the scheme of Planudes). The genitive covers the notion of 'from' as well as possessor and the dative includes locative and instrumental functions. According to Hjelmslev, Planudes was the first to see the cases from the point of view of the object rather than the subject. Note that the dative holds the central, neutral, pivotal position on a scale running from *rapprochement* (bringing nearer) to *éloignement* (taking away). The nominative is also neutral with respect to those two poles, but it is independent rather than dependent.

The dominant model for describing case systems in the Renaissance and right down to the present day has been the traditional method of listing a number of meanings and functions for each case as illustrated in section 2.3 above. However, in the early nineteenth century, a period famous for the development of comparative-historical linguistics, the notion of cases having a single, abstract meaning can be found in the work of linguists such as Rask, Bopp and Wüllner. Not surprisingly the notion of *Gesamtbedeutung* becomes prominent in the structuralist period of the twentieth century. The leading proponents are Hjelmslev and Jakobson, both of whom published important, influential works in the mid thirties.

Hjelmslev

For Hjelmslev, a case, like linguistic forms in general, does not signify several different things. It signifies 'a single abstract notion from which one can deduce the concrete uses' (Hjelmslev 1935: 85). The meaning of a case cannot be determined in isolation, but only from a consideration of the oppositions within the case system. Hjelmslev was a localist, in fact it was he who rescued Maximus Planudes from oblivion (see above), and he captured the oppositions within a case system in localist terms. The first dimension in a case system is direction of which the positive term is **rapprochement** (bringing nearer) and the negative **éloignement** (taking away) (1935: 128). To see how this works, let us look at Hjelmslev's

Table 2.10 *Planudes' case system of Ancient Greek*

(to)	+	0	-	(from)
dependent	acc	dat	gen	
independent		nom		

interpretation of Greenlandic Eskimo (Hjelmslev 1937: 65–75). In this language there are the following cases: nominative, ergative-genitive, equative (or predicative), instrumental, ablative, allative, locative and a 'through' case which is called perlative elsewhere in this text (Hjelmslev calls it prosecutive). The last four of these cases are clearly local, and Hjelmslev captures them in terms of rapprochement 'to' and éloignement 'from' as follows:

ablative	from
allative	to
locative	neither 'from' nor 'to'
perlative	both 'from' and 'to'

The second dimension in Hjelmslev's system is degree of intimacy: **coherence** versus **incoherence** (1935: 128). This is another local notion and Hjelmslev illustrates the distinction with prepositions. Coherence involves contact or penetration whereas incoherence merely involves proximity. *She went **into** the building* (coherent); *she went **to** the building* (incoherent); *she went **between** the buildings* (indifferent to coherence). With Eskimo Hjelmslev uses this dimension to capture the distinction between the local cases and the syntactic cases. The local cases were taken to be indifferent to the distinction and the syntactic cases to be incoherent. In Table 2.11 the local cases are shown as [+ coherent] since, for Hjelmslev, they represent the positive term of the opposition. He aligns the ergative-genitive with the ablative (the action proceeds from the agent) and the equative with the allative (*A is equal to B*). The nominative which is pivotal and which does not involve either the notion of 'to' or of 'from' is matched with the locative, and the instrumental with the perlative, an analogy which can be rationalised in terms of the action passing through the instrument to the patient. The tabloid summary is presented in Table 2.11 (after Hjelmselv 1937: 74).

Jakobson

Like Hjelmslev, Jakobson broke away sharply from the traditional practice of merely listing case uses or functions. As van Schooneveld describes the situation (1986: 374):

Table 2.11 *Hjelmslev's case system of Greenlandic Eskimo*

	[- coherent]	[+ coherent]
$\left[\begin{array}{l}\text{+ from}\\\text{- to}\end{array}\right]$	ergative	ablative
$\left[\begin{array}{l}\text{+ to}\\\text{- from}\end{array}\right]$	equative	allative
$\left[\begin{array}{l}\text{+ from}\\\text{+ to}\end{array}\right]$	instrumental	perlative
$\left[\begin{array}{l}\text{- from}\\\text{- to}\end{array}\right]$	nominative	locative

> The impact of such listings was that the majority of linguists considered the extraction, in a given language, of a semantic invariant of each case beyond reach. And suddenly, in the same decade [the thirties], appears this native speaker of Latin (because as far as case is concerned, Latin and Greek are similar to Russian) who states that to him, there is in his native language an invariant meaning for each case. Not only do these semantic characteristics of each individual case have elements in common but they constitute also a paradigmatic structure.

Jakobson distinguished between the invariant, **intensional** meaning of a case and its syntactically and/or lexically conditioned variants which make up the **extension** of the case (cf. (5), (6) and (7)). The *Gesamtbedeutung* of a case is independent of the environment and cannot be determined from the individual meanings (*Sonderbedeutungen*) nor from the principal meaning (*Hauptbedeutung*). Cases are correlative and take their value from their relation to other cases in a system of oppositions (Jakobson 1936/1971: 35–6).

Jakobson applied his theory to the case system of Russian. The cases are: nominative, accusative, dative, instrumental, genitive and locative, plus two rather restricted cases: genitive II or partitive (see section 2.2.2) and locative II. The locatives are also called prepositional. Jakobson takes the nominative to be unmarked. Opposed to it is the accusative, which is always subordinated to it and which signals direction or goal. The instrumental and dative are opposed to the nominative and accusative as marginal or peripheral cases (*Randkasus*) opposed to direct or central cases (*Vollkasus*).

(8) central nom acc
     marginal inst dat

The dative is aligned with the accusative in that both express the goal of an event. The instrumental is taken to be the unmarked marginal case just as the nominative is the unmarked central or direct case. In what most would take to be its core meaning, namely that of expressing an instrument in a sentence like *Petr rezal mjaso nožom* (Peter-NOM cut meat.ACC knife.INSTR) 'Peter was cutting the meat with a knife', the instrument is backgrounded relative to the subject and direct object, a backgrounding iconically reflected in its adjunct and marginal syntactic status (cf. Wierzbicka 1980). The instrumental case is also used to express back-grounded agents in the passive. The genitive and locative focus 'upon the extent to which the entity takes part in the message' (Jakobson 1958/1971: 179), the locative also being considered marginal. The genitive II (partitive) and locative II are taken to be marked with respect to genitive I and locative I respectively. Table 2.12 (from Jakobson 1936/1971: 65) shows the complete system. Within each opposition the marked case is to the right or below.

In his 1958 paper Jakobson presented the system in terms of a cube, with what are features serving as the dimensions: [± direction], [± marginal] (as in Table 2.12) and [±-quantification] (partial involvement). The feature [± directional] is extended from the accusative and dative to cover genitive I and locative I. It is also referred to as [±-ascriptive] since 'directional' is not so appropriate when it is extended to cover genitive and locative. I think it would be fair to say that Jakobson's characterisation of the Russian cases in terms of features is less than perspicuous and there is less than adequate demonstration of how the feature analysis can be exploited (see the discussion following Table 2.15). Neidle's representation of the system in terms of a matrix of distinctive features is shown in Table 2.13 (Neidle 1982: 397).

The notion that cases have a single, abstract meaning still has supporters such as Rubio (1966) and de Carvalho (1980). However, a description of meaning purely in terms of *Gesamtbedeutungen* has limitations. As Wierzbicka points out, the meanings Jakobson ascribes to the Russian cases are too broad to be predictive and one cannot learn to use the Russian cases from his formulas (1980: xv). The extension of a case is not always derivable from the generalised meaning. However, it does not follow from this observation that one should abandon generalised meanings or at least generalised characterisations. In section 2.2.1 the utility of the traditional cases was demonstrated. However, it was also pointed out that a description entirely in terms of distributional cases (the rows in the paradigms) neglected syncretisms (the vertical dimension). One thing generalised meanings or at least generalised characterisations are useful for is to serve as the basis for grouping cases into a hierarchy of sets, each set bearing one or more features in common. A syncretism between two or more cases is likely to be significant, especially if it recurs in a number of paradigms. In the Indo-European case languages there is

Table 2.12 *Jakobson 1936: Russian case system*

central	(nom	~	acc)	~	(gen I	~	gen II)
	∫		∫		∫		∫
marginal	(inst	~	dat)	~	(loc I	~	loc II)

Table 2.13 *Jakobson/Neidle: Russian case system*

	Marginal	Quantifying	Ascriptive
Nominative	-	-	-
Accusative	-	-	+
Genitive I	-	+	+
Genitive II	-	+	-
Locative II	+	+	-
Locative I	+	+	+
Dative	+	-	+
Instrumental	+	-	-

syncretism of nominative and accusative (and usually vocatives) for neuters no matter which declension or number they belong to. In Russian there is syncretism of accusative and genitive. This covers animate nominals of the first declension masculine singular or any animate plural or any personal pronoun. Significantly the syncretism covers all the different forms that occur in these paradigms, which would rule out phonological motivation: *sloná* (ACC/GEN) 'elephant', *slonóv* (ACC/GEN.PL) 'elephants', etc. Such syncretisms can be captured in terms of features of the type illustrated from a variety of linguists from Simon of Dacia (Table 2.8) to Jakobson (Table 2.13). The focus in such an analysis is more on shared formal properties than on meanings, but the idea of a generalised character-isation remains the same.

As in phonology, where the use of features rather than atomic phonemes becomes more attractive in proportion to the number of generalisations that can be captured, so in case the feature analysis becomes more convincing as cases are seen to exhibit shared behaviour across a range of areas. Here are some kinds of behaviour that cases share:

(a) Syncretism
   Syncretism in particular paradigms is the most readily observable and the most widespread example of shared properties between cases.

(b) Compound case
   In many languages semantic features shared between cases are reflected in the use of separate markers for the features yielding what

Mel'čuk calls compound cases (see section 4.4.3). Consider the case system of Kalkatungu (Table 2.14) which contains an unmarked nominative, plus four simple cases and four compound cases (only one marker for each of ergative, dative and locative I is shown).

The distribution of the marker *-thi* suggests that the locative and ablative have something in common and a comparison of *-thi* and *-thingu* identifies *-ngu* with the notion 'from'. The aversive is used to express what is to be avoided ('Keep away from the fire!') or the indirect cause ('sick from (eating) bad meat'). The marker *-thungu* is based on the ergative, which expresses agents and instruments, combined with *-ngu* expressing 'from'. Both components of the marking are clearly motivated. Similarly one can identify *-nha* as 'to' and see motivation for its distribution.

Naturally there can be shared features that are not revealed via compound marking, but the distribution of recurring markers would seem to be significant and worth pointing out.

(c)   Type of stem

In some languages cases can be distinguished according to the type of stem they attach to. In Tamil, for instance, the oblique cases of some singular nouns are suffixed to an oblique stem. The word for 'tree' has a nominative *maram*, but the other cases are suffixed to a stem *maratt-*. The accusative is *maratt-ai*, the dative *maratt-ukku*, and so on. This distinction in the stem serves to set the nominative off from the other cases (cf. section 4.4.2).

In some languages relator nouns with meanings like 'top', 'behind' and 'bottom' can appear only in the local cases.

(d)   Complement v. adjunct

Cases may group according to whether they express complements or not. In some languages there is a clear distinction between complement-marking cases and cases that mark adjuncts exclusively. In Pitta-Pitta, for instance, only nominative, ergative, accusative and dative mark complements.

(e)   Adverbal v. adnominal

Core cases such as nominative and accusative are not normally able to be used adnominally. In Latin the peripheral cases (genitive, dative and ablative) can be used adnominally, but the nominative, vocative and accusative cannot.

In some languages one case may be substituted for another. Such a substitution is a sign of a relatively close relationship and an indication of a markedness rela-

Table 2.14 *Kalkatungu cases*

nominative	Ø		
ergative	*-thu*	aversive	*-thungu*
dative	*-ku*	allative I	*-kunha*
locative I	*-thi*	ablative	*-thingu*
locative II 'facing'	*-ngii*	allative II 'towards'	*-ngiinha*

tionship between the two. In Latin, the nominative may be substituted for the vocative as in the following example from Livy where the vocative would have been *popule Albāne*.

(9)   *Audī   tū,   populus   Albānus*
        hear.IMP   thou   people.NOM   Alban.NOM
        'Hear, you people of Alba.'

This confirms what we know from syncretism, namely that the vocative and nominative are treated similarly. The fact that the nominative may be substituted for the vocative suggests the nominative is the unmarked member of the pair.

There can also be evidence for markedness with respect to particular functions. Ramarao 1976, for instance, notes that in Telugu a verb cannot take a dative or instrumental unless it has an accusative. He argues that the accusative is unmarked with respect to the dative and the instrumental as a means of encoding complements.

Across languages the distribution of syncretism, stem-forming suffixes, case-marking formatives and a consideration of the syntactic distribution of cases reveals that the nominative/oblique, core/peripheral and non-local/local groupings are widespread. In Table 2.15 these are applied to Latin with oblique, peripheral and local being taken as positive. The vocative is set off from all the other cases by the feature [+ addressee] and the genitive is distinguished from the other peripheral cases by the feature [+ possessor].

It is interesting to note that this system of features, which is largely derived from data in a large number of languages, facilitates not only the capturing of pervasive syncretisms in Latin, but also a number of other generalisations about syntactic distribution.

The feature specification [– addressee] captures the set of adverbal cases, i.e. all the cases that can mark dependents of the verb.

The feature [– oblique] captures nominative-vocative syncretism and [+ oblique] captures the set of cases that can be adjuncts to verbs and which can be modifiers of participles and adjectives. In Latin a genitive, dative or ablative

Table 2.15 *Feature analysis of Latin case system*

	voc	nom	acc	gen	dat	abl
addressee	+	−	−	−	−	−
oblique	−	−	+	+	+	+
peripheral	−	−	−	+	+	+
local	−	−	+	−	−	+
possessor	−	−	−	+	−	−

phrase can be adnominal (see (10) below) but with adjectives and participles there is an extra possibility. There are phrases such as *nūdae lacertōs* (nude.NOM.PL arm.ACC.PL) 'bare as to the arms' where an accusative phrase is dependent on an adjective. This accusative of respect is in imitation of the Greek construction illustrated in (6) above. The feature [+ oblique] is also relevant to the gerund or verbal noun. The gerund can only be [+ oblique].[14]

The feature specification [− peripheral] captures the syncretism of nominative, vocative and accusative found in all neuters and in the plural of the third, fourth and fifth declensions. The specification [+ peripheral] captures the cases that can be adnominal:

(10)   a. genitive
              vir   magnī   ingeniī
              man   great.GEN   talent.GEN
              'a man of great talent'
          b. dative
              locus   rēgnō
              place   kingdom.DAT
              'a place for a kingdom'
          c. ablative
              vir   summā   prudentiā
              man   highest.ABL   prudence.ABL
              'a man of the greatest prudence'

The syncretism of the dative and ablative is captured with two features [+ peripheral] [− possessor]. This syncretism is found in all plurals and in the singular of the second declension and third declension *i*-stems.

The genitive-dative syncretism can be captured with the specification [+ oblique] [− local]. It occurs only in the singular of the first and fifth declensions and is therefore somewhat marginal, i.e. closer to being an accidental rather than systematic syncretism. Nevertheless genitive-dative syncretism is not uncommon across lan-

guages and since the proposed system is based on widely distributed properties of
language it can capture this syncretism fairly economically.

In the third declension singular *i*-stems there is nominative-genitive syncretism.
This is isolated and therefore regarded as accidental. The feature system is not
designed to capture this syncretism which is not common across languages.

The feature [+ local] covers accusative (which expresses 'to' and 'through') and
the ablative (which expresses 'in/at' and 'from').[15] These are the two cases that can
be governed by prepositions, and which can complete the valency of a verb like
ponere 'to put down'. They are also the only cases in which the supine can appear.
The supine is a nominal form derived from a verb. In the following sentences
admonitum and *dictū* are supines.

(11)   a. *Vēnimus   tē   admonitum*
             come.PERF.1PL   you.ACC   remind.ACC
             'We have come to remind you.'
         b. *Facilis   dictū*
             easy   say.ABL
             'easy to say'

It is clear that an analysis of cases in terms of features can facilitate generalisations covering classes of cases. The value of a feature analysis will depend, in part,
on the overall grammatical framework adopted for description. Here is an example
of how feature notation can be exploited in a Lexical-Functional Grammar framework. The example is from Neidle's description of case in Russian (1988).

In this language the object of the verb may be in the accusative or the genitive.
(This is quite a separate matter from the accusative/genitive syncretism referred to
above.) Neidle treats object case marking as something that is assigned structurally. The rule expanding the verb phrase is annotated to show case assignment
on the object,

(12)   VP   →   V   NP
                            (CASE = [-, (-), +])

(12) says that a verb phrase (VP) consists of a verb (V) and a noun phrase (NP).
This noun phrase has a case specified in terms of three features. These three feature
specifications refer to [± marginal], [± quantifying] and [± ascriptive] as in Table
2.13. Actually Neidle uses a different set of features in her 1988 description, but
this does not affect the issue in hand. The notation in (12) says that the noun phrase
in the verb phrase has case with a minus value for marginal and a plus value for
ascriptive. The value for quantifying, which will distinguish accusative and geni-

tive, is left unspecified (hence the round brackets), but is given a default value neg-ative which characterises the accusative. This notation neatly captures the pair accusative and genitive and the fact that the accusative is the unmarked option. Oversimplifying the facts we can say that the genitive is used for a non-specific object and generally for the object in a negative clause. Interestingly the accusative/genitive case alternation also shows up on time expressions (Neidle 1988: 10, 167).

(13)   a. *On   ne   spal   odnu   minutu*
            he   not   slept   one.ACC   minute.ACC
            'He did not sleep (= was awake) for one minute.'
        b. *On   ne   spal   odnoj   minuty*
            he   not   slept   one.GEN   minute.GEN
            'He did not sleep (even) for a minute.'

Neidle suggests that the case assignment is structural and applies to post-verbal noun phrases irrespective of whether they are objects. However, word order in Russian is grammatically fairly free, so the notion of structurally assigned case involves a basic subject-predicate structure which can be captured with rules of the type 'Sentence → NP VP, VP → V NP' with subsequent scrambling rules. The notion of assigning case structurally comes up again in section 3.3.

2.3.5 *Summary*

Traditionally cases are described as having a number of functions or meanings. The Greek or Latin accusative, for instance, would be said to express the direct object and to express the meaning of extent in place or time. There is another approach in which cases are seen as a system, each one having a single, general meaning. These general meanings are not self-sufficient; one cannot pre-dict from the generalised meaning to the set of contexts in which a case can be used. However, generalised meanings, or at least generalised characterisations, can form the basis for a componential analysis of case which enables one to capture similarities between sets of cases.

3

Modern approaches to case

3.1 Introduction

This chapter deals with themes that have come to the fore over the course of the last thirty years. Since the early sixties linguistics has been dominated by the theories of Chomsky. His influence is evident not only in works couched in a Chomskian framework, but in the Case Grammar of Fillmore, the Relational Grammar of Perlmutter and Postal and the Lexical Functional Grammar of Bresnan. These theories and indeed most of the thirty-odd theories that have been advanced over the last few decades have been provoked by and are a reaction to some facet of Chomsky's theoretical approach.

At the beginning of chapter 1 case was described as essentially a system for marking dependent nouns for the type of relationship they bear to their heads. It was pointed out that the term case traditionally referred to inflectional marking (section 1.1), but could be extended to cover prepositions and postpositions (section 1.2). Other means of signalling the type of relationship dependent nouns bear to their heads, such as word order, were referred to as 'competing mechanisms' (section 1.3). In recent theories the view has emerged, foreshadowed in Hjelmslev (1935: 21), that all these mechanisms may be used to signal case, that case is abstract existing independently of the means of expression, that it is universal. This view is described in section 3.3 below.

While attention has been focussed on what constitutes the expression side of case, even more attention has been paid to the question of determining what the relations are that cases express. A prominent theme has been the view that there is a small list of universal semantic roles such as agent, experiencer, patient and instrument (see section 3.4).

A third theme of the recent literature has been the notion of the hierarchy. Case marking, cases, semantic roles and grammatical relations can all be arranged hierarchically. This notion is described in the final section of the chapter (section 3.5).

As a preliminary to this review of recent approaches to case some data from Kalkatungu is presented (section 3.2) since this language affords a neat example of how grammatical relations can be distinguished from cases, how conflicting systems of organising the core can co-exist, and the issue of whether SP rather than SA could be described as subject.

3.2   Grammatical relations

In the previous chapter cases were described as having functions (e.g. object) or meaning (e.g. source). In the recent literature it has become common to talk of morpho-syntactically distinct grammatical relations. Grammatical relations may be semantically heterogeneous (the subject, for instance, typically expresses a variety of semantic roles including patient (*He got run over*), agent (*She did it*) etc.) or they may be homogeneous. Peripheral grammatical relations tend to be semantically homogeneous; the locative case relation, for instance, may encode just locations.

The notion of grammatical relations that are not in a one-for-one correspondence with morphological cases is not new. Among the grammarians of the Roman empire the question of recognising different semantic roles (which they called cases) within the Latin ablative was raised, but the criteria used tended to be intuitive or based on historical or comparative grounds (Calboli 1972: 106ff). Quintilian, for instance, distinguished the source role of the ablative from the location and instrument roles, because in Greek, which had lost its ablative, source was expressed by the genitive, and location and instrument were expressed by the dative (*Institutio oratoria*: 1.4.26). Using the insights of structuralist and more recent approaches to morpho-syntax, it is now possible to demarcate grammatical relations on more objective grounds.

3.2.1   *Distinct grammatical relations within one case*

Kalkatungu affords some good examples of how grammatical relations can be distinguished from cases. In this language there are two core cases, the ergative and the nominative. Intuitively the ergative would appear to encode the A of a transitive verb and the instrumental function. By the use of paradigmatic oppositions, one can show that A and instrumental are in fact distinct grammatical relations. In Kalkatungu there is an antipassive construction, which is used instead of the transitive construction to express action that is ongoing, habitual or characteristic, or activity directed towards a non-specific or generic patient.[1] In this derived construction a nominative-marked S corresponds to A and a dative to P. A transitive clause with two tokens of the ergative is illustrated in (1a). (1b) is a corresponding antipassive. Note how this derivation differentiates A and the instrumental. The ergative phrase encoding A in (1a) corresponds to the nominative in (1b), but the ergative phrase encoding the instrumental is unaffected by the derivation.

(1)   a. *Marapai-thu   rumpa-mi   ithirr   matyamirla-thu*
       woman-ERG   grind-FUT   seed.NOM   grindstone-ERG
       'The woman will grind the seed with the grindstone.'
      b. *Marapai   rumpa-yi-mi   ithirr-ku   matyamirla-thu*
       woman.NOM   grind-AP-FUT   seed-DAT   grindstone-ERG
       'The woman will grind seed with the grindstone.'

The reflexive in Kalkatungu is also a derived intransitive. Here the A of the transitive verb is re-expressed as S and P is deleted. An instrumental is unaffected.

(2)   a. *Marapai-thu   karri-mi   pirlapirla   thupu-ngku*
       woman-ERG   wash-FUT   child.NOM   soap-ERG
       'The woman will wash the child with soap.'
      b. *Marapai   karri-ti-mi   thupu-ngku*
       woman.NOM   wash-REFL-FUT   soap-ERG
       'The woman will wash with soap.'

An instrumental can appear with underived intransitives, but in the nature of things there are only a few possibilities such as *tyanparra-thu ingka* 'to walk with a stick'.

There is a kind of converse to the antipassive and reflexive in which the instrumental phrase rather than A can be re-expressed in the nominative, though as P rather than as S. This is illustrated in (3), which should be compared with (1a). The verb is marked by *-nti-*, which signals the advancement of instrumentals and locatives to the nominative. Note that the ergative phrase for A is unaffected. Note too that the P of the transitive verb *rumpa* is demoted to the dative.

(3)   *Marapai-thu   rumpa-nti-mi   matyamirla   ithirr-ku*
      woman-ERG   grind-IA-FUT   grindstone.NOM   seed-DAT
      'The woman will use the grindstone for [to grind] the seeds.'

There is another means of distinguishing the two types of ergative phrase in Kalkatungu. The number and person of an A phrase (or S phrase) but not an instrumental phrase can be represented on the verb. The third person plural form for S and A is *-na*; the third person singular form for S and A is *-ø*. In (4a) the instrumental phrase but not the A phrase is plural, so the verb is not overtly marked. In (4b) the A phrase as well as the instrumental phrase is plural and the third person plural A is marked on the verb.

(4) a. *Papi-yi   kati-mba   pirlapirla   malhtha-yi*
fa's.mo-ERG   cover-PERF   baby.NOM   many-ERG
kulapuru-thu
blanket-ERG
'Granny covered the baby with blankets.'

b. *Papi-mia-thu   kati-mba-na   pirlapirla   malhtha-yi*
fa's.mo-PL-ERG   cover-PERF-3PL   baby.NOM   many-ERG
kulapuru-thu
blanket-ERG
'The grannies covered the baby with blankets.'

The above illustration involves isolating a case morphologically and then demonstrating that there are syntactic grounds for saying that it expresses more than one relation. This raises the question of whether, in the absence of such evidence, a case expresses a single relation, or, in other words, whether every morphological case expresses at least one case relation. Typically with peripheral cases there is no syntactic evidence beyond the morphology. Peripherally marked noun phrases do not normally control agreement or missing subjects of infinitives, for instance. The view taken here is that each morphological case expresses at least one grammatical relation except where a number of cases are co-hyponyms or where the meaning of one is included in the meaning of another. In Kalkatungu, there is a *to*-case (allative) and a *towards*-case (allative II) (see Table 2.14). These both express destination, but differ with respect to whether the journey is seen as completed or not. One would not want to say they represented separate grammatical relations.

3.2.2 *Conflicting systems of organising the core*

Interestingly the system of bound pronouns in Kalkatungu is in conflict with the case system. While the core case system is organised on a nominative-ergative basis, the bound pronoun system operates on an SA/P basis. This is illustrated in the following set of examples. Note first the inflectional case system on noun phrases. The second person singular is represented by *nyini* in S function (5) and in P function (7). It is represented by *nyinti* (< *nyin-tu*) in A function (6). Now note the forms of the bound pronouns. We find -*ni* in S function (5) and A function (6), and -*kin* in P function (7). In these examples the bound pronouns are enclitic to an auxiliary particle (or auxiliary verb perhaps) which marks the purposive/future aspect. The SA form is glossed as the subject form and the P form as the object form (see also Table 3.2 for the system of marking).

(5)   *Nyini*   *a=ni*   *ingka?*
       you.NOM(S)   PURP=2SG.SUBJ   go
       'Are you going?'

(6)   *Nyin-ti*   *a=ni*   *nuwa?*
       you-ERG(A)   PURP=2SG.SUBJ   see
       'Do you want to see him/her/it?'

(7)   *Nyini*   *a=kin*   *nuw*a
       you.NOM(P)   PURP=2SG.OBJ   see
       'S/he wants to see you.'

A number of languages, probably the majority, are like Kalkatungu in having some kind of bound pronominal representation, usually on the lexical verb or on a grammatical (auxiliary) verb. I refer to these markers as bound pronouns. In some languages they can be analysed as clitics, i.e. as elements that are words from the syntactic point of view but which attach to a host phonologically (see (13) in chapter 1). In other languages they are better analysed as inflection. This is the traditional analysis of the representation of the person and number of the subject found in most Indo-European languages. A sample of the person/numbering in Latin is presented in Table 3.1.

An important question that arises with bound pronouns is whether they alone represent the core grammatical relations or whether both they and the noun phrases they coreference represent them jointly. In the traditional interpretation of Latin and Ancient Greek the representation of the subject on the verb was referred to as agreement, even though this marking could occur without there being any coreferent noun phrase. In the Indian interpretation of Sanskrit, however, the marking on the verb was taken to represent the subject, and the nominative noun phrase was taken to be an adjunct in a kind of apposition with it (see section 3.4.1 below). It seems to be the agreed interpretation of many languages with pronominal representation of all core relations on the verb that any noun phrases expressing core arguments are adjuncts in a kind of apposition with the bound pronouns and that the bound pronouns bear the grammatical relations. In these languages the noun phrases expressing the core arguments are generally unmarked. However, this does not seem to be an appropriate analysis for Kalkatungu where nouns in A function bear ergative case and where the nominative-ergative case distinction rather than the subject-object bound pronouns can be shown to be relevant to a number of syntactic rules. Moreover, bound pronouns are not used at all in some clauses. In these clauses the core arguments are represented solely by noun phrases, yet there is no reason to distinguish these clauses syntactically from those

Table 3.1 *Person/number marking in Latin*

	singular	plural
1st person	*habitō*	*habitāmus*
2nd "	*habitās*	*habitātis*
3rd "	*habitat*	*habitant*

with bound pronouns for the core arguments. What we appear to have is dual representation of the core relations in two different systems, an SA/P system with bound pronouns and an SP/A system with nouns. One could try to avoid this conclusion by taking the clitics to represent a nominal paradigm, then one would have two non-isomorphic paradigms and an alignment of the two on the basis of function would yield a system of three core cases: nominative, ergative (distinguished in the free nominal paradigm) and accusative (distinguished in the clitic paradigm). This analysis would be the same as that obtained by applying the traditional analysis to a language with ergative marking on nouns and accusative marking on free pronouns (see Table 2.4). However, there are certain disadvantages with such an analysis applied to nominals and clitics.

Let us consider first of all whole-part constructions, in particular, constructions involving a person and their body parts. In Kalkatungu, as in Australian languages generally, the possessor and the body part appear in parallel, both marked with the case appropriate to their semantic role in the clause.[2] The English sentence *The snake is crawling towards your leg* would be translated literally as 'The snake is crawling towards you, towards leg', and *Ants are crawling on your leg* would be 'Ants are crawling on you, on leg.' If a possessor and their body part are the patient of a transitive verb, then the possessor may be represented by an object clitic. In the following example the possessor is encoded both as an object clitic and by a noun phrase.

(8) *Ngayi* *a=ngi-(i)na* *itya* *milthi* *milnga-ngku*
  me.NOM PURP=1SG.OBJ-3PL.SUBJ bite eye.NOM fly-ERG
  'Flies are biting me [in the] eye(s).'

If we treat the clitic pronouns as a nominal paradigm and recognise an accusative case on the basis of the bound form for the object, then *ngayi* in (8) would be accusative but not *milthi*. To make this clear some free and bound forms have been aligned on the basis of function in Table 3.2. Only one ergative marker is shown and only two clitic paradigms. The forms *ngayi* and *ngi* in (8) correspond with the row labelled P and the form *milthi* corresponds with the row labelled 'other'.

Table 3.2 *Kalkatungu case and clitics*

function	noun, pronoun marking	clitics 1SG	2SG
S	-Ø	*lhaa*	*n(i)*
A	*-ngku*	*lhaa*	*n(i)*
P	-Ø	*ngi*	*kin*
other*	-Ø		

* See (8), (9) and (10)

This approach has the disadvantage of throwing up an apparent exception to the general rule that possessors and their body parts match in case, and has the further disadvantage of requiring the recognition of an extra case, an unmarked case for the body part (see the row labelled 'other' in Table 3.2). Note that this example is not parallel to the Pitjantjatjara example presented as (3) in chapter 2 where it was argued that an accusative should be recognised for all nominals if accusative marking appeared on some.

A similar problem arises with the double object construction. Kalkatungu is like English in having two constructions with the verb *anyi* 'to give', one in which the recipient is expressed as a destination (9a), and the other in which both the recipient and the gift are expressed in the case appropriate for P (9b),

(9) a. *Yanyi-ngku*   *a=ina*   *awa*   *ntia*
        white.man-ERG   PURP=3PL.SUBJ   give   money.NOM
        nga-tyinha
        me-ALL
        'The white men are going to give money to me.'

      b. *Yanyi-ngku*   *a=ngi=(i)na*   *ngai*
        white.man-ERG   PURP=1SG.OBJ=3PL.SUBJ   me.NOM
        awa   *ntia*
        give   money.NOM
        'The white men are going to give me money.'

Since the recipient is cross-referenced by an object clitic, I take it to be the direct object and the patient to be a secondary object. As with constructions involving possessors and body parts, taking the clitics to be a nominal paradigm would mean taking the recipient object to be accusative and the patient object to be nominative. This would hold not only in clauses where there was an object clitic, but even in clauses where the objects are represented only by noun phrases.

At this point it might be worth considering again just what a case is. Cases are categories into which the relations nouns bear to their heads are classified. Cases are not always in a one-for-one correspondence with grammatical relations. If that were the situation, we would deal only in relations and the word forms or markers that express these relations. If, for example, the nominative forms in Latin expressed only subject, the accusative only direct object, the dative only indirect object, and so on through the whole system, then we would talk of subject forms, direct object forms and indirect object forms. There would be no need for the notion of case, just as there is no need for notional categories between tense markers and tense categories or aspect markers and aspect categories.[3]

The problem with integrating a clitic system into a case-marking system is that the clitic system picks out particular grammatical relations. If syntactic data can be imported into morphological paradigms, adpositional systems or systems involving both inflectional case and adpositions, then we are confusing two classifications and destroying the opportunity to explicate the relationship between the two classifications.

The effect of the cross-cutting of the two systems of core grammar is illustrated in Table 3.3. As can be seen S is expressed by a nominative noun or a subject-bound pronoun, A by an ergative noun or a subject-bound pronoun. As illustrated in (4), an instrumental is expressed in the ergative, but cannot be expressed by a bound pronoun. P is expressed by a nominative noun and an object-bound pronoun. Note the top right-hand box labelled 'adjuncts and complements in the nominative case'. Here are some of the possibilities it covers:

(a) the secondary (patient) object in the double object construction as in (9)

(b) the body part adjunct to P in transitive clauses like (8)

(c) the body part adjunct to S in clauses like (10)

(10) *Nyini   arnka   unu=n   putu*
      you.NOM   ail   LEST=2SG stomach.NOM
      'You might get sick [in] the stomach.'

As we shall see in section 3.4.3, Relational Grammar treats these complements and adjuncts as having been displaced from the absolutive relation.

Although a comparison of the case system and the bound pronominal system isolates S, A and P, it is not necessary to refer to S in the grammar. Most of the syntactic rules refer to the absolutive grammatical relation (SP) (see section 3.2.3). The subject relation and object relations are manifest only in the bound pronoun system.

Table 3.3 *Case and case relations in Kalkatungu*

functions	case	bound pronouns	grammatical relations
			adjuncts & complements in nominative case
P	nominative	object	absolutive
S		subject	
A	ergative		ergative
			instrumental

3.2.3   The status of SP as a grammatical relation

In an accusative language S and A are identified by such characteristics as case, control of agreement on the verb, word order, and the fact that they are not normally expressed with non-finite verb forms. The SA combination is described as bearing the subject relation. In an ergative language S and P are identified via case and the question arises of whether they should be described as bearing the subject relation. Although a number of suggestions to this effect have been put forward over the last hundred years or so, they have not been numerous over the last generation. Some eschew the idea of calling SP subject because it would be confusing. Others point out that in most languages with a nominative-ergative case system, there are identifications of S and A in other parts of the grammar, in the case marking of pronouns, for instance, or in the bound pronoun system (as we have just seen in the previous section). They prefer to use the term subject for an alignment of S and A wherever it is found.

Kalkatungu, from what we have seen, has a subject-object bound pronoun system along with a nominative-ergative case system. However, it should be noted that the SA alignment shows up only in the bound pronoun system; elsewhere it is the relation we are calling absolutive (i.e. SP) that prevails:

(a)   a purpose clause must be detransitivised if its A is coreferent with the absolutive of the governing clause (illustrated in (50) and (51) of chapter 4)

(b) in an infinitive clause it is the absolutive that is unexpressed (illustrated in (23) in chapter 6)

(c) only the absolutive can be relativised.

This last point is illustrated in (11), (12) and (13), at least as far as S, A and P are concerned. Each example contains a subordinate clause with a participial form of the verb. In (11) the relativised function in the subordinate clause is S which remains covert and is represented here by [ ],

(11) *Ngulurrmayi-nha nga-thu yurru*   [ ] *ngartathati-nyin*
      grab-PAST   I-ERG   man.NOM   sit-PARTICIPLE
      'I grabbed the man [as he was/who was] sitting down.'

In (12) the relativised function is P so P remains covert,

(12) *Ngulurrmayi-nha nga-thu yurru*   [ ] *thuku-yu itya-nyin*
      grab-PAST   I-ERG   man.NOM   dog-ERG   bite-PART
      'I grabbed the man [as he was/who was] being bitten by a dog.'

However, if any role that is not normally encoded as absolutive is to be relativised, then a derived verb must be used. In order to say 'I grabbed the man as he was hitting the dog', where the relativised function is an agent which would normally be expressed as A, an antipassive derivation must be used. In this construction S corresponds to the A of a transitive verb and a dative to P (See (1b) above). S in the following example is, of course, covert.

(13) *Ngulurrmayi-nha nga-thu yurru*   [ ] *thuku-u lha-yi-nyin*
      grab-PAST   I-ERG   man.NOM   dog-DAT hit-AP-PART
      'I grabbed the man [as he was/who was] hitting the dog.'

Clearly the absolutive (SP) plays a part analogous to that played by SA in an accusative language. Clearly SP is the primary grammatical relation, the privileged relation in that it is the only one that can be relativised. This being so, the antipassive is a derivation that allows A access to the privileged relation and indeed it was this that inspired Silverstein to choose the term antipassive; it is the analogue in an ergative system of the passive (Silverstein 1976).

Since ergative languages often exhibit SA alignments in parts of their grammar and since many ergative languages seem to be only superficially ergative in that they exhibit an SP/A alignment only in case marking, I do not use the term subject for the grammatical relation embracing S and P. I follow what is fairly widespread practice in calling it the absolute relation and I recognise that in some ergative languages the absolutive is the primary grammatical relation.

Although it has not been popular to use the term subject for SP even in languages where SP is not only in the unmarked case but clearly the privileged grammatical relation, there are formal analyses that effectively take SP to be subject. The first was Dixon's analysis of another Australian language Dyirbal (Dixon 1972). Casting the language into a Chomskian model, in which the sentence is first divided into NP (functioning as subject) and VP (functioning as predicate), Dixon took the NP immediately dominated by the sentence node in a transitive clause to be P and the NP immediately dominated by the VP to be A (Figure 3.1).

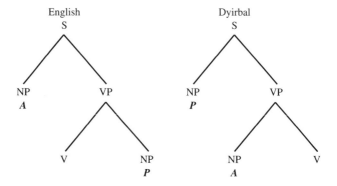

Figure 3.1 English and Dyirbal contrasted

The analysis offered for Dyirbal would be applied to any language in which S and P were identified syntactically, i.e. to any language which has ergative syntax. Analyses along similar lines have also been offered by Marantz (1984) and Levin (1987).

One last point about grammatical relations. I believe that the term double object construction can be applied in Kalkatungu, since a direct object can be picked out by the object series of clitics. I take the patient in examples like (9b) to be a secondary object, since it is marked like an object and it is a complement (as opposed to the similarly marked body-part noun phrases as in examples like (8)). For the purposes of most syntactic rules the direct object is subsumed under the larger relation of absolutive. In a language with a nominative-ergative case system, no object-bound pronouns, and syntactic rules based on the absolutive, the term object and more so the term double object is impossible to justify on internal grounds. Yalarnnga, Kalkatungu's southern neighbour, appears to have been such a language, although it must be admitted that the evidence for syntactic ergativity is meagre. It has a construction with *nguny-* 'to give' that is analogous to the Kalkatungu construction illustrated in (9b) but without the auxiliary.

3.3   Abstract case

Even in languages with inflectional case systems, case is quite often abstract in the sense that it is not always realised by a distinctive inflectional form or marker. In English there is an inflectional case system, which is confined to personal pronouns (*I/me, he/him,* etc.) and *who/whom* for some speakers. One could take the view that all nominals in English take case, but that it is realised morphologically only on personal pronouns. Under this view the abstract nature of case becomes quite apparent, because only a subclass of nominals show any marking. Some linguists take the view that case is universal. This involves taking all means of indicating the relationship of dependent nouns to their heads to be potential markers of case. However, as noted in section 3.2.2, one such mechanism, namely the use of bound pronouns on the head of a construction to mark grammatical relations, tends to involve systems in which there is a one-for-one correspondence between marking and relation. The notion of case is useful only where cases can express more than one relation. There is a danger in the notion of universal, abstract case of confusing case with grammatical relations.

Abstract case is found in a number of other recent theories. In Chomsky's Government and Binding model case theory, which is largely about abstract rather than morphological case, is an important module or component of the grammar. In this theory a distinction is made between **structural case** and **inherent case**.[4] Structural case is assigned to noun phrases according to their position in a structural configuration.[5] As we have seen in the previous section, Chomsky takes the basic structure of a sentence (S) to consist of a noun phrase (NP) functioning as subject and a verb phrase (VP) functioning as predicate.[6] The VP consists minimally of a verb (V) (Figure 3.2a). If the verb is transitive, there will be an NP within the VP functioning as its object (Figure 3.2b).

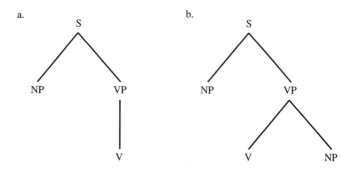

Figure 3.2 Basic clause structure

59

The verb assigns accusative case to the NP it governs, namely the object NP. Simplifying we can say that the finite verb assigns nominative case to the subject NP. The assignment is actually by an abstract element INFL (from INFLection), which is realised within the verb, but that is a complication we can avoid here.

Where there are case assignments peculiar to particular verbs or sets of verbs, these assignments are held to be inherent. In German, for instance, most two-place verbs take an accusative complement, but a few take a dative complement. The default assignment is accusative and this can be handled structurally, but the assignment of dative needs to be specified in the lexicon for particular verbs and therefore is taken to be inherent.

The contrast between structural and inherent case shows up in passivisation. If a verb with a structurally assigned accusative (as in (14a)) is passivised, the direct object is held to move from the VP to the subject position where it is assigned nominative case by the finite verb (14b). However, where a verb with a dative complement (15a) is passivised, the dative marking remains (15b) (Haegeman 1991: 174f).

(14)　　a. *Sie*　　　*sieht*　　*ihn*　　　b. *Er*　　　*wird*　　*gesehen*
　　　　　she.NOM　sees　him.ACC　　　he.NOM　is　　seen
　　　　　'She sees him.'　　　　　　　　'He is seen.'

(15)　　a. *Sie*　　　*hilft*　　*ihm*　　　b. *Ihm*　　　*wird*　　*geholfen*
　　　　　she.NOM　helps　him.DAT　　　him.DAT　is　　helped
　　　　　'She helps him.'　　　　　　　　'He is helped.'

Clearly there is a contrast, but in many analyses (15b) would be taken to be an impersonal passive with no overt subject and *ihm* in (15b) would be taken to hold the same grammatical relation as in the active (15a).

Verbs and adpositions regularly assign case, but rarely receive it.[7] Adjectives and nouns regularly receive case, but do not assign it in all languages. Van Riemsdijk has suggested that there is a hierarchy of case assigners (1983: 249),

(16)　　　　verb > preposition > adjectives > nouns

He also suggests that case assigners lower on the hierarchy are more likely to assign a case nearer to the oblique end of the hierarchy of cases. Where adjectives and nouns assign case, it is typically the dative or genitive rather than the accusative.

Nouns and adjectives are not considered to be structural case assigners normally. A phrase such as *proud John* as in **Dad is proud John* is considered ungrammatical because *John* has not been assigned case. All noun phrases must be assigned case. However, the phrase in question can be saved by the insertion of *of* to yield *Dad is proud of John. Of* is regarded as a meaningless case marker for the abstract genitive case. Note, however, that *of*, like all other prepositions in English, governs the accusative morphological case: *Dad is proud of him.*

Genitive case is held to be inherent rather than structural. Consider the following example,

(17)   **Dad is proud [John to be a winner]*

This cannot be turned into a grammatical English sentence by the insertion of *of*. Intuitively the reason is clear. Dad is not said to be proud of John, but of the content of the proposition [*John to be the winner*]. The adjective is taken to be an inherent case assigner rather than a structural case assigner. A structural case assigner is sensitive only to structure, whereas an inherent case assigner is sensitive also to semantic roles (called theta roles in Government and Binding Theory). An inherent case assigner can assign case only where it assigns a semantic role. In (17) the role for the complement of *proud* applies to the clause shown in brackets, not just to *John*.

In Government and Binding there are a number of levels of representation of which two need to be noted here: D-structure and S-structure. These correspond closely to the deep structure and surface structure respectively of Chomsky's earlier models of grammar (Chomsky 1965). The S-structure is pretty much the actual structure of a sentence and the D-structure is an hypothesised structure more closely reflecting semantic structure. It may differ from S-structure in order, for instance, or in the absence of meaningless elements like the preposition *of* in phrases like *proud of John*. Structural case assignment is made in S-structure and inherent case assignment in D-structure. Structural case assignment depends on a configuration of the kind shown in Figure 3.2 above, i.e. a structure with a VP (the order within VP is immaterial). However, such a structure cannot be found in the surface structures of various languages. In Welsh and the other Celtic languages, for instance, the basic word order is verb-subject-object where the verb and object are not adjacent to form a constituent. In many languages, including a majority of Australian languages, word order is pragmatically determined, i.e. rules order phrases according to their discourse status (focus, topic, comment) rather than relational status (subject, object, etc.) or categorial status (noun, verb, etc.). In Government and Binding the configuration shown in Figure 3.2 is held to be universal at least in D-structure. It can be modified or scrambled to form S-structure. Under the assumption of a universal D-structure structural assignment of case can be ascribed to any language, but the level at which the assignment is made would naturally differ.

In Government and Binding Theory an infinitive is considered unable to assign case to its subject, so a sentence like (18a) is held to be ungrammatical since *have* cannot assign case to *her*. (18a) can be rescued, however, by the addition of a preposition as in (18b) where *for* is considered to assign accusative case to *her*,

(18)   a. *[[*Her to have to chop the wood*] *was just too much*]
          b. [[*For* [*her to have to chop the wood*]] *was just too much*]

Where an infinitival clause functions as a complement, a noun phrase like *him* in (19) is taken to be the subject of the infinitive and to receive its accusative case from the finite governing verb.[8]

(19)   *We believed* [*him to be the culprit*]

(18b) and (19) are examples of **exceptional case marking** in that case is assigned outside the normal scope of government or, to put it another way, case is assigned across what is normally a barrier, in these instances the boundary of an infinitival clause. The assumed boundaries are shown by bracketing in (18a), (18b) and (19).

Latin provides a useful example of a verb assigning both inherent and structural case and making an exceptional case assignment. The verb *crēdere* 'to believe, to trust' takes a dative complement for the entity believed (in) or trusted and less frequently an accusative complement, i.e. a direct object, for what is believed or admitted. It also takes an 'accusative and infinitive construction' as a complement as in (20),

(20)   *Crēdidimus*   *Iovem*   *regnāre*
          believe.PERF.1PL   Jove.ACC   reign.INF
          'We believed Jupiter to reign.'

Crēdere would need to be allotted three lexical entries. In one a dative complement would be specified. This would be an instance of inherent case assignment. In a second an NP complement would be specified and in a third an infinitival clause complement. No case would be assigned in the second and third entries. The accusative would be assigned structurally as a default and where an infinitival clause complement occurred as in (20) the exceptional case-marking principle would apply to assign the accusative to the noun phrase functioning as the subject of the infinitive. Since Latin is a language where word order is determined largely by pragmatic considerations, this would be another example of a language where structural case assignment would take place in D-structure.

The discussion of case theory in Government and Binding is not as yet comprehensive and a number of points remain obscure or problematic.

A basic tenet of Government and Binding is that case is universal, but it is realised fully in morphological terms only in some languages. The degree of morphological realisation is said to vary from one language to another (Haegeman 1991: 144), and it is claimed that there should be no conflict between abstract case and morphological case (van Riemsdijk and Williams 1986: 230), though there is a kind of conflict in a phrase like *proud of John* if *of* is taken to be the realisation of an abstract genitive case, since *of* governs the accusative morphological case.

In the present work it has been assumed that cases can only be determined on the basis of marking of some kind. If we accept this assumption, then the notion of abstract case would appear to be incompatible. However, if we note that all idiosyncratic marking is assigned inherently, all we are left with is the structural assignment of nominative to the subject of a finite verb, accusative to the object of a verb and perhaps to the object of a preposition. Structural case emerges as a default case assigned where no inherent case has been assigned. Accepting the notion of structural case is then largely dependent on accepting the structure presented in Figure 3.2 as being universal at some level. The question remains, however, of how the default cases are determined. Is nominative always assigned to the noun phrase immediately dominated by the S node? What about a language with ergative case? If there is reason to believe the language is syntactically ergative, then such an assignment will make sense, but it will be the P rather than the A of a transitive verb that is realised by the NP immediately dominated by the sentence node (see Figure 3.1). A further question arises of whether the NP immediately dominated by VP will be assigned ergative (see section 3.2.3).[9]

And what of a superficially ergative language, i.e. one where S and A align in various rules of syntax, but where A bears ergative marking? Will the ergative be assigned inherently?

Examples of other data that will prove problematic for case assignment in Government and Binding are to be found in chapter 4. They include multiple case marking (25) to (29), concordial case replacing relational case (30) and special case marking in subordinate clauses (41).

3.4   Semantic roles and grammatical relations

Since the late 1960s a number of theories have been put forward claiming that the semantic relationships borne by nominal dependents to their governors make up a small, universal set. Since obviously there is a great deal of variation between languages as to how many cases and adpositions they have, the semantic relationships that are posited are not always reflected directly in the morpho-syntax. Theories positing a universal set of semantic relations include

Fillmore's proposal for Case Grammar (1968, 1971), John Anderson's Localist Case Grammar (1971, 1977), Starosta's Lexicase (1971, 1988) and Dik's Functional Grammar (1978).

All modern theories allow for some kind of semantic relations that are not always reflected directly in the morpho-syntax, but they differ in the extent to which they use syntactic rather than semantic evidence to isolate the semantic relations. There is also a lot of confusing variation in the terminology. Fillmore began by positing a universal set of relations with traditional case-like labels (agentive, instrumental, dative, factitive, locative, objective) (1968: 24–5), but later switched to agent, experiencer, instrument, object, source, goal, place and time, which, except for object, are more semantically transparent and less confusible with traditional case labels (1971). He called these 'syntactic-semantic relations' cases and his conception of grammar and its congeners came to be referred to as case grammar (1968: 19). It has become common over the last generation to refer to Fillmorean-type cases as deep cases and traditional cases as surface cases. The most widespread terms for purely semantic relations are semantic roles, case roles, thematic roles (Lexical Functional Grammar) and theta roles (as in Government and Binding).[10] I will use **semantic role** or simply **role** for a semantic relation.

These semantic roles need to be distinguished from **grammatical relations** (see section 1.1). On the basis of formal distinctions made in case, agreement, word order, adpositions and the like we can isolate a number of grammatical relations. Some of these relations are purely syntactic: subject, object, indirect object, ergative and absolutive, each of which subsumes a number of roles. Other relations are semantically homogeneous. It is not uncommon to find, for instance, that locative and instrumental are demarcated by case. In this situation grammatical relation and semantic role coincide. Some roles such as agent, experiencer and patient are normally subsumed under purely syntactic relations and can usually only be isolated by semantic tests. Some roles such as instrument and location, which are typically expressed outside the purely syntactic relations, can sometimes be expressed via a purely syntactic relation. An example of the instrumental being expressed via the absolutive relation in Kalkatungu was given in (3) above.

As noted in section 1.1 the term **case relation** also appears in the literature. For some it is synonymous with grammatical relation as described above (e.g. in Silverstein 1976), but it is perhaps more frequently used with reference to the syntactic-semantic relations posited in certain theories. In this text it will be confined to the relations of Localist Case Grammar (section 3.4.4) and Lexicase (section 3.4.5).

The notion of a set of 'syntactic-semantic relations' that have some independence from noun phrase marking is not entirely new. In fact relations of this type are to be found in the work of the ancient Indian grammarian Pāṇini, so it is appropriate to discuss these briefly before discussing the work of recent decades.

3.4.1 *Pāṇini and kāraka theory*

Pāṇini's grammar of Sanskrit is known as the Aṣṭādhyāyī ('eight books'). Its date is uncertain with estimates ranging from 600 BC to 300 BC. It is a work of great sophistication clearly deriving from a lengthy tradition and it has provided a model for the study of language in greater India down to the present day. Bloomfield described Pāṇini's grammar as 'one of the greatest monuments of human intelligence' (1933: 11). As is well known, the 'discovery' of Sanskrit by European scholars in the late eighteenth century and the realisation that it is genetically related to Greek and Latin provided great stimulus to comparative-historical linguistics. It has also been claimed that familiarity with Pāṇini and the ancient Indian tradition helped raise the level of sophistication in descriptive linguistics; however, the aspect of Pāṇini's theory that we are concerned with here, namely kāraka theory, has not been influential though discussed by various scholars (Cardona 1976a: 215ff).

Kārakas are semantic relations holding between nouns and verb. The verb is held to be the head of the clause and each nominal dependent is assigned to one of six kārakas. These kārakas are listed in (21) with their common translations. The term 'object' is unfortunate since it suggests a purely syntactic relation. A term like patient would have been more appropriate.

(21)   **kartṛ**   agent
               karman   object
               karaṇa   instrument
               sampradāna   destination
               apādāna   source
               adhikaraṇa   locus

To appreciate the significance of kārakas it is useful to compare them with the case system of Sanskrit, since the cases are obviously the main means of expressing kārakas. In Sanskrit there are eight cases, all of which are distinguished in the singular of masculine *a*-stems. In Pāṇini's grammar and in the Indian tradition generally they are numbered as in Table 3.4 and often referred to by their numbers.

The vocative does not mark a dependent of the verb and therefore a vocative-marked noun bears no kāraka. The genitive is held to be adnominal and so no kāraka is assigned to genitive-marked nouns. However, the genitive does have one adverbal function, namely to mark the complement of a small number of verbs as in: *mātuḥ smara-ti* (mother.GEN remember-3SG) 'S/he remembers his/her mother' (Filliozat 1988: 86). With the other six cases there are regular associations of case and kāraka as follows:

Table 3.4 *Sanskrit nominal declension as represented by deva- 'god'*

1	*devas*	nominative
2	*devam*	accusative
3	*devena*	instrumental
4	*devāya*	dative
5	*devāt*	ablative
6	*devasya*	genitive
7	*deve*	locative
8	*deva*	vocative

(22)

nominative	*kartṛ*	agent
accusative	*karman*	object
instrumental	*karaṇa*	instrument
dative	*saṃpradāna*	destination
ablative	*apādāna*	source
locative	*adhikaraṇa*	locus

This list is, however, misleading insofar as it suggests a one-for-one correspondence between case and kāraka and in that it suggests the nominative expresses a kāraka. A consideration of an active sentence and its passive counterpart demonstrates how the one-for-one association needs qualification.

(23)   *Devadatta   odana-m   paca-ti*
        Devadatta.NOM   rice-ACC   cook-3SG
        'Devadatta cooks the rice.'

(24)   *Devadatt-ena   pac-ya-te   odana-ḥ*
        Devadatta-INST   cook-PASS-3SG   rice-NOM
        'The rice has been cooked by Devadatta.'

The person marking on a finite verb is held to encode a kāraka, in the active the *kartṛ*. The nominative is held to encode only the denotation of the person marker on the verb. Since the nominative-marked noun refers to the same denotatum as the person marker in the verb (*-ti* in (23)), it names the referent holding the kāraka of *kartṛ* (agent). In the active the accusative encodes the *karman*. In the passive the person marker on the verb is interpreted as encoding the *karman*. The nominative in cross-reference with this person marker (*-te* in (24)) names the *karman*. The instrumental encodes the *kartṛ*.

A consideration of the passive then demonstrates that there is no one-for-one correspondence between case and kāraka and that the nominative does not encode a kāraka. However, Pāṇini's treatment of the passive can give the misleading impression that kārakas are like the deep cases or semantic roles of modern theories, which tend to remain constant under paraphrase. Consider now the following pair and their interpretation (Cardona 1976b: 22–4):

(25)   *Bhūmāv*   *ās-te*   *Devadatta-ḥ*
            ground.LOC   sit-3SG   Devadatta-NOM
            'Devadatta is sitting on the ground.'

(26)   *Bhūmi-m*   *adhy-ās-te*   *Devadatta-ḥ*
            ground-ACC   on-sit-3SG   Devadatta-NOM
            'Devadatta is sitting on the ground.'

Both these sentences can refer to the same objective reality in which *Devadatta* refers to the person sitting and *bhūmi* to the location. In (25) *bhūmi* is encoded in the locative and interpreted as expressing *adhikaraṇa* (locus). In (26) the transitive verb *adhyās-* (*adhi* 'on' + *ās* 'sit') is used. *Bhūmi* is in the accusative and interpreted as expressing *karman*. There are a number of examples like this available that show Pāṇini distinguished the linguistic encoding of events from objective reality, that is, he allowed for more than one semantic interpretation of an event. I have not been able to ascertain exactly what the difference in semantic interpretation is between (25) and (26), but there are similar pairs to be found in a variety of languages including Latin, English, Indonesian and Kalkatungu where the effect of advancing a locative to direct object is to add a sense of affecting an entity. English examples are given in (34) and (51) below. A Latin example is given in note 5 to chapter 6.

3.4.2 *Fillmore*

      Fillmore is responsible for bringing to the fore the notion that there is a universal set of atomic semantic roles. In his seminal paper *The Case for Case*, published in 1968, he proposed a set of six 'cases', which he later revised and extended to eight (see section 3.4). These 'cases' were deep-structure cases, described as being 'underlying syntactic-semantic relationships'. They were to be distinguished from 'case forms', which comprise the means of expressing cases: suffixes, suppletion, adpositions, etc. (Fillmore 1968: 21ff). Sets of roles similar to Fillmore's can be found in the writings of other linguists including Halliday 1967–8, Chafe 1970, Longacre 1976, Dik 1978 and Cook 1979.

      To establish a universal set of semantic roles is a formidable task. Although some roles are demarcated by case or by adpositions in some languages, in many instances they have to be isolated by semantic tests. There are no agreed criteria and there is certainly no consensus on the universal inventory. To a great extent establishing roles and ascribing particular arguments to roles involves an extra-linguistic classification of relationships between entities in the world. There tends to be agreement on salient manifestations of roles like agent, patient, source and instrument, but problems arise with the classification of relationships that fall between the salient ones. There are also problems with determining how fine the classification should be. Consider, for instance, an entity that is presented as the material from which something is made, as in *She made the bowl from clay*. The notion is conceptually distinct, but there is not normally any marking specific to this notion. On the other hand, since it is encoded differently in different languages, for instance, in the ablative or the instrumental, then it needs to be recognised in a cross-language comparison. It is not proposed to deal with these problems here, but the following list of roles is offered as a checklist of roles that have been frequently distinguished in the literature. It also represents a list of the roles mentioned in the present text, and on a few points it reflects my own preferences.

patient

Almost all inventories of semantic relations include a role that covers the following:

    (i)   an entity viewed as existing in a state or undergoing change:
        The sky *is blue*
        The flame *grew bright*

    (ii) an entity viewed as located or moving:
        The lion *is in the cave*
        The stone *moved*
        He moved **the stone**

    (iii) an entity viewed as affected or effected by an entity:
        The bird ate **the worm**
        The bird sang **a song**

Fillmore called this role object, later objective; Gruber called it theme; others have called it goal and patient.[11] The labels objective and object are unsatisfactory in that they are confusible with a case label and a label for a grammatical relation respectively. The label theme, which derives from Gruber's 1965 dissertation (see also Gruber 1976), is also unsatisfactory since the term had been established earlier in Prague School linguistics for a discourse-pragmatic function. The label goal is sometimes used for the role that I call destination, so it too is less than ideal. The label patient is the most widely used of the various alternatives, even if it is not appropriate for all the examples to which it is applied (like those in (i) and the first two in (ii)). A number of linguists in fact make a distinction between theme and patient using theme for (i) and (ii) and patient for (iii). Others combine them under the label patient/theme. In this text I use the term patient, qualifying it where necessary as affected patient, effected patient or neutral patient. It could be said that such a patient is more like a syntactic entity than a semantic one, but I doubt whether one needs to subdivide it to cater for a contrast within the clause (see also the discussion of (27) below). The patient, in the wider sense, is a fundamental role in that it has the closest semantic relationship with the predicate. A number of linguists including Gruber (1976: 38) have claimed that it is an obligatory role, though that would not appear to be true for a small number of one-place predicates such as SHOUT and URINATE. In the case of predicates of bodily emanation there is a patient (the emanated substance), but it is not expressed as an argument (Blake 1982).

agent
The entity that performs an activity or brings about a change of state.

> **The robots** *assembled the car*
> **The crowd** *applauded*
> **The sun** *melted the ice*
> *The race was won by* **the favourite**

instrument
The means by which an activity or change of state is carried out.

> *She squashed the spider with* **a slipper**

experiencer
The creature experiencing an emotion or perception.

> **They** *love music*
> **They** *see everything*

Some writers distinguish the perceiver or cogniser of verbs like *see* or *hear* from the experiencer of verbs like *love*. The perceiver is almost always aligned syntactically with the agent, whereas the experiencer is often treated differently (see the brief discussion of inversion in section 3.4.3). In some Northeast Caucasian languages the perceiver is treated differently from both the agent and the experiencer. See (6), (7) and (8) in chapter 5.

location
The position of an entity. The view taken here is that location and the other local roles can refer to time as well as place. Some linguists, however, including Fillmore and Dik, distinguish temporal and spatial roles.

> *The vase is on/under/near **the table***
> *Australia Day fell on **a Tuesday***

source
The point from which an entity moves or derives.

> *They got news from **home***
> *Since **June** everything has been all right*

path
The course over which an entity moves.

> *The dog chased the cat along the **path** and through the **conservatory***
> *They managed to survive through **the drought***

destination
The point to or towards which an entity moves or is oriented.

> *He turned to the **altar** and walked towards **it***
> *She slept till **dawn***

The terms **direction** and **goal** are alternatives, but the meaning of the former is not transparent and the latter has also been used for patient/theme and for recipient.

recipient
A sentient destination.

> *She gave her spare change to **the collectors***

purpose
The purpose of an activity.

> *He went to the Red Rooster for **some take-away***

beneficiary
The animate entity on whose behalf an activity is carried out.

> *She did the shopping for **her mother***

manner
The way in which an activity is done or the way in which a change of state takes place.

> *He did it with **great skill***

extent

The distance, area or time over which an activity is carried out or over which a state holds.

> *It lasted **the winter***
> *He ran (for) **three miles***

possessor

The entity that possesses another entity.

> *I saw **John's** golf clubs*

Although there is no consensus on the universal inventory of roles, linguists tend to adhere to a common set of practices in ascribing roles:

- (a) the inventory is kept small
- (b) a role can be assigned only once in a clause
- (c) no dependent can bear more than one role
- (d) roles remain constant under paraphrase.

Keeping the inventory small

All the inventories of roles that have been proposed are fairly small, usually about the same as the number of cases found in a typical case language, i.e. between six and ten or so. Where complements are concerned there is an obvious relationship between the meaning of the verb and the role of its arguments. The verb *hit* implies a hitter and a hitee, the verb *scrape* implies a scraper and a scrapee, and so on. No one, of course, suggests treating hitter and scraper as separate roles, rather one abstracts the notion of agent. Similarly no one suggests taking hitee and scrapee to be separate roles; one abstracts the notion of patient. The problem, however, is to determine how broad the roles are to be. Consider the verb *watch* as in *The pelican watched the fish*. The pelican can be described as an agent, but the fish is not a patient in the sense of an entity that is affected by an activity (at least it is not necessarily affected), and some would describe it as bearing the role of theme (see above). However, the affected patient of *hit* and the unaffected or neutral patient of *watch* do not contrast syntagmatically nor are they opposed paradigmatically, so one can treat them as sharing the same role. If one does this, one is exploiting a principle of complementary distribution, which is just what languages do. It is also efficient to take this step, since the only function the roles of complements can play in the grammar is to indicate the orientation of a verb.[12] Consider, for instance, the following sentence and its French translation:

(27)   a. *He misses   you   very   much*
        experiencer   patient
     b. *Tu   lui   manques   beaucoup*
        pat   exp

With the English verb *miss* the subject expresses the experiencer of the feeling of loss and the direct object expresses the neutral patient. With the French verb *manquer*, when used in the corresponding sense, the subject encodes the neutral patient and the indirect object (*lui*) encodes the experiencer. Obviously grammars need to indicate which grammatical relation encodes which role, but to do that they do not need certain distinctions such as the one between affected patient and unaffected patient or theme. Of course if one exploits the complementary distribution fully, one tends to wind up with syntactic entities rather than semantic ones.

While an exploration of the syntactic relations raises questions of how many distinctions are needed, an examination of adpositions raises the opposite issue of how few are required. The set of adpositions found in many languages runs to forty or so members and in some Fennic and Northeast Caucasian languages the case systems approach this figure. Most of the forms making up these sets are local, expressing notions such as 'above', 'below', 'near', 'on' etc. If one were to take these as expressing separate roles, the inventory would be much larger than it typically is. It is clear that one cannot take all these local forms to represent separate roles and maintain the notion of atomic roles. These local forms can be analysed in terms of the notions of source, location, path and destination plus markers of relative orientation such as 'above', 'below', etc. See also Table 5.4.

Once per clause

The notion that each role can be assigned only once per clause is generally agreed. However, it needs to be interpreted as allowing co-ordination (*Jack and Jill went up the hill*) and multiple specification of a particular location (*It is on the shelf, to the left, behind the door*). Where nominals stand in apposition they may share a role, but it could be argued that only one of the apposed nominals is in the clause proper. In any event apposed nominals are coreferent, so only one referent is understood as bearing the role assigned.[13] Multiple assignment of a role is, however, a feature of John Anderson's Localist Case Grammar. Examples are given in section 3.4.4.

No dependent with more than one role

Most linguists adhere to the principle that each dependent bears but a single role to its governor, but certain verbs have been discussed as providing a challenge. These include the pair *buy* and *sell*. Consider the following assignment of roles:

(28)   *Fred   bought   the   book   from   John*
         agent   patient   source

(29)   *John   sold   the   book   to   Fred*
         agent   patient   destination

In (28) Fred is an agent in that he initiates an activity; the book is a patient in that it passes from the possession of John to Fred, and John is marked as the source from whom the book passes. In (29) John is an agent in that he initiates an activity; the book is a patient, and Fred is marked as a destination. However, some have pointed out that Fred is a destination in (28) in that he receives the book and John is a source in (29) in that the book passes from him. But if one takes this view one would also have to consider the passage of the money in the opposite direction from the book.[14] It would seem superfluous to extract all these roles which are entailed in the definitions of the two verbs. The ascription of the role of agent to the subject and patient to the object, however, links *buy* and *sell* to the large class of activity verbs, but if these verbs are marked [+ activity] even the specification of agent and patients is predictable as the default role for the subject and object respectively of an activity verb.

Roles constant under paraphrase

In the generally accepted tradition roles may be identified across paraphrases and across translational equivalents; they are independent of expression (cf. Agud 1980: 456). Fillmore would identify an agent expressed as subject with a dative of agent or an ablative of agent (1968: 19). All these possibilities can be found in Latin where the dative is used with the gerundive[15] and the ablative with the passive (though the ablative can be used with the gerundive where ambiguity threatens and the dative is a possibility with the passive).

agent as subject
(30)   *Mīlitēs   hanc   provinciam   dēfendērunt*
         troops.NOM   this.ACC   province.ACC   defend.PERF.3PL
         'The troops defended this province.'

passive with the ablative of agent
(31)   *Haec   provincia   ā   mīlitibus   dēfensa   est*
         this.NOM   province.NOM   by   troops.ABL   defended.NOM   is
         'This province has been defended by troops.'

gerundive with dative of agent

(32)	*Haec*	*mihi*	*provincia*	*est*	*dēfendenda*
	this.NOM	1SG.DAT	province.NOM	is	defend.GERUNDIVE.NOM

'This province is to be defended by me.'

An active sentence and its passive counterpart are normally taken to be synonymous in terms of propositional content though different in terms of discourse-pragmatic structure. *Mīlitēs* would be taken to be agent in both (30) and (31), but in the active *mīlitēs* has no marking that is peculiar to a role; the nominative marks the subject grammatical relation encoding several roles such as agent, experiencer and patient. In the passive, however, *mīlitēs* appears in the ablative governed by *ā/ab* (the latter variant being obligatory before vowel-initial words) which means 'from': *ab eō locō* 'from that place'. In the normal practice of modern grammarians of virtually all schools the choice of case and/or adposition is disregarded in a situation like this. The preposition *ā/ab* is not interpreted as having its normal meaning, but is regarded as a grammatical marker.

The use of *ā/ab* plus the ablative to express the agent of the passive makes an interesting comparison with the following example where the clause with the ablative of agent is not passive (*De Bello Gallico* 1:20, 4 via Rubio 1966: 89).

(33)	*Sī*	*quid*	*eī*	*ā*	*Caesāre*	*gravius*
	if	anything	3SG.DAT	from	Caesar.ABL	more.serious.NEUT
	accidisset...					
	happen.PPERF.SUBJ.3SG					

'If anything drastic befalls him from/on Caesar's part...'

Here where there is no passive and therefore no possible active counterpart, it is difficult to avoid taking *ā Caesāre* at face value as a *from*-phrase. No agency is expressed, but an interpretation of what is meant entails agency on Caesar's part.

The situation with the dative of agent is rather similar. Although (32) refers to a situation in which *ego* will have to be an agent, (32) does not present *ego* as an agent. (32) could be translated as 'It is up to me to defend this province' or 'This province is for me to defend'. As Rubio points out (1966: 150), the term 'dative of agent' is inappropriate. The dative in a sentence like (32) can be considered a dative of the person indirectly involved, i.e. a typical indirect object, with the sense of agency merely being entailed by the context of the gerundive. The dative in (32) is rather like the ablative in (33). In both instances agency is not expressed directly.

There is a range of examples that presents problems for Case Grammar. One type, recognised by Fillmore as problematical (1968: 48–9), involves valency alternations with different choices of object. Suppose we are describing a situation in which an agent (John) moves an object (a smoking pipe) and causes it to come into light contact with another object (a wall). In English we could say either (34a) or (34b),

(34) a. *John tapped the wall with his pipe*
    b. *John tapped his pipe on the wall*

In Case Grammar deep cases remain constant under paraphrase. Either we consider that the wall in (34a) is a patient and the pipe an instrument and transfer these roles to (34b), or we take the pipe in (34b) to be patient and the wall to be locative and transfer these roles to (34a). Obviously we cannot do both and maintain that roles remain constant under paraphrase. If one recognises that (34a) and (34b) represent different encodings of the same physical event, the problem disappears. (34a) is likely to be our choice if, for instance, John is seen to be tapping the wall with his pipe to see if the wall is hollow. The wall is seen as a patient and his pipe an instrument. (34b) is likely to be chosen if John is seen to be tapping his pipe on the wall to dislodge some wet tobacco from the pipe. His pipe is seen as a patient and the wall as a location.[16]

Encoding an entity as an object rather than as a non-core dependent often adds a sense of affectedness. This can be seen in (34a) and (34b). In both sentences the tapping is aimed at affecting the object. There are numerous examples of this in the literature, including some parallelling Pāṇini's pair (25) and (26). I do not know if there is such a difference between the Sanskrit sentences, but such a distinction can easily be captured. The sense of affectedness can be related to the fact that *bhumim* is the direct object of an activity verb. The sense of location is attributed to the locative or stance feature of the verb.

These examples are not meant to imply that roles can never be tracked across paraphrases. Obviously one can identify a patient and a recipient in both *Mary gave a book to Martha* and the paraphrase *Mary gave Martha a book*, but allowance needs to be made for more than one perception of a situation (the 'wall tapping' examples) and roles that are implied but not encoded (the Latin dative-of-agent example).

Fillmore's case grammar and similar attempts by others to establish a small list of universal roles have fallen somewhat into disrepute largely because no one has been able to produce a definitive list. However, a number of major theories such as Government and Binding and Lexical Functional Grammar embrace the notion of semantic roles, but they remain uncommitted about the universal inventory.

3.4.3 *Relational Grammar*

Relational Grammar is a theory originally developed by Perlmutter and Postal in the early 1970s.[17] It is of particular relevance to the study of case since it has concerned itself almost entirely with grammatical relations. In this theory grammatical relations are taken as undefined primitives. A distinction is made between the grammatical relations subject, direct object and indirect object, collectively known as **terms**, and the **obliques** such as locative, benefactive and instrumental. The terms are pure syntactic relations whereas the obliques are semantic. The grammatical relations form a hierarchy as follows:

(35)   subject   direct object   indirect object   obliques
            1   2   3

The theory is multistratal, i.e. the dependents of the verb may bear different relations in different strata. The relations held at the initial stratum are determined semantically. An agent or experiencer will be a subject, a patient a direct object, a recipient an indirect object, and other roles such as locative will be encoded in the appropriate oblique relation. The following sentences reflect initial stratum relations directly. From here on the Relational Grammar convention of referring to relations by their position on the hierarchy will be adopted (1 = subject, 2 = direct object, 3 = indirect object):

(36)   *Cain   slew   Abel*
            1   2

(37)   *Eve   gave   the   apple   to   Adam*
            1   2   3

A passive sentence or a double-object construction, however, will be interpreted as involving two strata. In the passive *Abel was slain by Cain* the argument *Abel* is said to be advanced from 2 to 1. The argument *Cain* is said to have become a **chômeur**. The French word *chômeur* means unemployed person and is part of an extended metaphor relating to work that runs through a good deal of Relational Grammar terminology.

(38)   *Cain   was   slain   by   Abel*
            2   1   initial stratum
            1   chômeur final stratum

Chômeurs are not found in the initial stratum, but arise in multi-stratal clauses where a dependent is displaced from term status by a revaluation, as the initial 1 is displaced by the advancee from 2 in (38). A chômeur lacks some of the properties of the corresponding term and cannot be advanced back to term status. In Relational Grammar there are no revaluations to oblique status, i.e. to locative, instrumental, etc. The 1-chômeur in the passive may come to be expressed by a particular preposition, postposition and/or case, but this marking is never interpreted as indicating oblique status.

The following sentence illustrates the interpretation of a double-object construction. The recipient is taken to be an initial 3 which advances to 2. As a result of this advancement the initial 2 (the patient) is demoted to chômeur status.

(39)

Eve	*gave*	*Adam*	*the*	*apple*	
1		3		2	initial stratum
1		2		chômeur	final stratum

The principal piece of evidence for taking the recipient object to be the direct object is that this object can be advanced to subject by the passive:

(40)

Adam	*was*	*given*	*the*	*apple*	*by*	*Eve*
3				2		1
2				cho		1
1				cho		cho

In languages with bound pronouns for direct object, the recipient object in the double object construction is normally represented by the direct object series which suggests that the recipient object is in fact the direct object. The point was illustrated from Kalkatungu in (9) above. In English, however, the analysis of the double object construction is controversial. The recipient object has claims to being direct object in that it comes immediately after the verb and can be advanced to subject via the passive as shown in (40). However, where the first object in the double-object construction is a beneficiary (*I made her a cake*), it cannot be advanced to subject. Moreover, the first object, whether recipient or beneficiary, cannot be relativised freely (*?I saw the man who you gave/made a cake*) as the direct object can (*I saw the man who you admire*). Hudson (1992) argues that the second object in the double-object construction in English should be taken to be the direct object, but in the present work the recipient or beneficiary object will be taken to be the direct object since this analysis seems to hold across languages.

There is one other Relational Grammar analysis that is worth mentioning and that is possessor ascension, since it is relevant to the Kalkatungu examples involving body parts presented as (8) and (10) above. We will consider a sentence similar to (8), but cast in the future tense rather than the purposive modality, since this enables us to dispense with the complication of bound pronouns. It will be recalled that in (8) the possessor of a body part and the possessed body part appeared in parallel. (41b) presents the propositional content of (8) and it is paired with (41a), which shows a possessor expressed in the dative (the case that covers possessive function). In Kalkatungu the dative is not normally used to refer to the possession of one's own body parts, so (41a) would normally be taken to refer to the possession of an eye other than one's own.

(41)   a. *Milnga-ngku*   *itya-mi*   *ngatyi*   *milthi*
             fly-ERG   bite-FUT   1SG.DAT   eye.NOM
             'The fly/flies will bite my eye(s).'
      b. *Milnga-ngku*   *itya-mi*   *ngayi*   *milthi*
             fly-ERG   bite-FUT   1SG.NOM   eye.NOM
             'The fly/flies will bite me [in the] eye(s).'

In Relational Grammar these two sentences would be based on the same initial stratum, one directly underlying (41a), i.e. one in which the first person possessor is taken to be a POSSessor dependent within a 'possessor phrase' with the possessed body part (*milthi*) as head. (41b) would be held to reflect a revaluation, namely the ascension of the possessor out of the possessor phrase to become a dependent of the verb. In the revaluation the possessor assumes the relation borne by the possessed in the initial stratum (namely 2) and pushes the possessed into chômage.

(42)   *Milnga*   *itya-mi*   *ngayi*   *milthi*
             [1   P   [POSS   2]]
             [1   P   2   cho]

An analogous analysis would be provided for a sentence like (10) where the possessor of the body part is in S function.

If we consider (8), (9) and (10) together ((9b) is an example of the double object construction), we see that in each clause with two nominative-marked noun phrases one is interpreted as absolutive (S or P) and the other as a chômeur.

Relational Grammarians have not attempted to establish a universal set of semantic roles and their conception of terms (1, 2 and 3), which are semantically heterogeneous, and obliques (locative, instrumental, etc.), which are simply semantic roles, is a conventional one. Their main interest in the present context lies in the following:

    (a)   the Universal Alignment Hypothesis
    (b)   the treatment of the absolutive and ergative relations
    (c)   the concept of chômage

Universal Alignment Hypothesis

As mentioned above, initial stratum grammatical relations are determined semantically. Perlmutter and Postal proposed a Universal Alignment Hypothesis (1984: 97; orig. 1978). According to this theory agents, experiencers and cognisers are encoded as 1, patients as 2, and recipients as 3. The hypothesis is not entirely unproblematic. Consider, for example, the semantic role of the object in *She speaks French.* A survey of a number of languages reveals that the translational equivalent can appear in a great variety of cases and with a great variety of adpositions. In Australian languages alone the locative, instrumental, ablative, perlative, dative, accusative and nominative (in an intransitive construction) are used. This is hardly surprising. The relationship between the name of a language, dialect, etc. and a predicate meaning 'speak language X' falls between the salient roles of patient, location, instrument, etc. Languages encode it in different ways, some allowing alternatives as English does (*She speaks French, She spoke in French*) (Blake 1987: 27, Blake 1990: 24f). The Universal Alignment Hypothesis is recognised as not being tenable in its strict form (Rosen 1984), though it is unproblematic in most instances. Its main effect is to force a multistratal interpretation of clauses that do not exhibit the 'universal alignment'. Consider, for instance, the following English examples:

(43)   a. *That girl speaks to me*
            agent   recipient
      b. *That girl matters to me*
            patient   experiencer

(44)   a. *The prisoner escaped confinement*
            agent   source
      b. *The reason escapes me*
            patient   experiencer

In the (a) examples the default alignment of role and relation occurs, but in the (b) examples there is a marked alignment. In the Relational Grammar analysis of (43b) *me* is an initial 1, because it is an experiencer, which demotes to 3. *The girl* is an initial 2, since it is a patient, which advances to 1 to provide a subject. In Relational Grammar the final stratum must contain a subject.

(45)   *That girl matters to me*
             2   1
             2   3
             1   3

A similar analysis applies to (44b) except that the initial 1 demotes to 3 and then subsequently advances to 2 (Perlmutter and Postal 1984, orig. 1978):

(46)   *The   reason   escapes   me*

                       2   1

                       2   3

                       1   3

                       1   2

The (b) sentences cannot be passivised. Perlmutter and Postal attribute this to a principle to the effect that there can only be one advancement to 1 in a clause. These clauses already have an advancement to 1.

Predicates that encode a role normally associated with subject as an indirect object, or occasionally a direct object, are known in the Relational Grammar literature and elsewhere as **inversion** predicates. Inversion is common with the meaning 'to please', witness German *gefallen*, Latin *placēre*, Italian *piacere a*, Spanish *gustar a* and French *plaîre à* where the neutral patient is encoded as subject and the experiencer as indirect object. For examples see (48) and (55) in chapter 5.

Absolutive and ergative

As noted above, Relational Grammar recognises a set of primitive (undefined) grammatical relations comprising subject, direct object, indirect object and a yet to be determined number of obliques. It also admits absolutive and ergative as derived (defined) relations. The absolutive covers the 2 of a transitive verb and the 1 of an intransitive verb (but see below). The ergative is the 1 of a transitive verb.

The derived relations of absolutive and ergative provide a cross-cutting classification of the primitive relations of subject and object. The two classifications between them provide for any mixture of SA/P and SP/A alignments such as the one illustrated from Kalkatungu in section 3.2.2.

The definition of absolutive given above is adequate in a system that recognises only surface structure. However, Relational Grammar recognises underlying strata and it analyses some intransitive predicates as having an initial stratum 2, mostly predicates that take a patient argument such as *fall*, *die*, *be small*. The definitions of the derived relations are meant to be applicable to all strata, so the absolutive should be defined more strictly as covering the 2 of a transitive verb and the nuclear term (1 or 2) of an intransitive predicate. (See Figure 3.3.)

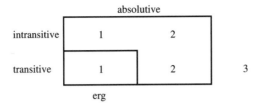

Figure 3.3 Nuclear relations in Relational Grammar

It should be noted in passing that most of the revaluations posited in Relational Grammar must be recognised in any theory. Although there are revaluations like those illustrated with *matter to* (43) and *escape* (44), which have no direct surface manifestation, most revaluations concern valency changing derivation: passive, antipassive, reflexive verb formation (see (2b) above), advancement to direct object (see (3) above), causativisation, etc.

Chômage

As noted earlier in the discussion of (38) and (39) where a dependent is displaced from term status by a revaluation (usually the advancement of another dependent) it becomes a chômeur. In some instances the chômeur retains its marking as in the double object construction (39); in others it assumes oblique marking as in the passive (38). It is the assumption of oblique marking that is relevant to case. In the Latin passive quoted above in (31) the displaced subject is marked by the preposition *ā/ab* meaning 'from' plus the ablative, one of the functions of which is to express 'from'. In the Relational Grammar interpretation the displaced subject takes on no more than the marking *ā/ab* plus ablative. It is not interpreted as being recategorised as the grammatical relation otherwise expressed by *ā/ab* plus the ablative and certainly not as being semantically recategorised. As noted in connection with (38) there are no revaluations to oblique relations.

3.4.4 *Localist Case Grammar*

In his Localist Case Grammar John Anderson (1977) establishes a set of universal 'case relations' comprising only four members:

(47)   absolutive
            locative
            ergative
            ablative

It is immediately obvious that these entities are not the generally accepted grammatical relations. The question arises of how the larger number of semantic roles recognised by scholars like Fillmore, Chafe and Cook can be accommodated. There are three characteristics of Localist Case Grammar that account for this:

    (a)   localism
    (b)   case relations interpreted according to syntagmatic contrast
    (c)   multiple assignment of case relations

(a) Localism

    As noted in section 2.3.4 a localist interpretation of case involves taking syntactic case categories to be extensions of local case categories into an abstract domain. For example, in a localistic interpretation the subject of a verb like *have* as in *She has it* in English will be [locative]. This can be rationalised by reference to the fact that the object is located in the possession of the subject. If this type of interpretation is exploited liberally, obviously the inventory of case relations can be reduced.

(b) Syntagmatic contrast

    The absolutive and the locative are interpreted as goal (destination) in the context of ergative and ablative respectively. For instance, the noun phrase *the stick* will be [abs] in both *The stick broke* and in *The teacher broke the stick*, but will be interpreted as a 'goal of action' (patient) only in the transitive clause. Similarly [loc] will be interpreted as a 'spatial goal' (destination) in (48a) but not in (48b) (cf. Anderson 1977: 115):

(48)   a.   *They   rode   from   Ghent   to   Aix*
                                [abl]   [loc]
     b.   *They   remained   in   Aix*
                                [loc]

(c) Multiple assignment

    In Localist Case Grammar an argument can bear more than one case relation. Combinations of case relations obviously have the effect of extending the inventory and the case relations effectively become features.

    Most systems of semantic roles would distinguish an agent subject in *She bit it* from an experiencer subject in *She knew it*. Anderson distinguishes them as follows (Anderson 1977: 45, 87, 145):

(49)   a. *She   bit   it*
        [erg]   [abs]

b. *She   knew   it*
   [erg]   [abs]
   [loc]

The case relation [loc] is motivated by a comparison with sentences such as the following where the 'knower' is [loc]:

(50)   *He   taught   English   to   migrants*
          [erg]   [abs]   [loc]
          [abl]

Clearly Anderson is motivated by a desire to maintain a fixed mapping of extra-linguistic roles to case relations. The localist nature of his interpretations also comes out in his interpretation of the 'teacher' as [abl] since the 'teacher' is the abstract source of the knowledge. Note that it is this [abl] that forces the spatial goal interpretation of the [loc] case relation in the same clause.

Anderson uses multiple case assignment to handle pairs of sentences like the following:

(51)   a. *He   sprayed   the   paint   on   the   wall*
             [erg]   [abs]   [loc]
          b. *He   sprayed   the   wall   with   paint*
             [erg]   [loc]   [abs]
                                    [abs]

As noted in section 3.3.2 (see (34)), pairs of sentences like these were discussed by Fillmore as being problematic for a theory that holds roles constant under paraphrase. In section 3.3.2 I suggested that the principle be abandoned and more than one conceptualisation recognised, but Anderson has a way of capturing the objective properties of the arguments and at the same time recognising the difference in perspective. The sentence in (51a) is allotted the typical roles for transitive subject, direct object and local phrase. The sentence in (51b) is interpreted as involving a marked relationship between semantic role and grammatical relation. *The wall* is now marked [abs] as well as [loc] and the *paint* retains its [abs] relation from (51a). Sentence (51b) has as its unmarked interpretation a holistic reading, i.e. the sentence would be used where the wall was wholly covered or at least substantially affected by paint. Anderson captures this by tying the holistic reading to the case relation [abs]. Every clause contains at least one exponent of [abs] and S and P will always be [abs], no matter what other relation either may hold. Note that Anderson effectively treats the preposition *with* as marking a demoted [abs] rather than an instrument. This is essentially the same treatment that would be found in Relational Grammar where *with* would be interpreted as marking a direct object chômeur (cf. the treatment of the agent in the passive discussed in conjunction with (38) in the previous section).

Undoubtedly the most interesting aspect of Anderson's approach is his belief that the core grammar of all languages is organised on an absolutive-ergative basis at an underlying level, even a language like English where the grammatical relation of subject is so prominent. Consider the assignment of case relations in the following (Anderson 1977: 82):

(52)   a. *The   stone   moved*
                [abs]
         b. *John   moved*
            [abs]
            [erg]
         c. *John   moved   the   stone*
            [erg]   [abs]

The semantic motivation is transparent. An agent is [erg] and a patient is [abs]. In a typical reading of *John moved* the subject *John* is agent (John instigates the movement) and patient (he is displaced).[18] Anderson believes that all languages have this assignment of case relations at an underlying level, but that many languages exhibit the phenomenon of subject formation which obscures the absolutive and ergative case relations. Languages of the type that Klimov (1973) calls active (see section 5.2.3) reflect the case relations directly in their morphological marking. Ergative languages collapse [abs, erg] with [abs], but otherwise reflect the case relations shown in (52). In a language like English it is possible to distinguish rules that are sensitive to the putative case relations from those that are based on the subject grammatical relation. The target of raising, for instance, is [abs], i.e. there is raising to S and to P, but not to A:[19]

(53)   *The patient seems [ ] better*

(54)   *The doctor expected the patient to [ ] recover*

On the other hand rules of case assignment (*he* v. *him* etc.), word order and verb agreement are sensitive to subject as are other rules such as the requirement that the subject remain unexpressed, in almost all circumstances, with a non-finite verb.

3.4.5 Starosta's Lexicase

Lexicase, a model of grammar developed by Starosta (1971, 1988), is similar to Localist Case Grammar in that it takes the core grammar of all languages to be organised on an absolutive-ergative basis. There are five atomic, syntactic-semantic case relations:

(55)   PATIENT

              AGENT

              CORRESPONDENT

              LOCUS

              MEANS

PATIENT covers S plus P, i.e. what we are calling the absolutive relation in this text. AGENT corresponds to A, i.e. the ergative relation. The other three relations have inner and outer sub-types. An inner sub-type has the PATIENT as its scope; the outer sub-type has the clause as its scope. A second (patient) object in a double-object construction would be an inner CORRESPONDENT, whereas an outer CORRE-SPONDENT would be marked by an adposition and/or oblique case. An outer CORRE-SPONDENT covers roles like purpose and beneficiary. LOCUS covers all local relations, differences between source, path, location and destination being attributable to case marking (inflection, adpositions, etc.) and choice of verb (*leave*, *cross*, *inhabit*, *approach*). MEANS covers roles like instrument and manner. Some illustrations follow:

(56)   *In   the   springtime   birds   nest*
                         [+LOC]   [+PAT]
                         [+outer]

(57)   *The   diner   gave   the   tip   to   the   waiter*
           [+AGT]   [+PAT]   [+LOC]
                                                      [+inner]

(58)   *The   diner   gave   the   waiter   a   tip*
           [+AGT]   [+PAT]   [+COR]
                                              [+inner]

(59)   *Lassie   caught   a   rabbit   for   us*
           [+AGT]   [+PAT]   [+COR]
                                              [+outer]

(60) *The kids smeared paint on the nursery wall*
    [+AGT]   [+PAT]   [+LOC]
                    [+inner]

(61) *The kids smeared the nursery wall with paint with their fingers*
    [+AGT]   [+PAT] [+MEANS] [+MEANS]
               [+inner] [+outer]

As can easily be seen, there is no attempt to keep case relations constant under paraphrase. Semantic roles may well remain constant under paraphrase, but these play no part in the theory except for the interpretation placed on the case relations according to marking and choice of verb. An AGENT, for instance, will be interpreted as an agent with activity verbs and as an experiencer with verbs of emotion.

Clearly the case relations are primarily syntactic rather than semantic, and the same question arises with Lexicase as with Localist Case Grammar, namely how can AGENT and PATIENT be justified in languages which obviously have a subject. In fact the PATIENT is exploited in much the same way as [abs] is in Localist Case Grammar. The PATIENT is the scope of inner case relations. In (62) and (63) the final local phrase is inner and refers to the location of the PATIENT:

(62) *In the summer they sit in the shade*
      [+LOC] [+PAT]   [+LOC]
      [+outer]   [+inner]

(63) *In the summer they put their meat in the ice chest*
      [+LOC] [+AGT]   [+PAT]   [+LOC]
      [+outer]   [+inner]

The inner/outer distinction applies to infinitival dependents. The PATIENT is the controller of the missing subject of an infinitival complement (Starosta 1988: 133–7). In (64) the missing subject of *swim* is interpreted as the PATIENT of the intransitive verb, namely *Mary*. In (65) the missing subject of *go* is interpreted as coreferential with the PATIENT of the transitive verb *tell*, again *Mary*.[20]

(64) *Mary tried to [ ] swim the river to [ ] impress John*
    [+PAT]   [-fin]   [-fin]
            [+inner]   [+outer]

(65) *John told Mary to [ ] go home to [ ] please his father*
    [+AGT] [+PAT]   [-fin]   [-fin]
             [+inner] [+outer]

The target for raising can be captured in terms of [+PATIENT]. A raising analysis is not used in Lexicase, but raising verbs such as *seem* (66) and *expect* as in (67) have the property that they do not impose selection restrictions on their PATIENT. The PATIENT will control the missing subject of an inner infinitival complement and this subject will fulfill the selectional requirements of the infinitive (cf. Starosta 1988: 158f):

(66)   *Cindy   seems   to   [ ]   speak   French*
        [+PAT]   [+PAT]

(67)   *I   expected   Cindy   to   [ ]   speak   French*
        [+AGT]   [+PAT]   [+PAT]

Rules of word order and verb agreement are based on case. In English, for instance, the verb agreement is controlled by the nominative-marked noun phrase. One other entity is needed. In some languages with a nominative-ergative system of case marking S and A are treated alike in terms of certain syntactic rules even though they are not both in the nominative. An example from Kalkatungu was given in section 3.2.2 where the case system was nominative-ergative, but where the bound pronominal elements operated in terms of SA versus P. To capture SA alignment Lexicase invokes the notion of [+actor] which is a feature independent of the system of case relations.

3.5   Hierarchies

Grammatical relations, cases and case markers do not form sets of equipollent entities. As we saw in the previous chapter, sets of cases share properties, and markedness relations can be found between cases. Shared properties and markedness can be captured in terms of a feature analysis (section 2.3.4); to some extent markedness can also be captured by means of hierarchical ordering. It is a moot point whether grammatical relations should be given a componential analysis and it partly depends on which set of relations one recognises, but there is no doubt grammatical relations can be ordered hierarchically. Case marking is an abstraction covering different types of exponent, e.g. adpositions and affixes. The various types of case marker can be ordered in terms of their formal properties (e.g. free vs. bound), and these formal properties can be shown to co-vary with the hierarchical ordering of cases and grammatical relations.

Semantic roles can be ordered hierarchically with respect to grammatical relations. Under some views this order is also relevant to the acceptability of certain constructions such as reflexives and passives.

3.5.1 *Grammatical relations*

As we saw in section 3.4.3 the following hierarchy of grammatical relations is posited in Relational Grammar:

(68)   1. subject
         2. direct object
         3. indirect object
         4. obliques (locative, instrumental, etc.)

The hierarchy manifests itself in various ways. In some languages the unmarked word order follows the hierarchy. This is true of English, French (clitic pronouns apart), Thai, Indonesian and Swahili, for instance. In some the hierarchy shows up in causativisation. If one causativises a verb, a new agent is added to the valency of the verb. This agent is encoded as subject and it displaces the old subject. In languages such as Turkish, French and Italian, the ousted subject takes up the first available relation on the hierarchy: direct object, indirect object, oblique. The following examples are from Turkish. In (69a) we have an intransitive clause. When the new agent is added as subject in (69b), the old subject is expressed as the direct object. In (70a) we have a transitive clause with a direct object. When the new subject is introduced in (70b), the old subject is expressed as an indirect object. In (71a) we have a ditransitive verb with a subject, direct object and indirect object. When the new subject is introduced in (71b), the old subject is expressed in a phrase governed by the postposition *tarafından* (Comrie 1976, 1989: 175–6).

(69)   a. *Hasan   öl-dü*
           Hasan.NOM   die-PAST
           'Hasan died.'
        b. *Ali   Hasan-ı   öl-dür-dü*
           Ali.NOM   Hasan-ACC   die-CAUS-PAST
           'Ali killed Hasan.'

(70)   a. *Müdür   mektub-u   imzala-dı*
           director.NOM   letter-ACC   sign-PAST
           'The director signed the letter.'
        b. *Ali   mektub-u   müdür-e   imzala-t-tı*
           Ali.NOM   letter-ACC   director-DAT   sign-CAUS-PAST
           'Ali got the director to sign the letter.'

(71)   a. *Müdür   Hasan-a   mektub-u   göster-di*
           director.NOM   Hasan-DAT   letter-ACC   show-PAST
           'The director showed the letter to Hasan.'

b. *Ali   Hasan-a   mektub-u   müdür   tarafından*
Ali.NOM   Hasan-DAT   letter-ACC   director   by
göster-t-ti
show-CAUS-PAST
'Ali got the director to show the letter to Hasan.'

The hierarchy also shows up in access to relativisation. English can relativise subjects (*the man who left*), objects (*the man I saw*) and oblique relations (*the gun with which I shot the intruder*). However, Keenan and Comrie 1977 have shown that some languages can relativise only subjects, some only subjects and direct objects, some only subjects, direct objects and indirect objects, and so on.[21]

Most languages allow for some verbal derivations that change the valency of the verb. The passive is a widespread example. On the basis of the hierarchy of grammatical relations, such verbal derivations can be described in terms of advancement (or promotion) and demotion. The passive involves the advancement of the direct object to subject and the demotion of the subject to a peripheral relation.

Except for the passive there are not many general valency-changing derivations in Indo-European languages, though there are some possibilities available through alternative lexical choice as with English *steal* and *rob*. However, in some languages, especially the Bantu languages, the Austronesian languages and some Australian languages, there are extensive verbal derivations available that allow a grammatical relation (and its associated role or roles) to be advanced up the hierarchy. There are two patterns of advancement. In accusative languages where the core grammar is organised on a subject/object basis, advancements to object feed the passive enabling an indirect object or oblique relation to be advanced to subject. In ergative languages like Tagalog, Dyirbal and Kalkatungu, where the core grammar is organised on an absolutive/ergative basis, advancements are to the absolutive, which is at the top of the relational hierarchy.[22] There is no passive, but there is an antipassive that enables an ergative to be advanced to absolutive (Table 3.5). An example of the advancement of a locative to direct object was given in (25) and (26) from Sanskrit. An example of the advancement of an instrumental to absolutive was given in (3) from Kalkatungu.

3.5.2 *Case*

At the end of chapter 5 (section 5.8) it is argued that inflectional case systems tend to be built up in the following order,

(72)   nom   acc/erg   gen   dat   loc   abl/inst   others

Table 3.5 *Pattern of advancements*

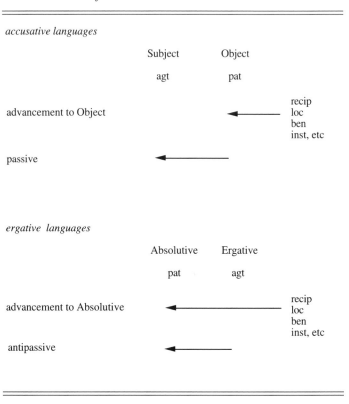

The hierarchy is to be interpreted as follows. If a language has a certain case, say locative, it will usually have a nominative, at least one other core case, a genitive and a dative. If it has an instrumental or ablative, it will usually have a nominative, accusative or ergative or both, genitive, dative and locative, and so on. Where there are gaps in the hierarchy it is usually because the higher grammatical relations are marked by bound pronouns or differentiated by word order. The hierarchy that emerges is a hierarchy of grammatical relations, an elaboration of the Relational Grammar hierarchy given in (68).

Pinkster has demonstrated that cases can be arranged hierarchically according to the extent to which they encode arguments of a predicate rather than adjuncts.. In Latin the hierarchy is as follows (after Pinkster 1985: 167):

(73)   nom > acc > dat > abl > gen

The order nom > acc > dat > other (or nom > erg > dat > other in ergative languages) would appear to hold generally, but it must be remembered that the label 'dative' is often allocated to a case because it is the favoured choice for complements after the core cases (see section 5.3).

Ramarao (1976) shows that in some languages, such as the Dravidian language Telugu, the priority of the accusative over the non-core cases can be established from the fact that the non-core cases cannot encode a complement unless an accusative-marked complement is present.

3.5.3   Marking

There are generalisations to be made about the distribution of morphologically unmarked forms, about synthetic-versus-analytic marking, and about head-versus-dependent marking.

If there is an unmarked (zero) case, and there usually is, this will normally be the nominative encoding SA (subject) in accusative languages and SP (absolutive) in ergative languages. Indo-European was unusual in having a positive marker *-s* for nominative. Some nouns, however, had a zero nominative, namely those of the *ā* declension: Greek *chōra* 'land', Latin *mēnsa* 'table'. In Modern Greek some accusative forms are unmarked: *logos* 'word' (nom), *loge* (voc), *logo* (acc), *logou* (dat). There are a few languages in which the accusative rather than the nominative is unmarked for all nominals. Wappo (Penutian) is an example (Li and Thompson n.d.).

There is a clear correlation between the type of marking employed for a grammatical relation and the position of that relation on the hierarchy. Analytic case markers (adpositions) are more likely for the non-core or peripheral relations, especially the semantic relations (see Table 2.7 for these distinctions). Conversely synthetic markers (inflection) are more likely than analytic ones for the purely grammatical relations, especially the core ones. English is an example to the extent that it has suppletive accusative inflection with pronouns and a genitive marker *'s* with nouns, but prepositions for most other functions.. The status of the genitive *'s* is unusual in that its scope is phrasal: *the man over there's dog*.[23]

Head marking, i.e. marking the head of a construction rather than the dependents to show grammatical relations (section 1.3.1), is practically confined to the purely grammatical relations. Some languages have cross-referencing bound pronominal forms, usually on the verb, for the subject only. This is the traditional Indo-European type exemplified by Latin (Table 3.1). Other languages have cross-referencing for the object as well (Swahili) and a smaller number cross-reference the indirect object too (Georgian). It is very common to cross-reference an adnominal noun phrase in possessor function on the head of the construction. An example was given from Turkish in section 1.1: *adam-ın ev-i* (man-GEN house-3SG.POSS) 'the man's house'.[24]

The distribution of inflection versus adpositions and the distribution of head-versus-dependent marking has implications for the interpretation of the historical development of case systems. These developments are described in chapter 6.

In some languages there is no marking for any core function, either on the noun phrases or on the verb, though there is marking for all the peripheral functions. In such languages a subject/object distinction is made via word order, usually subject-verb-object order as in Thai or Cambodian.

Case marking, particularly core case marking, may be sensitive to the category of the stem (common noun vs. proper noun, noun vs. pronoun, etc.) including other categories which may be marked on the stem such as number. The sensitivity of case marking to the category of the stem is discussed in section 5.2.6.

3.5.4 Roles

When Fillmore proposed the notion of semantic roles independent of the morpho-syntax, he also introduced the idea of a subject choice hierarchy (1968: 33). Most modern theories incorporate such a hierarchy, some adding an object choice hierarchy. The following example is to be found in Dik's Functional Grammar (with 'patient' substituted for 'goal') (Dik 1978: 74f).

(74)   agent > patient > recipient > beneficiary > instrument > location > temporal

This represents a hierarchy of accessibility to subject. Agent is most accessible to expression as a subject, patient next most accessible and so on. (74) also represents a hierarchy of accessibility to direct object except that the agent cannot be expressed as object. In Dik's view a continuous segment of the hierarchy has access to subject and another continuous segment has accessibility to direct object. Assignments of lower roles to subject and object are less frequent within languages and across languages; they are usually subject to lexical constraints and they typically involve marked constructions. In English, agent is the first choice for subject in the unmarked (active) construction (*I shouted, I ate it*), patient is the next choice (*I fell*), but a marked construction (the passive) must be used if it is to displace an agent argument (*He got shot by a madman*).

A recipient of the verb *give* may displace a patient in the choice for object (*I gave the book to him, I gave him the book*), but the double-object construction would have to be considered marked with respect to the construction with a prepositional phrase which is obviously much more common across verbs in general. The recipient can be promoted to subject via the passive (*He was given the book*). However, the advancement of a recipient to direct object is not possible with all three-place verbs (cf. *donate*). A beneficiary can be advanced to direct object with some verbs (*He built me a carport*), but not others (e.g. *construct*) and it is difficult to find felicitous examples of passives with beneficiaries as subject.[25]

English is highly unusual in allowing roles low on the hierarchy to be encoded as subject, at least with a few verbs. In *The first chapter contains the definitions* the subject would appear to be locative and in *The war years saw a reduction in the crime rate* the subject is arguably 'temporal', although one could take it to be a metaphorical perceiver.

Across languages the passive can be seen as a means of making a marked choice for subject. Similarly derived verbs of the type illustrated in (3) above allow a marked choice for object.

Dik does not recognise an experiencer role. If an experiencer were included, it would presumably outrank the patient, since it is more often expressed as subject than the neutral patient is (*I like/hate/fear him*). In a number of role hierarchies not only is the experiencer placed above the patient, but several other roles are as well (see, for instance, Jackendoff 1972: 43, Foley and van Valin 1984: 59 and Bresnan and Kanerva 1989: 23). To some extent these hierarchies in which the patient is ranked low are based on different premises and used for different purposes. Jackendoff, for instance, introduces the hierarchy in (75) and uses it as a basis for the Thematic Hierarchy Condition on passives and reflexives. In a passive the agent phrase is supposed to be higher than the derived subject and in reflexives the reflexivised argument may not be higher than its antecedent (Jackendoff 1972: 43, 148).

(75)   1. Agent
        2. Location, Source, Goal
        3. Theme.

The Thematic Hierarchy Condition could be invoked to show why the following sentences do not have passives. In both, the subject is a neutral patient or theme and the other argument an experiencer which Jackendoff would take to be an abstract goal.

(76)   *That girl matters to me*

(77)   *The reason escapes me*

These sentences were previously presented in the discussion of universal alignment of roles and relations in Relational Grammar (see (43) and (44)).[26]

4
Distribution of case marking

4.1 Introduction

This chapter describes the distribution of case marking within the sentence. The order of presentation is clause level (4.2), phrase level (4.3) and then word level (4.4). The distribution of case marking in subordinate clauses is treated in the final section (4.5).

4.2 Within the clause

In the clause case marks the relationship of various complements and adjuncts to the predicate. These complements and adjuncts are usually realised by noun phrases or adverb phrases, and the predicate is usually a verb. This function of case is the basis for the central definition of case given at the beginning of chapter 1, and numerous examples of this function are to be found throughout the text and do not therefore need further illustration now. However, as noted in section 1.2.1, case marking may also be found on dependents within a noun phrase or on words, mostly nouns and adjectives, in predicative function.

In a construction such as Virgil's *vēnit summa diēs* 'The last day came' the nominative case on *diēs* 'day' indicates that it bears the subject relation to the verb *vēnit* and this usage fits our central definition. However, the nominative on the adjective *summa* 'highest' does not indicate that *summa* is subject, but that it is a modifier of the subject. This usage is somewhat marginal to our central definition, since the nominative here is merely specifying that *summa* is a dependent of *diēs* without specifying a type of relation between *summa* and *diēs* (see also section 4.3).

Where there is concord between a predicative nominal and a subject, the case marking is even further from our central definition. In many languages a nominal may instantiate the predicate without there being any grammatical verb, at least in the unmarked tense and mood.[1] In Latin, for instance, a noun or adjective can instantiate the entire predicate as in *Nihil bonum* 'Nothing [is] good', where the adjective *bonum* is the predicate and it shows concord in case (nominative), number (singular) and gender (neuter) with the subject *nihil* 'nothing'. On the assumption that the predicate is the head of the clause, even when realised by a nominal, the concord is of a head with a dependent.[2]

If a verb is used with a predicative noun or adjective, then the verb will be the grammatical head of the clause and the concord will be between two dependents. In the following example from Pliny the verb *esse* 'to be' is used,

(1)   *Hominī   fidēlissimī   sunt   equus   et*
        man.DAT   most.faithful.NOM.PL   be.3PL   horse.NOM   and
        canis
        dog.NOM
        'To a human the horse and the dog are the most faithful.'

Here the concord is between the subject *equus et canis* and the predicative adjective *fidēlissimi*. *Fidēlissimi* is the predicate word that determines the valency (the subject and the dative complement) but *sunt*, the finite verb, is the head of the predicate phrase.

A noun or adjective can be predicative to nouns in cases other than the nominative. In Latin predicates controlled by an accusative object were common,

(2)   *Cicerōnem   cōnsulem   creāvērunt*
        Cicero.ACC   consul.ACC   made.3PL
        'They made Cicero consul.'

Here the noun *cōnsulem* is a predicate exhibiting accusative concord with the direct object. Under the traditional analysis it would be referred to as the object complement and considered part of the clause containing the object. In one modern analysis *Cicerōnem cōnsulem* would be taken to be a verbless clause serving as a constituent of the larger clause: [[*Cicerōnem cōnsulem*] *creāvērunt*]. In another analysis *Cicerōnem* would be taken to have been raised from the clause *Cicerō cōnsul* to become a constituent of the main clause, leaving the nominal predicate *cōnsul* as the sole constituent of a non-finite subordinate clause. The missing subject of this non-finite clause would be identified with the object *Cicerōnem* of the main clause.[3]

Besides nominals in predicate function exhibiting concordial case there are in any case language also phrases in predicate function bearing relational case. Consider the following Latin examples,

(3)   *Cicerō,   vir   capite   candidō,   dixit ...*
        Cicero.NOM   man.NOM   head.ABL   white.ABL   speak.PERF.3SG
        'Cicero, a man with white hair, said ... .'

(4) *Vir   est   capite   candidō*
     man.NOM   is.3SG   head.ABL   white.ABL
     'The man is white haired.'

In (3) the ablative in *capite* (which also shows up in *candidō* via concord) expresses the relation of the modifier *caput* to the head *vir* and thus fits our central definition. In (4) the ablative in *capite* expresses the same relation to *vir*, but *caput* is not a dependent of *vir*. It seems that we need to extend our definition of case to cover the marking of nominals in predicative function expressing their relation to their controller.

Now to return to concord. While concord of case, number and gender of predicative adjectives is the norm in Latin and Ancient Greek, in many other languages predicative adjectives display no concord. This is the situation in German where the predicative adjective consists of the bare stem and is distinct from the various case forms. The following sentences illustrate the difference between the attributive adjective in nominative forms and the predicative adjective. In the first three examples below the attributive adjective is in the 'weak' form following the definite article. In (8) it is the 'strong' form, since there is no definite article.

(5)   *Der alte Tisch ist sehr gut*
        'The old table (masc.) is very good.'

(6)   *Das gute Kind ist sehr nett*
        'The good child (neut.) is very nice.'

(7)   *Die nette Frau ist sehr alt*
        'The nice lady (fem.) is very old.'

(8)   *Alter Wein ist sehr nett*
        'Old wine (masc.) is very nice.'

Hjelmslev (1935: 120) took the predicative to be a fifth case separate from the four recognised cases (nominative, accusative, genitive and dative). The justification for this analysis is not strong, since the sole function of the predicative lies outside the central range of case functions. A better analysis would be to say that German predicate adjectives lack case altogether.

Hjelmslev also notes that in Tabassaran, a Daghestan language of the Caucasus, a language noted for having the largest case system (see section 5.6), there is a predicative case marked by *-u-*, *-ä-* or *-ö-*. The markers precede the markers for number and gender, whereas markers for other cases are word final as in *mu ǰeχr-*

ar sib-u-r-ar-u: 'These pears are green' where *sib-* 'green', 'not ripe' is suffixed by
-u-, Hjelmslev's predicative case, followed by *-r-*, the gender marker, and *-ar-*, the
plural marker (Hjelmslev does not gloss the final *u*:). Hjelmslev is not deterred by
the position of the markers for predicative case, since he sees the function as all
important (1937: 139). However, as stated above, the function is not a typical case
function. What Hjelmslev analyses as predicative case markers would appear to be
derivational affixes. The predicative case markers in Tabassaran are matched by an
attributive case marker, which is discussed in section 4.3.2 below.

Besides concord within the noun phrase and concord exhibited by predicative
nominals and adjectives, there is also apparent concord between what look like
separated parts of a noun phrase. In Latin, it is possible to take a word that would
appear to modify a noun and express it in a phrase separate from the noun. The following example is from Virgil (*Aeneid* II:3),

(9)   *Infāndum,*   *rēgīna,*   *iubēs*   *renovāre*   *dolōrem*
        unspeakable.ACC   queen.VOC   order.2SG   renew.INF   sorrow.ACC
        'Unspeakable, [O] queen, [is] the sorrow you order [me] to rekindle.'

Here the gerundive adjective *infāndum* is displaced from the word it might be
thought to modify, namely *dolōrem*. In Australian languages the non-contiguous
expression of words that would normally appear within a single noun phrase in
English is commonplace. The translational equivalents of English adjectives frequently appear late in the clause separated from their apparent heads. The following examples are from Warlpiri (Pama-Nyungan). In this language case marking is
phrase-final. In (10) the ergative suffix appears on the final word of the phrase
tyarntu wiri (dog big). In (11) *tyarntu* and *wiri* are separate phrases, and each takes
the phrase-final case marking. The form *=tyu* is an object clitic attached to the first
constituent of the clause (Hale 1973b: 314).

(10)   *Tyarntu   wiri-ngki=tyu   yarlki-rnu*
        dog   big-ERG=1SG.OBJ   bite-PAST
        'The big dog bit me.'

(11)   *Tyarntu-ngku=tyu   yarlku-rnu   wiri-ngki*
        dog-ERG=1SG.OBJ   bite-PAST   big-ERG
        'The big dog bit me.'
        'The dog bit me, big (one).'

4.3   Within the noun phrase

4.3.1   *Internal relations*

The relationship of dependent nouns to the head noun in a noun phrase can normally be expressed by a variety of non-core or peripheral cases. In English any preposition can be used (*the house on the corner, the strike over leave loadings*, etc.); in Latin any peripheral case,

(12)   a. genitive: *cōnsulis equus*   'the consul's horse'
        b. dative: *obtemperātiō legibus*   'obedience to laws'
        c. ablative: *vir praestāntī prudentiā* 'a man of outstanding wisdom'

Typically one case emerges as a specialised adnominal case with a variety of functions. In Latin the genitive is almost exclusively an adnominal case; it marks the complement of only a handful of verbs. One of its important functions is to provide a means of expressing the adnominal equivalent of an adverbal complement. Consider the following pairs,

(13)   a. *Catilīna*   *coniūrat*   *adversus*   *rem*
          Catiline.NOM conspire.3SG against   matter.ACC
          pūblicam
          public.ACC
          'Catiline conspires against the state.'
        b. *coniūrātiō*   *Catilīnae*
          conspiracy.NOM Catiline.GEN
          'Catiline's conspiracy'

(14)   a. *Metuit*   *calamitātem*
          fear.3SG   calamity.ACC
          'S/he fears calamity.'
        b. *metus*   *calamitātis*
          fear.NOM   calamity.GEN
          'fear of calamity'

In (13b) the genitive corresponds to the subject of the corresponding verb and is an example of the **subjective genitive**. In (14b) the genitive corresponds with the object of the corresponding verb and is an example of the **objective genitive**. The genitive could be used to express the adnominal equivalent of a complement in the dative, ablative or even genitive case, and it could also be used with nouns that are

not derived from verbs. In the following example there are two genitives dependent on the noun *iniūria* 'injury' which does not have a verbal analogue (cf.
English *injury/injure*). One genitive must be interpreted as a subjective genitive
and the other as an objective genitive, but this can only be done on the basis of
extra-linguistic knowledge, although where both genitives have human referents
there is a preference for a prenominal subjective genitive and a postnominal objective genitive (Torrego 1991: 284).[4] The following example is a standard one. It
comes from Caesar (*de Bello Gallico* 1, 30, 2).

(15)   *prō* *veter-ibus* *Helvēti-ōrum* *iniūri-īs*   *popul-ī*
          for   old-ABL.PL Helvetii-GEN injury-ABL.PL people-GEN
          Romān-ī
          Roman-GEN
          '... for the old injuries inflicted by the Helvetii on the Roman
          people.'

The emergence of a specialised adnominal case is common across languages
and such a case plays an important part in the nominalisation of clauses. For examples, see section 4.5.1.

4.3.2   *External relations*

The case relation of a noun phrase is typically marked by an affix, an
adposition or both. The position of the adposition, i.e. whether it is a preposition or
a postposition, is related to whether the language has the order verb-object (VO) or
object-verb (OV). Part of the reason for this is that adpositions frequently derive
from verbs and naturally tend to retain the same position with respect to their complement. In English, for instance, the participle *concerning* has become an adposition as in *concerning the students*; it has become a preposition rather than a postposition for the obvious reason that *concern*, like all other verbs in English, takes a
following object. Conversely the corresponding German participle *betreffend* has
become a postposition since participles in German, like most dependent verbs, take
a preceding object (Vennemann 1973: 31). If similar developments have occurred
generally in verb-final languages (German is verb-final only in subordinate
clauses), then this will mean an association of postpositions and verb-final syntax. It
may be true, as is commonly believed, that languages tend to maintain a consistent
head-modifier order at clause and phrase level. Since the verb is the head of the
clause and the adposition the head of the adpositional phrase, this would mean an
association of prepositions with verb-initial languages and of postpositions with
verb-final languages. Whatever the reason, there is such an association plus a strong
association of prepositions with subject-verb-object (SVO) order as in English.

It has been argued that affixes rather than stems are the heads of words. This is most obvious in derivation where the affix determines the part-of-speech. The addition of *-ish* to *fool* in English produces the adjective *foolish*; the addition of *-ness* to the stem *foolish* produces the noun *foolishness*. With inflection the principle it is not so clear, but it can be said that the part-of-speech category can be read from the inflection. If we accept this idea, then we could ask whether the consistent ordering of heads and modifiers extends to word structure. If it does, we would expect the following correlations:

(16)   *head-modifier   modifier-head*
          verb initial   verb final
          preposition   postposition
          prefix   suffix

Even if we reject the notion of affixes being heads, for after all they are semantically less important than stems, or if we reject the notion of there being a tendency for heads and modifiers to order themselves consistently, we should still expect the correlations in (16) to hold with respect to case since there is good evidence that many case affixes derive from adpositions (see also section 6.1). In fact it turns out that in verb-final languages (almost all SOV) affixes are indeed almost all suffixes, but in verb-initial languages (predominantly VSO) and in SVO languages there are not the expected prefixes. These languages tend to have suffixes. In a study of the distribution of affixes Cutler, Hawkins and Gilligan 1985 found no language with case prefixes (but see section 4.4.1 below). They posit a general tendency for languages to prefer suffixes and they advance a psycholinguistic explanation. It can be established independently of the data on affixation that the initial part of a word is the most salient. Cutler, Hawkins and Gilligan suggest that stems favour this salient initial position, because stems are processed before affixes. The contribution of affixes can only be determined after stems have been identified.

There are two common distributions for the case suffixes. In one type case appears not only on the head nominal in the noun phrase but also on the determiner and usually the adjective (word-marking languages). This system is familiar from Indo-European languages and can be illustrated from Ancient Greek. In (17) the determiner and attributive adjective show concord for case, number and gender with *bios* which is masculine.

(17)   *ho   anexetastos   bios*
          the.M.NOM.SG   unexamined.M.NOM.SG   life.M.NOM.SG
          'the unexamined life'

Case concord is also found in Balto-Finnic, Semitic, in some Pama-Nyungan languages and elsewhere, but it is a minority system.

In the other type, case marking appears on the final word in the noun phrase (phrase-marking languages). We can distinguish two sub-types. In the first the final word is the head noun in the noun phrase. This type is widespread. It is found, for instance, in Quechua. It is common among the Papuan languages and there is a concentration of the type in Asia including the Turkic, Mongolian and Tungusic families north of the Himalayas as well as the languages of the sub-continent whether they be Dravidian, Munda or Indo-Aryan (though a number of Indo-Aryan languages have vestigial concord). In this area most languages are consistent modifier-head languages with SOV order at clause level and determiner-noun, adjective-noun order at phrase level. The following example is from the Dravidian language Kannada (Giridhar 1987: 33):

(18)   *Naanu   ellaa   maanava   janaangavannu   priitisutteene*
          I.NOM   all   human   community.ACC   love.1SG
          'I love all mankind.'

In the other sub-type the final word in the noun phrase is not always the head. This is the situation in various Australian and Amazonian languages (Derbyshire and Pullum 1986, 1989, 1991). The phenomenon also occurs in Basque (Saltarelli et al. 1988: 77):

(19)   *etxe   zaharr-etan*
          house   old-PL.LOC
          'in old houses'

Besides these two common distributions, there are a number of minority patterns. Among Australian languages there are some where only one constituent of the noun phrase needs marking, not necessarily the head and not necessarily the last word in the phrase. In Nyigina and Gooniyandi[5] discourse principles play some part. In Nyigina, for instance, the marking is often on the first word: *gudyarra-ni wamba* (two-ERG man) 'two men', or frequently on the word that is most significant: *ginya marninga Wurrawurra-ni* (that woman Wurrawurra-ERG) 'that Wurrawurra woman' (Stokes 1982: 59f). In another Australian language, Uradhi, the case marking applies obligatorily to the head, but only optionally to the dependents (Crowley 1983: 371f).

(20)   *Utagha-mpu   amanyma(-mpu)   udhumpuyn   ighanhanga-n*
          dog-ERG   big(-ERG)   back.ACC   break-PAST
          'The big dog broke [the other dog's] back.'

In some languages case is marked on the determiner and the noun but not on the adjective. Traditionally the determiner is considered to be a dependent of the noun, but this should not be taken for granted. In Ancient Greek the definite article would appear to be a dependent (see (17)), since it cannot appear in a noun phrase on its own. However, in many languages the determiner is morphologically the same as or similar to third person pronouns or demonstrative pronouns, that is, certain forms can appear as the head of a noun phrase (pronoun usage) or they can appear with nouns in a noun phrase (determiner usage). Where these pronominal forms are used as determiners, it is not certain that they are dependents, they may be heads. One such language is Diyari (Pama-Nyungan) where the determiner, which comes first in the noun phrase, is inflected for case and so is the final word of the rest of the phrase (Austin 1981a).[6]

(21)   *Nhu-lu   karna   pirna-li   wama   thayi-yi*
         he-ERG   man   big-ERG   snake.ACC   eat-PRES
         'The big man eats snake.'

Yaqui (Uto-Aztecan) provides a straightforward example of a language with case marking on determiners and nouns but not adjectives (Lindenfeld 1973: 60).

(22)   *Ini-e   tu?i   usi-ta=u   noka-?e*
         this-OBL   good   child-OBL=to   speak-IMP
         'Speak to this good child.'

Another language in which only the determiner and noun take case marking is Hungarian (Abondolo 1987: 591). In this language there is an article separate from the determiner. It is not marked for case.

(23)   *ez-ek-ben   a   nagy   görög   ládá-k-ban*
         this-PL-in   the   large   Greek   crate-PL-in
         'in these large Greek crates'

A similar situation is found in Tabassaran where adjectives all bear a marker *-i* rather than the case marking found on the head noun: *sib-i več* 'green apple'. As noted in section 4.2 predicative adjectives in Tabassaran bear a predicative marker, which Hjelmslev considered to be a marker of predicative case. He also took the attributive marker to be a marker of attributive case (Hjelmslev 1937: 139–40), but the two markers could be considered derivational markers of their respective classes. This analysis would seem compelling in that there is a third marker in the set, namely *-d-*, which marks adjectives serving as heads of phrases. This *-d-*

would appear to mark the derivation of nouns from adjectives. It is followed by case suffixes: *bic'ur-d-i qap'ur* 'the little one said' where *-d-* is followed by the ergative-instrumental *-i*.

In the Indo-Aryan languages adjectives exhibit fewer case distinctions than nouns and in some, including Bengali (Klaiman 1987: 499), they exhibit no concord at all. In Germanic languages that exhibit a morphological case system it is noticeable that in noun phrases with a determiner, an adjective and a noun it is the determiner that displays the maximum amount of differentiation. A paradigm of German noun phrases is given in Table 4.1. It shows a masculine singular noun of the strong declension with an adjective and determiner.[7]

In Maba (Nilo-Saharan) a nominative-accusative distinction is made by tone only on the determiner: *àmárà-gù* 'lion-NOM' versus *àmárà-gú* 'lion-ACC' (Tucker and Bryan 1966: 199).

In some Balto-Finnic languages there is concord with some case markers and not with others. Kilby relates this difference to the age of the case markers. The older ones display concord, the newer ones do not. In the following examples from Estonian, the elative shows concord (24), but not the comitative (25) (Kilby 1981: 115).

(24) *Puu   on   murtud   tugev-ast   tuul-est*
      tree   be   broken   strong-EL   wind-EL
      'The tree was broken by a strong wind.'

(25) ... *iseäralise   elavuse-ga*
           unexpected   liveliness-COM
      'with unexpected liveliness'

In a few languages such as Georgian and Hurrian concord extends from the head of a noun phrase to dependent noun phrases bearing adnominal case marking (Plank 1990). The effect of this is to produce double case marking. (26) is from Old Georgian (Mel'čuk 1986: 69).

(26) *sarel-ita   man-isa-jta*
      name-INST   father-GEN-INST
      'with father's name'

Double case marking is not uncommon in Australia. It is found not only in languages with concord but in languages that mark case phrase-finally. In (27), which is from Alyawarra, *-kinh* marks the relationship of *artwa ampu* to *ayliyla*, and *-ila* marks the external relationship of the phrase as a whole (after Yallop 1977: 117f).

Table 4.1 *German case inflection*

nominative	*der liebe Mann*	'the dear man'
accusative	*den lieben Mann*	
genitive	*des lieben Mannes*	
dative	*dem lieben Mann(e)*	

The suffix *-(i)la* represents a syncretism or merger of the ergative and the locative. It expresses A, instrument and location, and is glossed OBL(ique).

(27)　*Artu-la　ayliyla　　artwa　ampu-kinh-ila　atu-ka*
　　　man-OBL　boomerang　man　old-GEN-OBL　hit-PAST
　　　'The man hit [him] with the old man's boomerang.'

Quechua is a typical subject-object-verb (SOV) language with pre-posed modifiers in noun phrases and phrase-final case marking. A dependent genitive precedes the head noun and is cross-referenced on it (Weber 1989: 254).

(28)　*Hwan-pa　wasi-n-ta　　　rika-a*
　　　John-GEN　house-3SG-ACC　see-1SG
　　　'I see John's house.'

If the genitive appears on its own either because the head noun has been elliptically deleted (29) or because the possessor and possessed are represented as separate phrases (30), then the genitive case marker can be followed by an adverbial case marker.

(29)　*Hwan-pa-ta　rika-a*
　　　John-GEN-ACC　see-1SG
　　　'I see John's (house).'

(30)　*Hipash-nin-ta　　　kuya-a　　Hwan-pa-ta*
　　　daughter-3SG-ACC　love-1SG　John-GEN-ACC
　　　'I love John's daughter.'

Double case marking in noun phrases is logical in that it arises naturally from the operation of two independent case-marking strategies, namely the marking of dependents and the use of concord. The fact that it is relatively unusual suggests that languages tend to employ some special principle to bar it. In Indo-European languages generally there can be no second or outer layer of case marking; concordial case marking is suppressed where it would give rise to double case marking. In Latin, for instance, if a noun in, say, the accusative has a dependent genitive, then there is no extension of the accusative to the genitive-marked dependent: *Vīdī cōnsulis uxōrem* (saw.1SG consul.GEN wife.ACC) 'I saw the consul's wife.'

Another way of suppressing double case marking in noun phrases is to allow concordial case to supplant the expected genitive. This happens in Armenian where the genitive is supplanted by both the ablative and instrumental (Hübschmann 1906: 479),

(31) *bazmnt'eamb zarauk'n Hayoc*
  mass.INST troops.INST Armenian
  'with the mass of Armenian troops'

For an analogous example of concordial case marking replacing relational case marking at the clause level see (55) and (56) below.

4.4 Within the word

4.4.1 *Types of marking*

As noted in the previous section case is most often realised via suffixes. The almost total absence of prefixes is striking.[8] One solid example of case prefixing is to be found in Nungali, a Northern language of Australia (Hoddinott and Kofod 1976: 397). In this language there are noun classes. Prefixes mark case and class cumulatively (Table 4.2).

In some languages the case marking is not linearly separable from the stem. This is true of the classical Indo-European languages though the fusion of stem and case/number suffix is not too great. One can almost separate stem and suffix as a perusal of the Latin case forms in Table 1.2, which are fairly typical, reveals. An example of greater fusion can be found in the umlauted datives and plurals of Germanic. In Old English the dative of *fōt* 'foot' is *fēt* which derives from *fōti via *fǣti* and *fǣt*, the original *-i* suffix having induced an assimilatory fronting in the stem vowel before being lost. In the Slavonic languages case is basically marked by suffixation, but certain distinctions in some languages are realised by suprasegmental phonological properties. In Serbo-Croat the genitive/dative and locative of *i*-stems are distinguished by tone: *stvâri* 'thing' (GEN/DAT) versus *stvári* (LOC) (Corbett 1987: 398f). In Russian the genitive singular and nominative plural are distinguished in some instances by stress: *rukí* (GEN.SG) versus *rúki* (NOM.PL) (Comrie 1987: 333). The ultimate union of stem and case is suppletion as evidenced, for example, in the pronouns of Indo-European languages, witness English *I* (nominative) versus *me* (accusative).

Table 4.2 *Nungali class/case prefixes*

		absolutive	oblique	
Class	1	*di-gal*	*nyi-gal*	water
	2	*nya-ngarrung*	*nganyi-ngarrung*	woman
	3	*nu-ngulud*	*nyu-ngulud*	camp
	4	*ma-yadayn*	*nyi-yadayn*[9]	skin

Another category of inflection found frequently on nouns is number. The marking for number, like case marking, is usually via suffixation, and the number suffix normally precedes the case suffix as in Tamil: *āRu-kaḷ-ai* (river-PLUR-ACC) 'rivers' (Steever 1987: 737).[10] A partial exception is to be found in Classical Armenian where in some paradigms the number marking follows the case marking: *am* 'year', *am-k'* 'years'; *amaw* (INSTR.SG), *amaw-k'* (INSTR.PL) (Coleman 1991: 206).

Where pronominal possessors are marked on the noun these usually appear before the case marking, as in Turkish, where they appear between the number marking and the case marking: *adam-lar-ɪm-la* (man-PL-1SG.POSS-LOC) 'with my men'; similarly in Hungarian: *hajó-i-m-on* (ship-PL-1SG.POSS-LOC) 'on my ships' (Abondolo 1987: 584). In the Balto-Finnic languages, however, the possessor marking usually follows the case marking. In Finnish, for instance, we find: *kirko-lla-mme* (church-ADESSIVE-1PL.POSS) 'at our church' (Branch 1987: 610). The adessive case expresses the sense of 'near' or 'at'.[11]

Another category sometimes marked on nouns, and often on their dependents, is gender or class. Where there is a separable suffix as in Dravidian or Semitic, this usually appears before the case marking as in Arabic: *mudarris-at-u-n* (teacher-FEM-NOM-INDEF) 'a female teacher' (cf. Kaye 1987: 672). This example also illustrates a further category that can be marked on nominals, namely a specification of definiteness or indefiniteness. Dyirbal (Pama-Nyungan) is exceptional in marking noun class by post-case suffixation on determiners: *ba-gu-l* 'that-DAT-MASC' versus *ba-gu-n* 'that-DAT-FEM' (Dixon 1972: 44).

4.4.2 Stem formatives

In quite a number of languages some case marking is added to stems that include a stem-forming element, often identifiable as a case marker. This is not uncommon in the Daghestan languages. The paradigm displayed in Table 4.3 is a partial paradigm from Archi (Kibrik 1991: 256). The genitive and dative are representative of all the other cases in that they are based on a stem which coincides with the ergative. One can say that they are built on the ergative stem, but it needs to be noted that the forms *-i* and *-čaj/-če* do not function as ergatives when

Table 4.3 *Archi case marking*

	singular	plural
nominative	*qlin*	*qlonn-or*
ergative	*qlinn-i*	*qlonn-or-čaj*
genitive	*qlinn-i-n*	*qlonn-or-cě-n*
dative	*qlinn-i-s*	*qlonn-or-cě-s*

another case suffix follows. The ergative would appear to be the unmarked oblique case (see also Mel'čuk 1986: 63).

In Yuwaalaray (Pama-Nyungan) the dative and ablative of the pronouns are built on a genitive stem. A typical noun paradigm and typical pronoun paradigm are displayed in Table 4.4 (Williams 1980: 38, 47). The formative *-ngu(n)-* in *ngalingunda* and *ngalingundi* does not function as a genitive and *-ngunda* and *-ngundi* can be taken to be unanalysable case markers. That is not to say that the presence of *-ngu(n)-* is insignificant. It marks all the non-core cases. Such a generalisation can be captured in a feature analysis of the cases (see Table 2.15), but such an analysis is not dependent on the presence of any marker.

In Tamil, singular nouns have a stem distinct from the nominative to which all oblique case marking is added, but the stem-forming element does not appear without a following case marker. *Maram* 'tree', for example, has a nominative *maram* and an oblique stem *marratt-* to which the case markers are suffixed: *marratt-ai* ACC, *marratt-ukku* DAT, etc. (Steever 1987: 737).

Sometimes the differentiation between nominative and oblique is the result of phonological processes as with the consonant stems of several of the older Indo-European languages. In Ancient Greek, for instance, the oblique stem is original and the nominative results from cluster simplification, e.g. *elpis* NOM 'hope' has an oblique stem *elpid-* as in *elpida* ACC, *elpidos* GEN, *elpidi* DAT. In the nominative the final *d* of the stem has been lost before *s*.

4.4.3 Compound case marking

It is possible for a stem to bear more than one inflectional case marker. In some languages, especially the Daghestan languages, there are numerous local cases the marking for most of which is segmentable into a component for location, destination, path or source on the one hand, and a component for relative position on the other. In Avar, for instance, *-de* indicates 'to the top of' and may be broken down into *-d* indicating 'on' or 'over' and *-e* representing 'away from'. A fuller exposition is included in section 5.6.

As Mel'čuk points out, the stem-forming use of case markers and compound case marking are logically independent. They co-occur in a number of northeast

Table 4.4 *Yuwaalaray case marking*

nominative	*dhayn*	*ngali*
ergative/instrumental	*dhayndu*	*ngali*
genitive	*dhayn.gu*	*ngalingu*
dative	*dhaynda*	*ngalingunda*
ablative	*dhayndi*	*ngalingundi*

Caucasian languages including Lezgian where, for instance, the word *vaxa-q^h-di* 'moving to behind the sister' consists of a base *vax* 'sister' augmented by the ergative *-a* used as a stem-forming case, plus *q^h* 'behind' and *-di* 'to' (Mel'čuk 1986: 64).

4.4.4 Multiple case

Multiple case is not a common phenomenon. It involves two or more cases with different scope and often with different functions. Most but not all instances involve an inner layer of adnominal case plus an outer layer of adverbal case, as in the examples from Old Georgian, Alyawarra and Quechua quoted in section 4.3.2 (see (25) to (30)). However, some Australian languages evince double adverbal case. In Warlpiri, for instance, a locally marked adjunct may take ergative case marking in a transitive clause (Hale 1982: 266). Consider the contrast between the following sentences. In (32a) the noun phrase in the role of destination is marked for allative case as one would expect. However, if a verb for 'carry' is substituted for a verb meaning 'send', then it is possible to further mark the allative-marked phrase for ergative,

(32) a. *Ngarrka-ngku   ka   maliki   ngurra-kurra   yilya-mi*
          man-ERG   PRES   dog.NOM   camp-ALL   send-NPST
          'The man is sending the dog to the camp.'
      b. *Ngarrka-ngku   ka   kuyu   ka-nyi*
          man-ERG   PRES   meat.NOM carry-NPST
          ngurra-kurra (-rlu)
          camp-ALL(-ERG)
          'The man is carrying the meat to the camp.'

An inner local phrase normally has the patient as its scope (and this is normally encoded in the absolutive relation, i.e. as S or P (Blake 1982: 76)). In Warlpiri the use of the ergative on the locally marked phrase is to indicate that the agent (A) is also within its scope. With carrying, the agent moves to the same destination as the patient.

Where a local phrase occurs with a two-place intransitive verb that takes a nominative subject and dative complement, the locally marked phrase can show dative concord (Hale 1982: 269),

(33) *Ngaju   ka-rna-rla   kurdu-ku   mari-jarri-mi*
      I.NOM   PRES-1SG-IO[12]   child-DAT   sorry-INCH-NPST
      ngurra-kurra-ku
      camp-ALL-DAT
      'I feel sorry for the child (who is on its way) to camp.'

Another Australian language, Kayardild, has what look like spectacular examples of multiple case. In this language there is adnominal case, adverbal case, and two outer layers of what are etymologically case marking. In the following example the outer layers are glossed as M(odal) ABL(ative) and OBLIQUE (Dench and Evans 1988: 34).

(34) *Maku-ntha   yalawu-jarra-ntha   yakuri-naa-ntha*
      woman-OBL   catch-PAST-OBL   fish-MABL-OBL
      dangka-karra-nguni-naa-ntha   mijil-nguni-naa-ntha
      man-GEN-INST-MABL-OBL   net-INST-MABL-OBL
      'The woman must have caught fish with the man's net.'

The adnominal case is the genitive realised by *-karra* and the adverbal case is the instrumental realised by *-nguni* which appears on *mijil* 'net' and via concord on *dangka-karra*.

Of the two outer layers the modal ablative appears on all the dependents within the verb phrase and the oblique appears on every word in the clause. These markers do not mark the relationship of dependent nouns to their heads, or even of dependent verbs to their heads; they have a modal value. They are not case markers, but they derive from case markers. Their historical derivation involves the following steps:

(a) case is marked on a dependent verb
(b) case spreads from the head of the dependent clause (the verb) to its dependents via concord
(c) the governing clause is omitted and the formerly dependent clause becomes an independent clause.

Consider, for instance, the ablative, which means 'from'. It can often be marked on a verb, or at least a nominalised verb, where it will normally refer to the domain of time. Compare English *From working as a waiter he graduated to becoming one of the city's leading restauranteurs.* In many Australian languages case marking on a dependent verb will spread to the dependents of that verb, often producing multiple case marking. An example from Yukulta, which is closely related to Kayardild, is given as (53) below. It is also common in Australian languages for dependent clauses to come to be used without their governing clauses, i.e. they develop into independent clauses (an example is given in (24) in chapter 6). When this happens the case in the formerly dependent clause no longer marks the relationship of a dependent to a head, since there is no longer any head. An ablative, which formerly marked the subordinate clause as referring to an event prior to the activity or state described in the governing clause, comes to mark an event as prior to the speech act.[13]

In (34) the oblique, which may once have shown concord with an oblique constituent in a higher clause, marks the clause as if it were a clausal argument of a perception verb like SEE. The oblique has the effect of presenting the proposition as an inference (Evans 1985: 450 ff, Dench and Evans 1988: 34–5). It should probably be treated as a feature of the verb which spreads to the dependents via concord. Like modal case it is synchronically ungoverned (see section 1.2.4) and therefore it lies outside the scope of our original, central definition of case and our broader definitions (see section 4.2). Nevertheless, the derivation of this marginal use of case marking is clear.

Multiple case differs from compound case marking in that it cannot be captured in terms of a selection of unordered features from a particular set. This is particularly obvious in examples involving two tokens of the same case. Following Stephen Anderson (1982: 598ff) we could suggest that each layer of multiple case be assigned to a different layer of word structure, so that a word like *ngurra-kurra-ku* in (33) would be described in terms of a bracketed structure of the form [[*ngurra*-ALLATIVE]DATIVE] (Anderson 1982: 598 ff).[14]

4.5   Within the subordinate clause

Where a clause is subordinate the notion of case is relevant to the marking of relations within the clause and the marking of the relation of the clause as a whole to its governing predicate.

Broadly the following strategies are employed within a subordinate clause:

(a)   no change from the schema used in an independent clause
(b)   a non-finite predicate
(c)   nominalisation

Nominalisation may be partial or complete. Where it is complete, the result is a noun phrase. Such a nominalisation is not a subordinate clause but the functional equivalent of a subordinate clause.

Subordinate clauses, including their reduced equivalents, serve a number of functions:

(a) outer adjunct (not closely related to the meaning of the governing predicate)

(b) inner adjunct (e.g. a purpose clause where the subordinate clause makes sense only with certain governing predicates)

(c) complement (e.g. complement of verbs of saying, wishing, etc.)

(d) core functions such as subject and object

There is a correlation between function and form. The further one goes from outer adjunct along the function scale, the greater the likelihood of formal reduction towards nominalisation.[15]

(35)   form: finite > non-finite > partial nominalisation > full nominalisation

              function: outer adjunct > inner adjunct > complement > core function

4.5.1 *Internal relations*

A non-finite predicate is significantly different from a finite one in that it usually lacks any specification of subject either within the verb or via a noun phrase.[16] The missing subject of a complement clause is normally interpreted as being coreferential with the S of an intransitive governing verb or the P of a transitive one, and the subject of an infinitival adjunct clause is supplied by pragmatic principles.[17] Another possibility is for the expected subject of the non-finite verb to be expressed as the object of the governing verb. These distinctions can be illustrated from Imbabura Quechua (Cole and Hermon 1981 via Foley and van Valin 1984: 275–6). In (36) the complement of *yacha* 'know' is expressed by a clause with the normal valency, nominative for subject and accusative for object, though the verb has a marker (*j*) sensitive to tense, which replaces any representation of the subject in the verb (compare *yacha-n*) and forms a stem to which case can be added. It is glossed as a nominaliser (PRES.NM), but there is no syntactic reflection of any nominalisation.

(36)   *Juzi*   *yacha-n*   *ñuca*   *Maria-ta*
        Jose-NOM   know-3SG 1SG.NOM Maria-ACC
        juya-j-ta
        love-PRES.NM-ACC
        'Jose knows that I love Maria.'

In (37) the subordinate clause lacks an overt subject, the missing subject being interpreted as being coreferential with *Juzi*.

(37)	*Juzi*	*muna-n*	*lichi-ta*	*ufya-na-ta*
	Jose-NOM	want-3SG	milk-ACC	drink-FUT.NM-ACC

'Jose wants to drink milk.'

In (38) the first person singular is understood to be the experiencer of *juya* 'love'. However, it is expressed as the direct object of *yacha* 'know'. In some modern frameworks it would be described as having been raised from the lower clause to the higher clause.[18]

(38)	*Juzi*	*ñuca-ta*	*yacha-wa-n*	*Maria-ta*
	Jose-NOM	1SG-ACC	know-1SG-3SG	Maria-ACC

juya-j-ta
love-PRES.NM-ACC

'Jose knows me to love Maria.'

Full nominalisation allows the propositional content of a clause to be expressed as a phrase. The process can be illustrated from English:

(39) a. *John read the book to the students quickly*
      b. *John's quick reading of the book to the students*
      c. *He read the book to the students quickly*
      d. *His quick reading of the book to the students*

The subject is re-expressed as a determiner and the object is re-expressed as a complement marked by the preposition *of*.[19] The adverb is re-expressed as an adjective. Adjuncts like the *to*-phrase in (39a) carry over to the nominalised phrase.

As we can see from (39b) English has genitive-like phrases to express both the subject and the object of the nominalised verb. Where both genitive-like phrases are used the *'s*-phrase must be used to correspond to the subject and the *of*-phrase to correspond to the object. Where only one of the complements of the verb is to be re-expressed with the nominalised verb, there is some possibility of using the *'s*-phrase for either the subject or the object; the interpretation of a phrase like *the robot's delivery* is dependent on context. There is also some possibility of using either the *'s*-phrase or the *of*-phrase to encode the subject of a nominalised intransitive though *'s* is normal with animate agents (*The baby's crawling*) and *of* with inanimate patients (*the dripping of the tap*). However, English is unusual in having two genitive-like possibilities; most languages have only one.

As we saw in section 4.3.1 Latin uses the genitive case in both subjective and objective senses, which can lead to ambiguity where both occur in the one sentence. A feature of nominalisation is that it typically involves a reduction in the

range of possibilities found with verbs. In Latin the genitive used with a nominalisation can correspond to any adverbal case including prepositionally marked
complements. Thus one can have *imperium provinciārum* 'command of the
provinces' where the base verb *imperāre* governs the dative, and *reī pūblicae
dissēnsiō* (matter-GEN public-GEN disagreement) 'disagreement on political matters' where the corresponding verb and its complement is *dē rē pūblicā dissentīre*
with the complement of the verb marked by the preposition *dē* which governs the
ablative.

Although in general there is a reduction of the range of case possibilities there
are extra prepositional possibilities mainly used to resolve ambiguities which
would result if two genitives were used. The phrase *amor dominī dominae* could
mean 'the love of the master for the mistress' or 'the love of the mistress for the
master' although the first mentioned genitive tends to be taken to be subjective.
The ambiguity can be resolved by providing a prepositional alternative for the
objective genitive: *amor dominī erga dominam* means 'the love of the master
towards the mistress'.

The use of a nominalised verb does not always mean a wholesale switch to noun
phrase structure. In English, for instance, alongside *John's reading of the book* as
in (39b) there is partial nominalisation as in *John('s) reading the book surprised
me* or *His reading the book surprised me* where the nominalised verb still takes a
direct object though it can take a determiner.

In Latin the present participle behaves morphologically as a noun in that it takes
case and number marking and syntactically as a non-finite verb in that it takes the
same range of complements and adjuncts as the underlying verb less the subject
(Virgil, *Aeneid* 2, 49):

(40)   ...   *timeō*   *Danaōs*   *et*   *dōna*
                fear.1SG   Greek.ACC.PL   and   gift.ACC.PL
          fer-ent-ēs
          bear-PRPART-ACC.PL
          '... I fear Greeks even bearing gifts.'

In (40) *ferentēs* agrees in case and number with *Danaōs* and takes an accusative
object, *dōna*. However, some participles used with reference to ongoing states or
permanent properties came to be regarded as adjectives and then took a complement in the genitive which reflects full nominalisation. The following example is a
standard one (Cicero, *pro lege Manilia* 3):

(41)   *Semper*   *appetentēs*   *gloriae*   *atque*   *avidī*
          always   seeking.NOM.PL   glory.GEN   and   avid.NOM.PL

> *laudis   fuistis*
> praise.GEN   were.2PL
> 'You have always been thirsty for glory and eager for praise.'

Latin is unusual in allowing the genitive to encode both the subject and the oblique complement in nominalisations, and, as we have seen, English is unusual in having two genitive-like dependents available in a noun phrase to encode subjects and objects of nominalised verbs. Most languages have only a single genitive strategy. In some languages the genitive encodes the object of the verb; in others it encodes the subject. According to Givón the latter is more common (Givón 1990: 504).

In Dhalandji (Pama-Nyungan) the dative, which is the main adnominal case in this language, is used to mark the complement of transitive verbs in non-finite relative clauses. Contrast the accusative on *kanyara* and the dative on *murla* in (42) (Austin 1981c: 222). It is significant that the dative is the specialised adnominal case in this language corresponding to the genitive in Latin.

(42)   *Ngatha   nhaku-nha   kanyara-nha   murla-ku   warni-lkitha*
        I   see-PAST   man-ACC   meat-DAT   cut-REL.DS
        'I saw the man (who was) cutting meat.'

The verbal suffix *-lkitha* 'relative, different subject' marks a qualifying clause the covert subject of which must be interpreted as being distinct from the main clause subject (see also section 6.4).

In Turkish the genitive is used to mark the subject of a nominalised verb. The object of such a verb if present takes the normal case marking (Kornfilt 1987: 640).

(43)   *Ahmed-i   ben-i   sev-diğ-in-i   bil-iyor-um*
        Ahmed-GEN 1SG-ACC love-NM-3SG.POSS-ACC   know-PRES-1SG
        'I know that Ahmed loves me.'

The form *-in* is a third singular possessive form in cross-reference with *Ahmed-i*. In Turkish noun possessors are cross-referenced on possessed nouns: *Biz-im heykel-imiz* (we-GEN statue-1PL.POSS) 'our statue'. The accusative on the nominalised verb marks it as the complement of *biliyorum*, and the accusative on *ben* marks it as the complement of *sevmek* 'to love'.

In Finnish the subject of an infinitive is expressed in the genitive. There are a number of different infinitives used for different purposes. The following examples involve an infinitive marked for the inessive ('inside') case to express action contemporaneous with that of the governing verb. In (44) the subject of the infinitive is not expressed by a noun phrase since it is the same as the subject of the governing verb *sanoa* 'to say', but it is represented by a possessive pronominal suffix which follows the inessive case marking on the infinitive (Whitney 1956: 142).

(44)   *Tule,   sano-i   täti   kahvi-a   kuppe-i-hin*
         come   say-IMPF.3SG   aunt   coffee-PAR   cup-PL-ILL
         kaata-e-ssa-an
         pour-INF-IN-3SG.POSS
         '"Come", said aunt, as she poured coffee into the cups.'

In (45) the understood subject of the inessive-marked infinitive is different from that of the governing verb *tuijotta* 'to stare' and it is expressed in the genitive.

(45)   *Tädi-n   kaata-e-ssa   kahvi-a   kuppe-i-hin,*
         aunt-GEN   pour-INF-IN   coffee-PAR   cup-PL-ILL
         tuijo-tti   Eeva   ikkuna-sta   ulos
         stare-IMPF.3SG   Eeva   window-EL   out
         'While aunt was pouring coffee into the cups, Eva stared out of the window.'

Besides these widespread strategies of using non-finite verbs and nominalisation there are various other more particular strategies of which two will be described. The first is the accusative and infinitive found in Ancient Greek and Latin. The second is the use of detransitivisation to indicate certain patterns of coreference. This strategy is found in a number of Australian languages including Dyirbal and Kalkatungu.

In Ancient Greek and Latin there is a subordinate clause type known as the 'accusative and infinitive' used to complement verbs of speaking, thinking, believing, etc. The verb is in the infinitive, but whereas non-finite verbs do not normally have overt subjects, the infinitive in this construction takes an accusative noun phrase expressing S and A. If the verb is transitive, it still takes a direct object in the accusative, so there can be two accusative noun phrases as in the following Latin version of a prophecy from the priestess at Delphi to Pyrrhus, king of Epirus:

(46)   *Aiō   tē   Rōmānōs   vincere   posse*
         say.1SG   you.ACC   Romans.ACC   conquer.INF   be.able.INF

Since word order is an uncertain guide in Latin, the string in (46) can be interpreted as 'I say that you can conquer the Romans' or 'I say that the Romans can conquer you.' Pyrrhus optimistically chose the first alternative, which proved to be the wrong choice.[20]

In a handful of Australian languages a detransitivised construction is used in purpose clauses and in certain other dependent clauses to signal coreference between the A of a lexically transitive verb and the absolutive of the governing clause. The best-known exemplar of this phenomenon is Dyirbal (Dixon 1972). The following examples are from Kalkatungu (cf. Blake 1979a). As illustrated in section 3.2, the core case-marking operates on an ergative-nominative basis. (47) illustrates an intransitive clause and (48) a transitive clause.

(47)   *Kaun*   *muu-yan-ati*
            dress.NOM   dirt-PROP-INCH
            'The dress is dirty.'

(48)   *Kuntu* *wampa-ngku* *kaun*   *muu-yan-puni-mi*
            not   girl-ERG   dress.NOM   dirt-PROP-CAUS-FUT
            'The girl will not dirty the dress.'

There is a detransitivised alternative to the transitive construction, namely the antipassive. In this construction the A of the transitive verb is re-coded as S (in the nominative) and P is re-coded in the dative (also illustrated in (1b) in chapter 3). In independent clauses the antipassive signals reduced semantic transitivity, in this instance habitual activity.[21]

(49)   *Kuntu* *wampa* *kaun-ku*   *muu-yan-puni-yi-mi*
            not   girl.NOM dress-DAT   dirt-PROP-INCH-AP-FUT
            'The girl will not dirty [her] dresses.'

In dependent clauses the use of the antipassive is determined by syntactic rather than semantic factors. The following illustrations involve 'lest' clauses introduced by the subordinating particle *ana*. In (50) the antipassive is used in the first 'lest' clause signalling that the A of the transitive verb *muuyanpuni* is coreferential with the S of the governing verb. This contrasts with the second 'lest' clause where the absence of the antipassive indicates that the covert A is referentially distinct from the S of the governing verb.

(50)   *Wampa* *rumpi* *ana*   *kaun-ku*   *muuyanpuni-yi* *ana*
            girl.NOM fear   LEST   dress-DAT   dirty-AP   LEST
            lhaa
            hit
            'The girl is frightened in case [she] dirties her dress and [someone] hits her.'

If we substitute a transitive governing clause with *wampa* as P, the antipassive will operate in the 'lest' clauses with the same effect.

(51)   *Wampa*   *nga-thu*   *yarrka-puni-mi*   *ana*   *kaun-ku*
      girl.NOM   I-ERG   far-CAUSE-FUT   LEST   dress-DAT
      muuyanpuni-yi   *ana*   *lhaa*
      dirty-AP   LEST   hit
      'I'll send the girl away in case [she] dirties her dress and [someone] hits her.'

The antipassive is used to indicate that the A of a lexically transitive verb is coreferent with the absolutive (S or P) of the governing verb.

4.5.2   External relations

The relationship of a subordinate clause to its governing predicate is more often than not signalled by the normal case marking found in the language, i.e. suffix, preposition or postposition. In English this is partly true in that prepositions like *before* and *after* can function as subordinating conjunctions (*Before I go, I'll phone. After you get there, phone me*), but there are subordinating conjunctions such as *when*, *although* and *while* that are peculiar to that function.[22] In a large number of languages the local case markers are used with nominalised verbs to refer to time. In Quechua, for instance, the ablative is used to indicate 'since' and the limitative ('as far as') to indicate 'until' (Weber 1989: 291). In Pitta-Pitta the ablative indicates 'since', the locative 'while' and the allative 'until'. An example of the Finnish inessive ('in') case used to indicate 'while' was given in (43) above, and an example of the translative appears in (52) immediately below.

Where a clause rather than a noun phrase is a dependent, the same possibilities for the distribution of case marking arise. In most instances the case marker appears only on the head of the clause, namely the verb, as in the following example from Finnish, where the translative case is found on the infinitive. The translative means 'into', mainly metaphorically as in 'You'll turn into a pumpkin', and purpose as in *mi-ksi* 'what for'. With a nominalised verb it indicates purpose. The actor of the nominalised verb is expressed by the possessive pronominal suffix (compare (45) above) (Branch 1987: 615).

(52)   *Osti-n*   *karttakirja-n*   *suunnitella-kse-ni*   *automatka-n*
      bought-1SG   atlas-ACC   plan-TRANS-1SG.POSS   car.trip-ACC
      'I bought an atlas in order to plan a car journey.'

Another possibility is for the case marking of a dependent verb to spread to its dependents by concord. The following example is from Yukulta (Northern Australian). Note that the dative, which is appropriate to the verb *warratj-*, spreads to the allative-marked complement to yield a second layer of case marking (Keen 1972: 270).

(53)　　*Taamitya=ngandi*　　*tangka*　　*natha-rul-ngkurlu*
　　　　ask=1SG.3SG.FUT.AUX　man.NOM　camp-ALL-DATIVE
　　　　warratj-urlu
　　　　go-DATIVE
　　　　'I'll ask the man to go to the camp.'

This spreading may also occur where a clause modifies a noun phrase. In the following example from the Pama-Nyungan language Panyjima all words in the modifying clause show concord with the accusative-marked object of the main clause (Dench and Evans 1988: 28).

(54)　　*Ngatha*　　*wiya-rna*　　*ngunha-yu*　　*marlpa-yu*　　*paka-lalha-ku*
　　　　I.NOM　　see-PAST　　that-ACC　　man-ACC　　come-PERF-ACC
　　　　nharniwalk-ku　　*warrungkamu-la-ku*
　　　　hither-ACC　　　morning-LOC-ACC
　　　　'I saw that man who came this way this morning.'

In Vedic Sanskrit the case marking of nominalised verbs traditionally described as infinitives spread to the complement of the infinitive (Burrow 1955: 365):

(55)　　*dr̥śáye*　　*súry-āya*
　　　　see.NM.DAT　sun-DAT
　　　　'to see the sun'

(56)　　*Trā́dhvam*　　*kartā́d*　　*avapádah*
　　　　save.IMP　　pit.ABL　　fall.NM.ABL
　　　　'Save [us] from falling into a pit.'

These examples illustrate two principles. The first is case concord in a subordinate clause (cf. (53)) and the second is the use of special case marking for the complement of a nominalised verb (cf. (42)).

5
Survey of case marking

5.1 Introduction

This chapter provides a global perspective of case systems and their marking. It is divided broadly into two parts. In section 5.2 the organisation of the core or nuclear relations is surveyed and in section 5.3 the organisation of the peripheral relations is described. As Nichols 1983 points out, it is difficult to maintain a strict distinction between core grammatical cases, which encode S, A and P, and semantic cases like locative, allative and instrumental. A single case may cover A and instrumental function or P and allative (destination) function. Nevertheless there are significant generalisations that can be made about cases that encode S, A and P, even if they sometimes cover peripheral grammatical relations as well.

5.2 Organisation of the core

As noted in section 3.5.3, noun phrases bearing core relations are often unmarked altogether, while noun phrases in peripheral relations are marked by inflectional cases, adpositions or both. In languages like this the burden of distinguishing subject (SA) from object (P) or the absolutive relation (SP) from the ergative (A) is borne by cross-referencing bound pronouns or word order. On the other hand there are languages with inflectional case only for the core relations, or for these together with possessor function (genitive), with adpositions for other grammatical relations.

In the majority of languages the core grammar is organised on an SA/P basis (accusative system). In a minority of languages the core is organised on an SP/A (ergative) basis. A few languages have a system which could be described roughly as distinguishing agents from patients irrespective of transitivity (active system) and a few others are mixed.

5.2.1 Accusative system

The familiar languages of Europe, whether Indo-European or Uralic, exhibit accusative systems. In Latin, for instance, the subject is encoded in the nominative and the object in the accusative. Moreover, the subject is represented pronominally in the verb. In Romance languages like French and Spanish the unmarked word order also picks out the SA alignment, the order being subject-verb-object as in English. In the Bantu languages typically there is no case marking, but the cross-referencing agreement system and the word order operate in an accusative system. Both subject and object are represented by prefixes on the verb and the basic word order is subject-verb-object.

Pure accusative systems of marking noun phrases where the marking of the object is always distinct from the marking for subject are rare. Korean provides an example, but, as pointed out in section 1.2.5 (see (12)), the status of the grammatical case markers vis-à-vis the postposition/suffix distinction is controversial. Japanese, which employs postpositions as case markers, provides another example (see (9) in chapter 1). With most languages, however, some qualification is required with respect to animacy and/or definiteness. In Latin and the other Indo-European case languages there is no nominative/accusative distinction with neuter nouns. This is related to animacy in that virtually all neuter nouns are inanimate, though inanimate nouns are also plentiful in the masculine and feminine genders. In the Slavonic languages the accusative is not always distinct from the nominative, but it tends to be the same as the genitive and distinct from the nominative for animate nouns. In Russian, for instance, animate nouns of the masculine *o*-class and all animate plurals take the accusative-genitive form.

In many languages accusative case marking is not used if the direct object is 'indefinite'. It would probably be more accurate to say 'non-specific', but even that requires some qualification. Consider the following examples from Turkish.[1]

(1)   a. *Hasan*   *öküz-ü*   *aldı*
          Hasan.NOM   ox-ACC   buy.PAST.3SG
          'Hasan bought the ox.'
       b. *Hasan*   *bir* *öküz* *aldı*
          Hasan.NOM   an   ox   buy.PAST.3SG
          'Hasan bought an ox.' (non-specific)
       c. *Hasan*   *bir* *öküz-ü* *aldı*
          Hasan.NOM   an   ox-ACC   buy.PAST.3SG
          'Hasan bought an ox.' (specific)

In (1a) the accusative case marker appears indicating that the direct object is definite. A definite referent is one that is taken to be identifiable by the hearer. In English the definite article is used with common nouns when they are used with definite reference. In (1b) and (1c) the direct object is indefinite as indicated by the indefinite article *bir*. However, it is possible to use the 'definite accusative', as it is sometimes called, with the indefinite article. The accusative, as in (1c), is likely to be used where the reference is to a particular (specific) ox identifiable by the speaker. Where there is no accusative marker, as in (1b), the reference is more likely to be to a non-specific ox (*I was looking for an ox, but I couldn't find one*). It might be thought that if buying is the activity involved, then a specific entity must pass into the possession of the buyer, but where the identity of this item is unimportant, no accusative would be used.

In other languages the direct object is marked only if it is both specific and animate. In Hindi, for instance, a postposition *ko* marks specific, animate patients, a usage with parallels in other languages of the sub-continent (see also (26) to (29) below). In Spanish the preposition *a* is used to mark specific animate patients. Compare (2a) and (2b).

(2)   a. *Deseo   un   empleado*
            want.1SG   an   employee
            'I want an employee.' [Anyone will do.]
        b. *Deseo   a   un   empleado*
            want.1SG   an   employee
            'I want an employee.' [I can't think of his name for the moment.]

The preposition *a* (from Latin *ad*) means 'to', though not in this context. In Rumanian *pe* 'on' (from Latin *per* 'through') performs an analogous function (Mallinson 1987: 315–16).

Personal pronouns are definite and mostly animate and typically share any marking for animate and/or specific patients. In some languages only pronouns bear accusative marking. English is, of course, an example.

In all the examples discussed up to this point the marking of P is sensitive to properties of P alone, but in a few languages the accusative is sensitive to the relative status of A and P on a person hierarchy of the form 1, 2 > 3 or 1 > 2 > 3 (> means 'is higher than'). In the Australian language Rembarnga the proclitic representing P on the verb is suffixed with *-n* only when the person/number of P is higher than the person/number of A. In this language the hierarchy is of the form 1 > 2 > 3 plural > 3 singular. Compare (3a) where A is lower than P with (3b) where A is higher than P (based on McKay 1976).

(3)   a. *Nga-n-pa-na*
            1SG-OBJ-3PL-see
            'They saw me.'
        b. *Pa-nga-na*
            3PL-1SG-see
            'I saw them.'[2]

5.2.2 *Ergative system*

Ergative systems are often considered rare and remote, but in fact they make up at least twenty per cent of the world's languages. Ergative systems are to be found in all families of the Caucasian phylum, among the Tibeto-Burman languages, in Austronesian, in most Australian languages, in some languages of the Papuan phylum, in Zoque and the Mayan languages of central America and in a number of language families in South America: Jê, Arawak, Tupí-Guaraní, Panoan, Tacanan, Chibchan and Carib.[3] Outside these phyla and families where ergative systems of marking are common ergativity is also to be found in some other languages including Basque, Hurrian and a number of other extinct languages of the Near East, Burushaski (Kashmir, Tibet), Eskimo, Chukchi (Kamchatka peninsula), and Tsimshian and Chinook (these last two being Penutian languages of British Columbia).

In an ergative system of case marking there is normally zero marking for SP (absolute) and positive marking for A. The morphologically unmarked case is referred to by some as the nominative and by others as the absolutive. In this text the term nominative is used, the term absolutive being reserved for the grammatical relation embracing S and P. The Daghestan language Avar provides an interesting example because the SP/A system shows up also in the cross-referencing bound pronouns (Ebeling 1966: 77).

(4)   *W-as*   *w-ekér-ula*
       M-child.NOM   M-run-PRES
       'The boy runs.'

(5)   *Inssu-cca*   *j-as*   *j-écc-ula*
       (M)father-ERG   F-child.NOM   F-praise-PRES
       'Father praises the girl.'

The nominative is unmarked. The case marker glossed as erg(ative) is the one that also indicates instruments. It is common to find that in ergative languages the so-called ergative marks a peripheral function such as genitive, locative or instrumental as well as A. In fact in Avar A is peripheral relative to P. P is represented generically on the verb by a prefix for masculine, feminine or neuter. In (5) *j-* is the pronominal prefix for feminine. It also appears on the noun *as* 'child'. A, on the other hand, is not represented on the verb and is omissible. Note that S in (4) is represented on the verb by *w-*, the pronominal prefix for masculine.

In most languages the perceiver of verbs of seeing and hearing aligns syntactically with the agent, and the experiencer of verbs of loving, hating, etc. often does too. Avar is interesting in lacking such a conflation. While agents are put in the ergative, experiencers are put in the dative (as in (6)), perceivers in the locative (7) and possessors in an adverbal genitive (8).[4]

Experiencer

(6)   *ínssu-je   j-as   j-óx̃'-ula*
       father-DAT   F-child   F-love-PRES
       'Father loves the girl.'

Perceiver

(7)   *ínssu-da   j-as   j-íx-ula*
       father-LOC   F-child   F-see-PRES
       'Father sees the girl.'

Possessor

(8)   *inssu-l   j-as   j-ígo*
       father-GEN   F-child   F-be
       'Father has a daughter.' [lit. Of father is a girl]

In a few languages the core case marking is sensitive to the relative positions of A and P on a hierarchy. An example was given above from Rembarnga (see (3)) where the bound pronoun in P function was marked only if A was third person and P was second or first, or A was second and P first. In Fore (Papuan), the use of the ergative case is determined by the following hierarchy: pronoun, personal name, kin term > human > animate > inanimate. If A is higher than P, no case marking is used, but if A is lower than P, then A appears in the ergative. So if a man kills a pig, then no ergative is used, but if a pig kills a man, then the ergative marker *-wama* is used (Scott 1978: 100–17).[5]

(9)   *Yagaa   wá   aegúye*
       pig   man.NOM   3SG.hit.3SG
       'The man kills the pig.'

(10)   *Yagaa-wama   wá   aegúye*
        pig-ERG   man.NOM   3SG.hit.3SG
        'The pig kills the man.'

Where A and P both occupy the same position on the hierarchy, the use of *-wama* is optional. In the absence of marking, the first noun phrase will normally be interpreted as A.

In languages with ergative case marking on nouns it is true more often than not that the ergative marking is lacking from first and second person pronouns and sometimes from third. This latter situation is found in Yup'ik Eskimo, for instance, where nouns exhibit nominative-ergative marking but pronouns remain unmarked for all core functions (Reed et al. 1977). In Kiranti and Gyarong (both Tibeto-Burman) first and second person pronouns lack ergative marking, but all third persons exhibit it (Delancey 1987: 806).[6]

Only a very small number of languages have an ergative system of cross-referencing. Examples are to be found among the Caucasian languages, the Austronesian languages and the Mayan languages. In Avar (see (4) and (5) above) only the absolutive is represented on the verb, but in Abaza and Abkhaz (both northwest Caucasian) both A and SP are separately represented and there is no case marking on noun phrases (Hewitt 1979).[7] A similar configuration is found in the Mayan languages (Larsen and Norman 1979) and the South Sulawesi languages of Indonesia. The following paradigm (Table 5.1) and sentence examples are from the south Sulawesi language Konjo (Friberg 1991). In this language the ergative and absolutive relations are distinguished by both form class (Table 5.1) and order class, the ergative bound pronoun preceding the verb and the absolutive following. Note in passing that the ergative series of bound pronouns is the same as the possessor series except in the second person honorific where the system distinguishes a direct or core form from a possessor form.[8]

(11)   *A'-lampa-a*
         INT-go-1.ABS
         'I go.'

(12)   *Na-itte-a*
         3.ERG-see-1.ABS
         'S/he sees me.'

(13)   *Ku-itte-i*   *balla'-na*
         1.ERG-see-3.ABS   house-3.POSS
         'I see his/her house.'

(14)   *Na-itte-i*   *balla'-ku*
         3.ERG-see 3.ABS   house-1.POSS
         'S/he sees my house.'

Only a very small number of languages identify S and P in word order. One is Kuikúro, a Carib language of Brazil, where the neutral word order is SV, PVA. SP is also distinguished from A by stress and in the clitic system (Franchetto 1990:

Table 5.1 *Konjo clitic pronouns*

	erg	abs	poss
1.	ku-	-a	-ku
2 familiar	nu-	-ko	-nu
2 honorific	ki-	-ki	-ta
3	na-	-i	-na

407–9). In Balinese the word order with basic, underived verbs is SV, PVA thereby identifying P with S. There is a derivation yielding verbs with an AVP order (Artawa 1992 and personal communication).

5.2.3 Active system

Some languages, perhaps no more than a few score, organise their core grammar so that the argument of some one-place predicates is marked like the A of a two-place verb while the argument of the other one-place predicates is marked like the P of a two-place verb. Such languages have been called **active** languages (Klimov 1973), split-intransitive languages or split-S languages (Dixon 1979: 80–5). Examples can be found in the Kartvelian languages of the Caucasus. The following sentences are from Laz (Harris 1985: 52f). Note that the suffix -*k*, glossed ergative on the basis of its appearance on A in transitive clauses like (17), also appears on the 'agent' of the intransitive verb in (15). On the other hand the subject of the intransitive verb in (16) is unmarked like the P of (17).

(15)   *Bere-k   imgars*
        child-ERG   3SG.cry
        'The child cries.'

(16)   *Bere   oxori-s   doskidu*
        child.NOM   house-DAT   3SG.stay
        'The child stayed in the house.'

(17)   *Baba-k   meçcaps   skiri-s   cxeni*
        father-ERG   3SG.give.3SG.3SG   child-DAT   horse.NOM
        'The father gives a horse to his child.'

This pattern also occurs in Georgian, but it applies only to certain classes of verbs in the aorist tense group. In the present tense all subjects are in the nominative case and the direct object in the dative (Harris 1981: 46).[9]

The active system is also found in the Americas where it usually shows up in the bound pronouns on the verb. It has been reported from Guaraní (Andean); Lakhota and other Siouan languages; the Pomoan languages; Caddo, Arikara and other Caddoan languages; and Mohawk, Seneca and other Iroquoian languages. It also occurs in Acehnese (Austronesian) where 'agent' clitics precede the verb and 'patient' clitics follow; the A of a transitive clause is marked by a preposition *lê* (Durie 1985: 180–95). The position of the clitics with respect to the verb in this language obviously invites comparison with the Konjo examples in (11) to (14) above.

The semantic motivation for splitting the one-place predicates into two groups varies from language to language. In Guaraní predicates meaning 'go', 'walk', 'dance', 'swim', 'fall' and 'die' take agent pronominal prefixes (e.g. *a-xá* 'I go'), whereas one-place predicates with meanings such as 'be sick', 'be dead', 'be wise' and 'be grey-haired' take patient pronominal prefixes (e.g. *šé-rasĩ* 'I am sick'). The distinction, according to Mithun (1991: 513), is primarily one of lexical aspect or Aktionsart. Verbs in the 'agent' group denote activities, accomplishments and achievements. They involve change over time. Verbs in the 'patient' group denote states. In Lakhota, on the other hand, the marking is sensitive to whether the argument is one that performs, effects and instigates an activity or not. The verbs for 'walk', 'dance' and 'swim' take agent-pronominal prefixes, but verbs for 'fall' and 'die' take patient pronominal prefixes (Mithun 1991: 515–16).

5.2.4   Mixed systems

Some languages employ both ergative and accusative case, though it is rare for a language to have both across-the-board ergative marking and across-the-board accusative marking, i.e. a full tripartite system with S, A and P distinguished for all classes of nominal. The only example reported in the literature is the Australian language Wangkumara (Breen 1976). The more common situation is for ergative or accusative or both to be lacking from some classes of nominal. This is the situation in Nez Perce (Penutian) where first and second persons lack ergative marking. The following examples illustrate the nominative-ergative-accusative opposition (Rude 1985: 83, 228).[10]

(18)   *Hi-páay-na   háama*
       3SG-arrive-PERF   man.NOM
       'The man arrived.'

(19)   *Háamap-im   'áayato-na   pée-'nehne-ne*
       man-ERG   woman-ACC   3SG.3SG-take-PERF
       'The man took the woman away.'

In the Hokan language Eastern Pomo (McLendon 1978) there is an interesting variation on the active theme with complementarity between agent and patient in that pronouns, kinship nouns and personal names may take patient marking and other nominals may take agent marking (see Table 5.2) (I eschew the terms absolutive and ergative in light of the distribution to be described below). Verbs fall into five classes with respect to whether they take one argument or two and whether they take agent marking or patient marking:

1. One argument marked for agent and optionally a second argument marked for patient: ('kill', 'bite')
2. One argument marked for patient: ('fall', 'be burned', 'bleed', 'sneeze','become sick')
3. Two arguments both marked for patient: ('love', 'hate')
4. One argument marked for agent or patient: ('slip/slide')
5. One argument marked for agent with pronouns, kin and proper nouns and for patient with common nouns (i.e. no overt marking): ('sit/dwell', 'go/walk', 'stand up').

This distribution is interesting with respect to the distinction between case and case marking. If we follow the traditional method of taking a case to be the set of forms that together express one or perhaps more than one relation, then the columns in Table 5.2 are cases. When it comes to describing the marking with class 5 verbs, we can say that the 'patientive' is used with common nouns and the 'agentive' with pronouns, kinship nouns and personal proper names.

An alternative would be to call the overt patient-marking forms patientive, the overt agent-marking forms agentive and the unmarked forms nominative. This would mean recasting all the statements made above about marking with the various verb classes. Class 2 verbs, for instance, would have to be described as taking patientive with pronouns, kinship nouns and personal names and nominative with common nouns. The statements about marking would all be more complicated except with class 5 where one could now say class 5 verbs take the nominative case.

In a number of languages there is a split in the core case-marking system along tense/aspect lines. Georgian has the same active pattern of marking as its fellow Kartvelian language Laz (see (15), (16) and (17) above), but only in the past tense (Harris 1981).[11] In the present it has a 'nominative/accusative system', though it should be noted that P is in the dative not the accusative. It is common to refer to a system that operates on an SA/P basis as a nominative-accusative system, but it would probably be preferable to talk of an SA/P system, since there is not necessarily any accusative case.[12] The Pama-Nyungan language Pitta-Pitta has an unusual three-way system of marking in the past and present with an

Table 5.2 *Case marking in Eastern Pomo*

	patient	agent
pronouns	-*al*	-
kin	-*al*	-
personal proper names	-*yiy*	-
other	-	-*la*

unmarked nominative for S, an ergative for A and an accusative for P. In the future, however, there is an SA/P system with a marked form for SA and another marked form for P, namely the dative. Sentences (20) and (21) illustrate the nominative-ergative-accusative system in the non-future (based on Roth 1897, Blake 1979b).

(20)   *Muyutyu*   *nhan-pa-ka*   *nyunukana-ya*
        old.woman.NOM   she-NOM-HERE   tired-PRES
        'The old woman is tired.'

(21)   *Muyutyu-lu*   *nhan-tu-ka*   *watyama-ka*
        old.woman-ERG   she-ERG-HERE   wash-PAST
        nhan-(nh)a-ka   *takuku-nha*   *thupu-lu*
        she-ACC-HERE   baby-ACC   soap-ERG
        'The old woman washed the baby girl with soap.'

The following pair illustrate the future-tense versions of these same sentences. Note that there is a common form -*ngu* for S function, A function and instrumental function. It is glossed as F(uture) A(ctor) which is an ad hoc label for a case with an unusual range of functions. P appears with dative marking (compare (24) below). The future tense is morphologically unmarked.

(22)   *Muyutyu-ngu*   *nhan-ngu-ka*   *nyunukana*
        old.woman-FA   she-FA-HERE   tired.FUT
        'The old woman will be tired.'

(23)   *Muyutyu-ngu*   *nhan-ngu-ka*   *watyama*
        old.woman-FA   she-FA-HERE   wash.FUT
        nhan-ku-ka   *akuku-ku*   *thupu-ngu*
        she-DAT-HERE   baby-DAT   soap-FA
        'The old woman will wash the baby with soap.'

One would naturally wonder whether a sentence like (23) should be taken to be intransitive since the patient is in the dative. However, there is another construction in which the patient appears in the dative, namely the antipassive, and there is a syntactic opposition between a future-tense sentence with a dative-marked patient and an antipassive with a dative-marked patient in that the antipassive allows the patient to be deleted but the future does not. For this reason I suggest that the future construction is transitive and the antipassive intransitive. The dative in Pitta-Pitta is the case used to express 'through' or 'across', in other words it has the perlative function. Its claim to be called dative rests on the fact that it marks the patient complement of a handful of two-place verbs such as *yatha-* 'to like', *tiwa* 'be jealous of' and *wapa-* 'to look for'. Example (24) illustrates one of these verbs, *wapa-* 'to look for'. The subject is in the unmarked nominative and the other complement in the dative. Example (25) illustrates the antipassive version of (21) above. The effect of the antipassive in this language is to express desiderative modality.

(24)   *Muyutyu*   *nhan-pa-ka*   *wapa-ya*
        old.woman.NOM   she-NOM-HERE   seek-PRES
        nhan-ku-ka   *takuku-ku*
        she-DAT-HERE   baby-DAT
        'The old woman is looking for the baby girl.'

(25)   *Muyutyu*   *nhan-pa-ka*   *watyama-li-ka*
        old.woman   she-NOM-HERE   wash-AP-PAST
        nhan-ku-ka   *takuku-ku*   *thupu-lu*
        she-DAT-HERE   baby-DAT   soap-ERG
        'The old woman was wanting to wash the baby girl with soap.'

The motivation for using the dative for two-place verbs that are low in semantic transitivity like *wapa-*, for the future tense and for the desiderative modality, is clear. In each of these usages the transitivity is 'unfulfilled', i.e. there is no carrying over of the activity to the patient. With the future and the antipassive this notion of non-impingement is morphologically marked; with verbs like *wapa-* the notion is inherent or lexical.[13]

A number of Indo-Aryan languages including Hindi-Urdu, Marathi and Punjabi and some Iranian languages such as Pashto and Kurdish are described as having an ergative construction only in the perfect. Typical Indo-Aryan languages are described as having a direct/oblique case system where the direct case encodes S, A and P and the oblique is governed by postpositions. However, if P is animate and specific, it is usually marked by a postposition. There is also subject-verb agreement as in the following examples from Marathi (Rosen and Wali 1988: 4f).

(26)   *Ti*   *keeḷ*   *khaa-t-e*
             she banana eat-PRES-3SG.F
             'She eats a banana.'

(27)   *Ti*   *Ravi* *laa*   *chaḷ-ḷ-a*
             she Ravi ACC   torture-PRES-3SG.F
             'She tortures Ravi.'

In the perfect, however, A is marked by a postposition. The verb agreement is with P unless P is marked by the postposition for specific, animate nouns, with the verb then remaining in its neutral form. In Marathi the ergative postposition is *ni* (Rosen and Wali 1988: 5).

(28)   *Ti*   *ni*   *keḷi*   *khaa-ll-it*
             she ERG banana.PL eat-PERF-3PL
             'She ate bananas.'

(29)   *Ti*   *ni*   *Ravi* *laa*   *chaḷ-ḷ-a*
             she ERG Ravi ACC   torture-PERF-NEUT
             'She tortured Ravi.'

The postposition *laa*, glossed as ACCusative, marks indirect as well as direct objects.

The typical Indo-Aryan patterns of core case marking and agreement are summarised in Table 5.3.

5.2.5 Direct-inverse system

There is one other system that needs to be mentioned in this context and that is the direct-inverse system of marking. In this system, which is characteristic of the Algonquian languages, the marking on the verb indicates whether an activity is in line with the person hierarchy or contrary to it. In the examples given earlier of marking that is sensitive to the relative positions of A and P on the person hierarchy the marking is identifiable as accusative (as in Rembarnga, see (3)) or ergative (as in Fore, see (9) and (10)). In the Algonquian languages, however, the marking can simply be identified as **direct** (in line with the hierarchy) or **inverse** (contrary to it). Compare the following example from Plains Cree.[14]

Table 5.3 *Core case marking in Indo-Aryan*

	non-perfect	*perfect*
S	agreement	agreement
A	agreement	ERG
P [+specific][+animate]	ACC	ACC
P [-specific] or [-animate]		agreement

(30)   a. *Ni-wāpam-ā-w*
          1SG-see-DIRECT-3SG
          'I see him.'
       b. *Ni-wāpam-ik*
          1SG-see-INVERSE.3SG
          (*ik* < **ekw-w* INVERSE.3SG)
          'He sees me.'

In transitive clauses with two third person participants the direct and inverse markers distinguish whether a more topical participant (**proximate**) is A, which gives a direct combination, or a less topical participant (**obviative**) is A, which gives an inverse combination. A 'more topical participant' will be chosen on the basis of discourse principles and will tend to be the last-mentioned person or the discourse topic. The 'less topical person' is marked by the obviative suffix -*wa*.

(31)   a. *Nāpēw   atim-wa   wāpam-ē-w*
          man   dog-OBV   see-DIRECT-3SG
          'The man saw the dog.'
       b. *Nāpēw-(w)a   atim   wāpam-ik*
          man-OBV   dog   see-INVERSE.3SG
          'The man saw the dog.'

(32)   a. *Atim   nāpēw-(w)a   wāpam-ē-w*
          dog   man-OBV   see-DIRECT-3SG
          'The dog saw the man.'
       b. *Atim-wa   nāpēw   wāpam-ik*
          dog-OBV   man   see-INVERSE.3SG
          'The dog saw the man.'

As can be seen, there are two ways of expressing the same propositional content according to which participant is chosen as topic.

5.2.6 *Interpretations of core marking*

In many languages where there are local cases such as locative, alla-tive and ablative, there is a straightforward relationship between case marking, case and role or function. Typically there will be a marker peculiar to a case (though the marker may have variant forms determined by the shape of the stem), and the case will have a clear semantic function. With the grammatical cases, how-ever, the function is not always so clear, and the case marking, as we have seen, is often not in a one-for-one correspondence with the cases. The first point that we need to discuss is the meaning or function of the core grammatical cases and then the significance of the distribution of the marking.

Obviously the core grammatical cases express the core grammatical relations, so the first question that needs to be answered is why these relations exist. Basically the core relations of subject and direct object in an accusative (SA/P) system and absolutive and ergative in an ergative (SP/A) system are syntactic rather than semantic, though, with the exception of subject, they could be said to have a semantic basis (see below). Languages do not mark the roles of their com-plements directly. Apart from anything else it would be extremely uneconomical, since the roles are predictable from the meaning of the predicate, though with two-place predicates there needs to be some way of indicating which complement encodes which argument (compare the discussion of (27) in chapter 3). So irre-spective of whether the core grammar groups S with A or with P, we can expect purely syntactic relations simply because of the redundancy that exists between predicates and the roles of their arguments.

Subject

The most common system for organising the core is the SA/P or nominative/accusative system. This system has a discourse-pragmatic basis rather than a semantic one. It is clear that the subject is not a semantic entity since it embraces diametrically opposed semantic roles, agent in examples like *It bit me* and patient in examples like *I got bitten*. On the other hand one can show that the subject is characteristically associated with 'given' as opposed to 'new' material, and that where there is a referential subject a clause can normally be described in terms of being a predication about the subject even where the subject is new.

Let us take the association with given information first. Cross-language studies of the distribution of given and new information reveal the following givenness hierarchy,[15]

(33)   A > S > P > peripheral

This is to be interpreted as indicating A is more often given than S which is more often given than P which is more often given than the peripheral relations. The basis for the association of A and to a lesser extent S with given information is the fact that discourse, particularly narrative, typically involves the successive actions of humans and animals. In fact, if one splits S into animate and inanimate or actor (agent, perceiver, experiencer) and patient, then the hierarchy becomes,

(34) $A > S_{actor} > S_{patient} > P >$ peripheral

which points even more clearly to the fact that discourse involves higher animates being involved in a succession of clauses.

The subject treats the first two positions on hierarchy (33) alike and some of the grammatical characteristics of the subject can be related to its association with givenness. The most common form of agreement is subject agreement and it is generally accepted that the bound pronouns that figure in agreement derive from unstressed pronouns that have become attached to the verb. If A and S are most frequently represented by given information, one would expect them to be represented very frequently by pronouns, in particular, unstressed pronouns.

The subject is typically used to encode what the clause is about. This is clearest with symmetrical predicates such as *resemble, collide with* or *be opposite* in English. If a cathedral and a kiosk stand on opposite sides of the city square, we can describe this as in (35a) or (b).

(35)   a. *The kiosk is opposite the cathedral*
            b. *The cathedral is opposite the kiosk*

(35a) is a statement about the kiosk, about its position in relation to the cathedral. Conversely (35b) is a statement about the cathedral, about its position in relation to the kiosk. Of course (35b) is an odd sentence from the discourse point of view, but that is because we do not normally take an insignificant kiosk as a reference point for saying something about the position of a large building, which highlights the fact that (35b) is a statement about the cathedral.

The fact that a sentence typically embodies a predication about its subject is also evident in co-ordination. It is the subject that can be deleted from a non-initial sentence and the identity of the deleted subject is established by reference to the nearest preceding subject in the sequence of co-ordinated clauses. This is true even where the subject of the preceding clause represents new information as in the first clause of (36b).

(36)   a. *What happened to the worms [for fishing]?*
            b. *A kookaburra took them and flew off with them*

In some languages there are constraints on what can appear as subject; in particular, there are bans on indefinite subjects. In English there are circumstances where an indefinite subject is strongly disfavoured as in the following stock example,

(37)   *Waiter! There's a fly in my soup*

Grammatically one could say *A fly is in my soup*, but this would be to say something significant about a fly, and this is not a likely sentiment in the situation referred to. English grammar demands a subject, so the non-referential pronoun *there* is used as a subject, which allows the situation to be described without making a statement about *a fly* or about *my soup*. For the latter perspective *My soup's got a fly in it* would be appropriate.

In sum the subject is a purely syntactic relation characteristically associated with presenting given and topical information. In a language with a case system the subject is in the nominative case.

Objects

The accusative is the case that encodes the direct object of a verb. It will encode both the objects where there is a double-object construction and it may mark the object of some or all adpositions. The direct object has both semantic and discourse-pragmatic properties:

(a)   Its core function is to express the role of patient in a two-place construction.

(b)   Where a non-patient is expressed as direct object the activity is presented from the point of view of its effect on the direct object.

(c)   The direct object holds a position on the givenness hierarchy intermediate between the subject and the peripheral relations.

The direct object encodes the patient by definition. To identify a direct object we need first to identify the patient of a two-place verb, providing it is treated differently from the sole argument of a one-place verb; in other words we want to identify a P that is distinct from S. Not all two-place verbs treat the patient alike. If we want to identify the relation that matches up with the direct object of Ancient Greek and Latin, the reference point for our labelling, we need to specify two-place predicates of maximum semantic transitivity, predicates like SMASH, KILL or DESTROY, which take an affected patient, rather than semantically weaker two-place predicates like HELP or TRUST, which take a patient nearer to the neutral or unaffected end of the patient spectrum. This will ensure that we identify a relation comparable to the direct object of the classical languages. If we deal in verbs of lower semantic transitivity we frequently find that some of these take complements that are not comparable to the direct object of the classical languages. In Latin and Ancient Greek some verbs with meanings like HELP or TRUST took an indirect object in the dative case, and this treatment of two-place predicates of lower transitivity has parallels in other languages (see section 5.3).

The significance of the direct object can be appreciated if we contrast it with the non-core or peripheral relations. Consider, for instance, the difference between (38a) and (b),

(38)   a. *The old man walked in the streets of the village*

         b. *The old man walked the streets of the village*

(38a) tells us where the old man did some walking, but (38b) tells us that the man traversed a lot of streets, perhaps most of the streets. Where a role other than patient is expressed as P there is often an added sense of affectedness, or a holistic interpretation becomes likely (compare the discussion in sections 3.4.2, 3.4.4 and 3.4.5).

The difference between expression as direct object and expression as a peripheral relation is even more apparent in three-place constructions. Consider, for instance, the following pair,

(39)   a. *The vandals*   *stripped*   *the branches*   *off the tree*

          agent   patient   source

         b. *The vandals*   *stripped*   *the tree*   *of its branches*

          agent   source   patient

The roles appropriate for (39a) are non-controversial. The vandals are clearly the agent, the branches patient and the tree source. Of the two sentences (39a) would appear to be unmarked, since it exhibits a normal association of role and relation: patient with direct object and source with a non-core or peripheral relation. The ascription of roles in (39b) is more problematic. Under a common interpretation of constructions like this the tree in (39b) would still be the source and the branches the patient. But note the difference in meaning. (39a) presents the situation from the point of view of the effect of the activity on the branches, whereas (39b) emphasises the fate of the tree. In fact, the phrase *of its branches* can be omitted from (39b). This makes it problematic for those who claim that every clause has a patient. The problem could be avoided by claiming that the tree in (39b) has been reinterpreted as a patient, but that creates the further problem of finding a different role for the branches. As with the previous example it seems that the role normally associated with the direct object is patient and that the encoding of another role as direct object may involve some added sense of affectedness.

In the double-object construction, where one could say that a recipient or beneficiary is advanced to direct object, the patient object remains as a secondary object; it is not demoted as *the branches* is in (39b). It is clear in these constructions that the recipient or beneficiary object is not reinterpreted as a patient, but the effect of using the double-object construction is to present an activity from the point of view of its effect on the recipient or beneficiary.

(40)   a. *I gave her a fiver and she was pleased as punch*
         b. *I made her a new frock for the party and she was ever so pleased*

These sentences are appropriate ways of reporting the effect on the recipient and beneficiary respectively.

It is significant that in most languages the passive allows as its subject only the direct object of the corresponding active. The main function of the passive is to allow a non-subject of the active to be promoted to subject where it can serve as topic (the subject almost always has the function of topic in the passive). Only noun phrases expressing an entity that is seen to be of central concern, like *the branches* in (39a), *the tree* in (39b), or *her* in (40a) are suitable choices for promotion.

Part of the motivation for the double-object construction as an alternative to the single object plus prepositional phrase is to allow a redistribution of roles in terms of given and new. The recipient or beneficiary object tends to be given and the patient object new, whereas in clauses with a direct object and a prepositional phrase there is a tendency for the direct object to be given and the prepositional phrase new.

Outside the roles of recipient and beneficiary the association of new information and prepositional phrases remains strong. Entities in roles such as instrument and location tend not to recur much in discourse. They come up an odd time as new information expressed as a peripheral relation and languages do not provide for the possibility of advancement to direct object nearly so often as they do with recipient and beneficiary. The direct object, on the other hand, is more frequently given and this is reflected in the the fact that languages often have a series of bound pronouns for direct object.

Absolutive and ergative

At first blush it might seem difficult to find a semantic basis for an SP/A system, since the absolutive relation (SP) will include agents as in *I swim* and patients as in *It grabbed me*. However, a number of linguists including John Anderson (1977, 1979), Kibrik (1979) and Wierzbicka (1981) have in fact claimed that the SP/A distinction has a semantic basis. A is seen as an entity acting on or towards an entity external to itself, while the absolutive complements this. It encodes a range of patients from strongly affected (*The meat was eaten*), through weakly affected (*The spear was taken*) to unaffected or neutral (*The spear lay there*) and, for a few verbs, agents who do not impinge on another entity (*John swam*). Since the absolutive also encodes various non-patients that are advanced to the absolutive through various verbal derivations (see, for instance, (3) in chapter 3 where an instrumental is advanced to P), it would be best to recognise that the absolutive is a purely syntactic grammatical relation with the expression of patient being its core function. This interpretation is similar to the interpretation of direct object offered above, the difference being that the direct object encodes the patient when there is an A in the clause, whereas the absolutive encodes the patient irrespective of the presence of A.

It is interesting to note that in languages where there is number marking in the verb, this marking almost always refers to the absolutive irrespective of the organisation of the core grammar. The marking referred to here is pure number marking, which is often marked suppletively, not the more familiar person/number marking. In Dyirbal, for instance, the suffix *-dyay* added to the verb *nyinya* 'to sit' refers to the plurality of the sitters, but when added to a transitive verb like *gundal* 'to put' it refers to the plurality of the items put.[16] Dyirbal is a morphologically and syntactically ergative language, but the point is that this pattern holds irrespective of any other manifestation of ergativity. This would appear to reflect the fact that the absolutive is the relation most intimately connected with the verb and conversely that the ergative is not so closely connected with the meaning of the verb. It should also be noted that in many ergative languages the ergative relation is very much an agent. There is often not much conflation of other roles with the agent, often only a conflation of the perceiver of a few verbs like SEE/LOOK AT and HEAR/LISTEN TO, and in no language is there is any possibilty of other roles being advanced to A.

To claim that an SP/A system has a semantic basis does not entail claiming that the distinction is devoid of discourse-pragmatic significance. In fact it would appear that all the points made above about the difference between encoding a participant as a direct object rather than in a peripheral relation apply to encoding a participant in the absolutive as opposed to a peripheral relation. The significant difference seems to be P versus peripheral. Moreover, the distribution of marking in an ergative system has discourse-pragmatic significance. If we accept that A > S > P > peripheral as in (33) is a universal hierarchy of givenness, then ergative systems present a pattern of marking that is in conflict with this hierarchy insofar as they have positive marking for the function that is at the top of the hierarchy and unmarked forms for the middle of the hierarchy.

The marking

Now we come to the question of the distribution of core case marking. There are two aspects of this that are remarkable. The first is that languages with simple across-the-board ergative or accusative systems are a distinct minority. As noted earlier in this chapter, a majority of languages have partial ergative marking, partial accusative marking, or both partial ergative marking and partial accusative marking. The second remarkable aspect of core case marking is that partial ergative and partial accusative marking define a hierarchy of nominal categories (pronoun, kinship term, etc.).

Linguistically naive common sense would predict the occurrence of accusative and ergative systems. If we have three entities, S, A and P, with two of them in syntagmatic contrast, namely A and P, then the simplest marking system is one that provides positive marking just for P (accusative system) or positive marking just for A (ergative system). An S/AP system would obviously be dysfunctional and an S/A/P system though functional is uneconomic. This discriminatory view of the function of case marking fares fairly well. Accusative systems are common; ergative systems are reasonably common; three-way S/A/P marking is rare, and no across-the-board S/AP system has been reported. What this logical approach fails to predict is the high frequency of partial marking.

Silverstein 1976 demonstrated that the distribution of partial ergative marking and partial accusative marking defined a hierarchy of lexical content. The hierarchy is as follows:

(41)   1st person (speaker)
         2nd person (addressee)
         3rd person pronoun
         personal name, kin term
         human
         animate
         inanimate[17]

Partial accusative marking will always run from the top of the hierarchy covering a continuous segment. Partial ergative marking on the other hand will always run from the bottom of the hierarchy. A language may have accusative marking only on first and second person pronouns (Dyirbal), only on personal pronouns (English), only on pronouns, kin terms and personal names (Nhanda), and so on. All the positions on the hierarchy can be defined on the basis of the distribution of accusative marking, i.e. seven different cut-off points are attested. Ergative case marking tends to be found on all nouns or all nouns and third person pronouns.[18] In languages with a mixture of ergative and accusative marking, the two may overlap in the middle of the hierarchy giving a three-way nominative-ergative-accusative opposition for some category such as third person pronouns.

If this hierarchy is to have any explanatory value with respect to case marking, it needs to be established on an independent basis. It has been referred to as an agency hierarchy, but this is only applicable to part of the hierarchy, namely human > animate > inanimate where we can safely assume that humans act on animates (in effect animals) and inanimates, more than the other way round, and similarly animals act on inanimates more than the other way round. It has also been characterised as an animacy hierarchy, but this too applies only to the last three categories in the hierarchy. Mallinson and Blake suggest the hierarchy reflects a relative centre of interest, that events tend to be seen from the point of view of the speech act participants (1981: 86). With respect to the lower end of the hierarchy, what is involved is the interest of categories for humans in general. Humans are most interested in other humans, and more interested in animals than inanimates. With respect to the top of the hierarchy, the degree of interest is related to the speech act.

Silverstein 1981 claims that the hierarchy represents the extent to which entities are given or presupposed in language use. The act of speaking presupposes a speaker, and communication presupposes an addressee. Anaphoric pronouns are presupposed on the basis of reference earlier in the discourse and demonstrative pronouns presuppose the presence of entities in the ambit of the speech event. Personal names (*Maria, John*) and kin terms (*mother's brother, grandpa*) are known to the speech act participants. All the categories down to this point are definite. The last three categories are hardly presupposed on the basis of inherent features, but where accusative marking extends to these categories it is usually only where they are definite or at least specific.

The hierarchy manifests itself in a number of areas besides case marking. These include the following:

(a) rules of order
(b) number marking
(c) agreement
(d) advancement

(a) Order

In some languages the order of bound pronominal elements is sensitive to the hierarchy. In Gunwin^{y}gu (Northern Australian) a first or second person bound pronoun always precedes a third irrespective of whether it is subject or object (Carroll 1976).

(42)   a. *Nga-be-n-bun*
           1SG-3PL-OBJ-hit.FUT
           'I'll hit them.'
        b. *Nga-n-di-bun*
           1SG-OBJ-3PL-hit.FUT
           'They'll hit me.'

In French a direct object clitic generally precedes an indirect object clitic: *Marie les lui donne* 'Mary gives them to him.' But if the indirect object is first or second person, the indirect object clitic precedes the direct object clitic: *Marie me les donne* 'Mary gives me them.'

Kalkatungu (Pama-Nyungan) is an ergative language with pragmatically determined word order. In transitive clauses the orders APV and AVP predominate, but where P is first or second person and A inanimate it is unusual not to have P first as in (43).

(43)   *Ngai   unthayi-nha   kuu-ngku*
         me   soak-PAST   water-ERG
         'I got soaked by the rain.'

(b) Number

In many languages there are obligatory number distinctions with pronouns, but not with nouns. In Chinese, for instance, pronouns are obligatorily marked for plural (*tā* 's/he', *tā-men* 'they'), but there is no bound form for plural that can be used with nouns, though *-men* can be used with human nouns providing the stem is polysyllabic: *lǎoshī-men* 'teachers'. In some languages number distinctions are made only with pronouns and kin terms (e.g. Kalkatungu. See (4) in chapter 3). In some noun-classifying languages of northern Australia a human plural class occurs, but there is no corresponding non-human plural class. In Wappo (Penutian) plural marking is obligatory for human nouns but only optional for non-human nouns; adjectives show number concord only with human nouns (Li and Thompson n.d.). In Turkish the third person plural pronominal agreement is dropped if the subject is inanimate.

(c) Agreement

Agreement is normally on the basis of grammatical relations: subject only (Indo-European, Uralic, Altaic, Dravidian), subject and object (Chukchi, numerous Australian, Turkana), absolutive (Avar) or absolutive and ergative (Mayan). However, in some languages agreement is with the argument higher in the hierarchy irrespective of grammatical relations. In Dargwa (Northeast Caucasian) the verb agrees with first or second person not third irrespective of whether first or second is A or P. Where both A and P are speech act participants, agreement is with P. In Sora (Munda) a first or second person object is marked on the verb but not third. In Pintupi and Walmatjari (Pama-Nyungan) the subject and object are represented by bound pronouns enclitic to the first constituent of the clause. Non-core relations may be represented too provided that they are animate.[19]

In most languages with clitic pronouns for P only specific objects can be represented by the clitic. The Swahili example given as (14) in chapter 1 implies that Ali loves a specific beautiful woman. Without the object clitic it would mean that Ali loves any beautiful woman.

(d) Advancement

Verb derivations such as passive are normally based on grammatical relations, but in some languages the pronoun-animacy hierarchy is involved. In the Wakashan languages the passive is obligatory where the agent is third person and the patient first person. In Tiwa (Aztec-Tanoan) only a third person can appear as the agent of a passive and the passive is obligatory where a third person is agent and first or second person patient.

The relevance of the hierarchy is also apparent with the double-object construction. In English, for instance, it is practically confined to constructions with an animate recipient or beneficiary: *He sent the refugees food* but not **He sent the station food*; *He made his guest a weak cocktail* but not **He made the lemon tree a weak emulsion of white oil*. In Relational Grammar the double-object construction is considered to be derived and to reflect the advancement of an indirect object or a beneficiary to direct object (see section 3.4.3). Not everyone would agree with this analysis, but the construction certainly involves two object-like noun phrases as opposed to a direct object and a prepositional phrase and it is certainly true that the extra object is almost always animate. The double-object construction and its counterpart in syntactically ergative languages (see section 3.2) is not uncommon across languages and it is true that it is generally confined to animate advancees. In languages where there are bound pronouns for P but not for indirect object, it is almost always true that in the double-object construction the P series represents the recipient or beneficiary, a fact that supports an advancement analysis.

Case marking apart, these manifestations of the hierarchy are consistent with the view that events are seen from the point of view of the speaker and hearer. In most languages the subject, which typically encodes the topic, precedes the object either as the result of a discourse-pragmatic strategy or a grammatical rule. Rules placing first and second person ahead of third can be interpreted as reflecting a topic-first principle. Rules of advancement favouring the top end of the hierarchy can be given a similar interpretation, as can preferential treatment in agreement since representation by a bound pronoun reflects givenness. The tendency to have more number marking at the top end of the hierarchy is surely an example of speakers making more distinctions in categories of greater interest to them.

If we have then a hierarchy based on the point of view of the speech act participants, how is it that partial accusative marking is regularly distributed from the top of this hierarchy and partial ergative marking from the bottom? Silverstein and Comrie see language as taking as most natural an event in which the agent is the speaker or addressee and the patient a non-specific inanimate.

Silverstein comments on the naturalness of the distribution as follows (1981: 243):

> It would appear that ... language structure is grammaticalising (with characteristic asymmetry) the perspective from which a state of affairs is predicated of referents, the most 'natural' being that which grows out of the configuration of the ongoing speech event, the informational givens of which, the maximally presupposable entities, are of course the same orderings as above [see (41)]. Hence, speaker 'Agent-of' and 'Subject-of' in direct (as opposed to inverse) predicate schemata.

In similar vein Comrie talks of the most natural kind of transitive construction being one in which A is high on the pronoun-animacy hierarchy and P low and non-specific. He sees deviations from this pattern as leading to a more marked construction (1989: 128). On this interpretation accusative marking at the top of the hierarchy reflects the fact that it is less than maximally natural for a category such as a pronoun or a personal name to be the object than for lower categories such as non-specific animates or inanimates. Conversely the confining of ergative marking to nouns reflects the fact that it is less natural for a noun to be an agent of a transitive verb than for a pronoun. This might seem strange outside the context of discourse; after all, sentences of the pattern *The man hit the dog* are common as linguistics examples. But in discourse sentences with nouns in A function are not so common as one might think (see the givenness hierarchy in (33)). The A function will be filled by a noun only where A is new, but in any coherent text most of the activities will be carried out by an A (or S) that is given on the basis of prior mention or because it is a speech act participant. In both these circumstances A will be represented by an unstressed pronoun, by a bound pronoun if one is available. Where ergative-marked noun phrases occur, they are often encoding non-specific agents or the forces of nature (as in (43) above).

In most languages with partial ergative or accusative case marking, A and P are marked independently, i.e. simply according to the category of nominal instantiating them, e.g. A is marked ergative if it is a noun and P is marked accusative if it is a pronoun. In a few languages, as we have seen, the marking is determined by the relative positions of A and P on the hierarchy and these are the most convincing examples of the sensitivity of marking to hierarchical considerations. The examples given in previous sections include the following types:

(a)   accusative marking used only where A is lower than P. See examples (3a) and (b) involving bound pronouns in Rembarnga.

(b)   ergative marking used only where A is lower than P. See examples (9) and (10) involving noun phrases in Fore.

(c)   marking for direct combinations (A higher than P) or inverse combinations (A lower than P) that cannot be linked either to A or P. See examples (30) to (32) from Cree.

The notion that partial ergative and partial accusative marking appear where there is a deviation from a kind of ideal transitive predication has the advantage of supplying a single explanation for both ergative and accusative marking. There are, however, some other attempts at explanation, one relevant primarily to accusative marking and one relevant primarily to ergative marking.

Hopper and Thompson make cross-language generalisations about the way greater semantic transitivity is reflected in formal transitivity. Full semantic transitivity involves an agent affecting a patient. There is less than full transitivity if the predicate is one of perception (SEE) or emotion (LOVE) or if the tense is future, the polarity negative, the aspect imperfective and so on. Languages usually have two ways of treating two-place predicates. There will normally be a large class of transitive verbs and another smaller class of intransitive verbs and adjectives that take their complement in a non-core relation. The formally transitive verbs will encode the predicates of greater semantic transitivity and the intransitive verbs and adjectives will naturally correlate with less than full semantic transitivity. Hopper and Thompson consider that there is greater semantic transitivity where a patient is specific rather than non-specific, definite rather than indefinite, human or animate rather than inanimate. They see positive marking for P, whether it be signalled by cross-referencing, position or case marking, to be indicative of greater semantic transitivity.

A view particularly relevant to ergative case marking is to be found in Wierzbicka (1980: 129f, 1981: 66ff). She sees ergative constructions as ones in which the action is seen from the point of view of the patient rather than of the agent; the patient is presented as the central, unmarked entity and the agent as a peripheral, marked entity. First and second persons especially and pronouns in general are most likely to drop their 'peripheral' marking, since they are given and topic-worthy. One could note that in English and various other languages passives with pronominal agent phrases are generally disfavoured. The ergative construction, which is transitive, and the passive, which is intransitive and in marked opposition with an active transitive construction, cannot be fully identified. Nevertheless there is some analogy between the marked A of the ergative and the marked agent of the passive.

The approaches to ergative marking of Comrie and Silverstein on the one hand and Wierzbicka on the other are perhaps not too far apart. In the former pronouns do not bear ergative marking because they are the most natural exponents of A and languages tend to leave what is most natural least marked. In the Wierzbicka view pronouns, especially first and second person pronouns, are natural topics and it is therefore appropriate that they be encoded as central, unmarked entities.[20]

One last point. Where there is an SA/P system and an SP/A system in the one clause, then it is always true that the SA/P system is found with bound pronouns, which naturally will be carrying given information rather than new. It should also be noted that inter-clausal rules of syntax such as the marking of switch-reference usually operate on an SA basis even where the case-marking system is nominative-ergative. These rules involve given information in at least one clause.[21]

5.3 Dative

In Ancient Greek the case used to express the indirect object with verbs like *didonai* 'to give' was called the *ptōsis dotikē* or 'giving case'. The label *dative* is the Latin translation applied to the Latin case with the corresponding function: *Cassius Brūtō librum dat* (Cassius.NOM Brutus.DAT book.ACC give.3SG) 'Cassius gives a book to Brutus'. However, in both Greek and Latin the dative also marked the non-subject complement of certain intransitive verbs. These complements were taken to be indirect objects like the dative complements of three-place verbs. Here are some examples of intransitive verbs that take an indirect object in the dative:

(44)   Greek   Latin
           boēthein   *auxiliārī*   help
           peithesthai   *parēre*   obey
           pisteuein   *fidere*   trust
           orgizesthai   *īrāscī*   be angry with

Cases are not isomorphic across languages, i.e. we do not find that languages generally have the same number of cases with each case in one language matching the extension of a corresponding case in other languages. The dative in Greek, for instance, covers a greater range than the dative in Latin. Greek does not have an ablative as Latin does and the Greek dative covers the instrumental and locative functions of the Latin ablative.[22] This lack of isomorphy can lead to difficulties in applying case labels. What does one do in describing language x if one case encodes the recipient of giving and another case the complement of some intransitive verbs? This problem confronted me in describing Kalkatungu (Blake 1979a). One case marked by -*ku* encoded the complement of a handful of intransitive verbs as well as the roles of purpose and beneficiary. Another case marked by -*kunha* encoded the recipient of the verb 'to give' as well as the role of destination. I chose to call the -*ku* case dative since it marked the complement (indirect object) of verbs analogous to verbs in Ancient Greek and Latin like those illustrated in (44) and the -*kunha* case allative (see Table 2.14). This strategy for identifying a dative gives good cross-language comparability. The dative under this interpretation emerges as the main non-core case used to mark complements. Its range of functions will typically include those listed as (a), (b) and (c) in (45) and quite frequently functions (d) to (h).

(45)   a. indirect object of some two-place verbs low on the transitivity scale (e.g. verbs such as HELP, SEEK or LIKE)

          b. indirect object of a few three-place verbs such as GIVE and SHOW

          c. the roles of purpose (*She went for fish*) and beneficiary (*She went for (on behalf of) her mother*). In a few languages there is a separate purposive case (e.g. Irula). Basque has a purposive case and a benefactive case (Saltarelli et al. 1988: 156–66)

          d. possessor (frequently expressed by the genitive)

          e. destination (sometimes expressed by a separate allative case as in many Australian languages)

          f. the indirect object of a detransitivised construction as in the antipassive of various languages (see (25) above from Pitta-Pitta)

          g. the direct object in certain aspects or tenses (see (23) above from Pitta-Pitta and (53b) below from Georgian)

          h. the indirect subject of certain verbs or of all verbs in certain aspects. This usage is somewhat different from the rest and is described at the end of this section. See (51) , (52) and (53).

The accusative is a syntactic case which can encode a variety of semantic roles, but one could take the central and defining function to be that of encoding the affected patient of activity verbs. The dative is likewise a syntactic case that can encode a variety of roles, but I would suggest that its central function is to encode entities that are the target of an activity or emotion. Traditional definitions refer to the entity indirectly affected as opposed to the entity directly affected, which is encoded by the direct object (at least in the active).[23] The accusative and the dative may be in syntagmatic contrast or in paradigmatic opposition. With verbs like

Latin *dāre* 'to give', *monstrāre* 'to show' and *mandāre* 'to entrust', the two cases are in syntagmatic contrast with the accusative encoding the entity that is directly affected in the sense that it is moved or transferred to new ownership and the dative encoding the sentient destination, the one to whom the transfer is directed.

(46)   *Brūtus*   *rem*   *mihi*   *mandāvit*
       Brutus.NOM   matter.ACC me.DAT   entrust.PERF.3SG
       'Brutus entrusted the matter to me.'

With a two-place verb like *auxiliārī* 'to help', *parēre* 'to obey', *fidere* 'to trust' or *īrāscī* 'to be angry with' the dative complement is in paradigmatic opposition with the accusative with verbs like *necāre* 'to kill', *tractāre* 'to pull' and *movēre* 'to move'. The accusative encodes entities that are directly affected whereas the dative encodes entities that are not directly affected. It should be added that one cannot predict the case from the role, since while it is true that entities directly affected by activities are always encoded in the accusative (at least in the active voice), entities that are not affected are encoded as accusatives with some verbs and datives with others. *Amāre* 'to love', for instance, is a transitive verb which takes an accusative direct object encoding the neutral (unaffected) patient, so is *vidēre* 'to see'. This generalisation about accusative-dative alternation carries over to a great number of other languages, although it needs to be reinterpreted some-what for languages that lack a dative case. In English, for instance, some predi-cates low on the transitivity scale are instantiated as verbs that take prepositional complements (*look for, look like,* etc.) and others are instantiated by adjectives that take prepositional complements with *of* as the unmarked or default choice (*be jeal-ous of, be supportive of*).

In many languages some verb roots appear both as transitive verbs with a direct object and as intransitive verbs with an indirect object in the dative. A few verbs in Latin are like this; *temperāre* 'to temper' or to 'restrain' is one; *moderor* which has much the same meaning is another. When these verbs refer to restraining or con-trolling an entity external to the agent, they are used transitively (47a), but where they refer to exercising self-restraint they take a dative complement (47b).

(47)   a. *Ego*   *moderor*   *equum*   *meum*
          I.NOM   moderate.1SG horse.ACC   my.ACC
          'I control my horse.'
       b. *Ego*   *moderor*   *ōrātiōnī*   *meae*
          I.NOM   moderate.1SG speech.DAT   myDAT
          'I moderate my speech.'

With self-restraint the restraint is directed towards oneself and the entity specified in the dative is only indirectly involved. In some Australian languages a particular verb root may cover 'look for' and 'find'. When such a verb takes a dative complement, it means 'look for', but when it is used transitively it means 'find'. Here the difference seems to be between activity directed towards a target and successful achieving of the target.

In many languages alternations between a transitive construction and a detransitivised antipassive-type construction are not confined to particular roots, but express some general difference of aspect or modality. Many of these detransitivised constructions involve the dative case. Examples from two Australian languages, Kalkatungu and Pitta-Pitta have been given earlier. In Pitta-Pitta the dative is used as follows:

(a)   the indirect object of a handful of verbs such as *wapa-* 'to look for', *yatha* 'to like' and *tiwa* 'to be jealous of' (24),

(b)   the indirect object in the antipassive construction which expresses desiderative modality (25),

(c)   the direct object in the future tense. A tentative example from Pitta-Pitta was given as (23) above. A stronger example from Georgian is given as (53b) below.

As noted in the discussion of the Pitta-Pitta examples the use of the dative across this range makes sense. It marks entities that are unaffected either because of the lexical meaning of the predicate (as with *tiwa* 'be jealous of') or because of a modality (desiderative) or a tense (future) that logically overrides any sense of direct impingement inherent in a particular predicate. Of course it should be added that this 'logic' is not normal language practice. More often than not case marking is simply insensitive to tense, aspect, modality and the like.

In the examples discussed up to this point the clause containing the dative has also contained a subject expressing an agent or an experiencer. In these examples the alignment of roles and relations has been normal. However, it is also possible to find examples where the dative encodes the roles normally assigned to subject. In many languages the dative is used to express the experiencer with a handful of verbs often including the translational equivalent of English *please*. This can be illustrated from Latin where *placēre* takes an experiencer in the dative. It may be used with a referential subject (48) or impersonally (49).

(48)   *Nōn   placet   Antōniō   meus   cōnsulātus*
         not   please.3SG   Antonius.DAT   my.NOM   consulship.NOM
         'My consulship does not please Antonius.'

(49)   *Venerī   placet   mittere   ...*
        Venus.DAT   please.3SG   send.INF
        'It pleases Venus to send ... .'

Latin also affords examples of a dative that is not limited lexically, but which can apply to any verb. This is the so-called dative of agent. It is used with the gerundive, a passive-like participle with a modal force of obligation. An example was given in chapter 3 in connection with identifying the role of agent across different cases (see (32)). It is repeated here as (50b) with its active counterpart (50a).

(50)   a. *Ego   hanc   provinciam   defendō*
           I.NOM   this.ACC   province.ACC   defend.1SG
           'I defend this province.'
        b. *Haec   mihi   provincia   est*
           this.NOM   me.DAT   province.NOM   is.3SG
           defendenda
           defend.GER.NOM
           'This province is to be defended by me.'

In (50b) the direct object of the active verb has been re-expressed as the subject of the gerundive. If we use the gerundive construction with a dative-taking verb like *moderor* in (47), the dative complement cannot be re-expressed as subject, so an impersonal construction must be used. In (51) the verb has a third person singular neuter non-referential subject expressed in the verb. Note that the original dative of the base verb is retained so that putting the subject of the base verb into the dative results in two datives with a syntagmatic contrast between an indirect object and what is sometimes referred to as an indirect subject.

(51)   *Moderandum   est   mihi   ōrātiōnī*
        moderate.GER.3SG.NEUT   is.3SG   me.DAT   speech.DAT
        meae
        my.DAT
        'I must moderate my speech.'

The constructions illustrated in (48), (49) and (50b) are all examples of inversion constructions. The label **inversion** implies that the alignment of role and relation is inverted, in particular it implies that the roles normally encoded as subject are encoded in the dative (see also the discussion of inversion in section 3.4.3).

These indirect subjects, as they are sometimes called, are not uncommon; they are an areal feature of the Indian subcontinent. The following example is from Malayalam (Dravidian) (McAlpin 1976: 191):

(52)   *Avaḷkku   avane   itikkaam*
         her.DAT   him.ACC   can/may.hit
         'She can hit him.'

In the Malayalam example the dative in conjunction with the potential marker *-aam* on the verb signals physical ability or permission. In some Kartvelian languages such as Georgian the use of the dative to mark the agent indicates the evidential mode: 'Evidently she did so-and-so' (Harris 1984). The following group of examples illustrate the ergative construction used in the past tense (53a), the accusative construction with dative-marked direct and indirect object used in the present tense (53b), and the inversion construction used to indicate lack of direct evidence (53c) (Harris 1984: 263).

(53)   a. *Rezo-m   gačuka   samajuri   (šen)*
            Rezo-ERG   you.gave.3s.it   bracelet .NOM   (you-DAT)
            'Rezo gave you a bracelet.'
         b. *Rezo   gačukebs   samajur-s   (šen)*[24]
            Rezo.NOM   you.give.3s.it   bracelet.DAT   (you.DAT)
            'Rezo gives you a bracelet.'
         c. *Turme   Rezo-s   učukebia   samajuri*
            apparently   Rezo-DAT   gave.3s.it.evid   bracelet.NOM
            šen-tvis
            you-BEN
            'Apparently Rezo gave a bracelet to you.'

Indirect subjects are rather like ergative-marked dependents in lacking the superficial properties of subject such as case, obviously, and control of agreement. However, they often exhibit syntactic properties of subjects. In Italian the dative complement of *piacere* 'to be pleasing to' can control the understood subject of a non-finite complement just as an unequivocal subject of a non-inversion verb can. In (54) which contains a normal non-inversion verb, the subject *Giorgio* is understood as the subject of the infinitive *far(e)*. In (55) it is still *Giorgio* that is understood as the subject of the infinitive *lasciar(e)*, even though *Giorgio* is not the subject of the main verb, *una compagna d'ufficio* is (examples adapted from Perlmutter 1982: 316–18).[25]

(54) Giorgio mi   ha   rimproverato tante   volte   da
     George   me has   reproved   so.many   times   to
     farmi   *paura*
     make.me   fear
     'George rebuked me so many times that he scared me.'

(55) A   Giorgio è   talmente piaciuta   una   compagna d'ufficio
     To   George   is   so   pleased   a   companion-of-office
     da   *lasciarci*
     to   leave.us
     [lit.] 'To George was so pleasing an office co-worker that he left us.'
     'George was so taken with a woman at the office that he left us.'

In Old and Middle English there were inversion verbs where the dative complement could be treated as a subject from the point of view of co-ordination. In the following example from Chaucer *'thoughte'* (< O.E. *thyncan* 'to seem'), which is an inversion verb, is conjoined with *granted*, which is a normal verb. The pronoun *us* is an oblique form, as it is in modern English. It represents a syncretism of accusative and dative. The subject of *granted*, if it had been expressed, would have been *we* (*Canterbury Tales*, the Prologue A 785–7).

(56) *Us thoughte it was noght worth to make it wys*
     And graunted him withouten more avys,
     And bad him seye his verdit, as him leste.

The verb *leste* (< O.E. *lystan* 'to please') is also an inversion verb used impersonally, literally 'as to-him it lusted', i.e. 'as it pleased him'.

It is quite common for the dative to be used to express the possessor. In languages where there is a dative but no separate genitive the dative is used adnominally. A dative of possession occurred in Latin as well as a genitive of possession and a possessive adjective (examples from Woodcock (1959: 46)).

(57) *Illi*   *duae*   *fuere*   *filiae*
     that.DAT   two.NOM   were.3PL   daughters.NOM
     'He had two daughters.'

(58) *Illius*   *duae*   *fuere*   *filiae*
     that.GEN   two.NOM   were.3PL   daughters.NOM
     'The two daughters were his.'

With the dative the existence of the daughters is asserted; with the genitive the existence of the daughters is taken as given and the identity of the possessor asserted.

5.4 Genitive

A genitive case is widespread. On the basis of Latin one would normally ascribe the label genitive to the most common or unmarked adnominal case, although one would not expect such a case to be exclusively adnominal. In Latin the genitive marks the complement of a handful of verbs such as *oblīvīscī* 'to forget' and *misererī* 'to pity'. In other languages, Old English for instance, the genitive marks the complement of some scores of verbs and vies with the dative as the case used to encode the complement of intransitive verbs. In such a situation the adnominal function would be crucial for allotting the label genitive. The unmarked adnominal case normally covers the sense of possessor, and the label **possessive** case is a common alternative. A genitive is found not only in Indo-European languages, but also in Uralic, Caucasian, Altaic, Dravidian and Semitic languages. In some Australian languages a single case covers the range of the Latin dative and genitive cases and the label dative is preferred.

In a few languages there is a case common to A function and possessor function. These include Zoque (Mexican), a number of Caucasian languages and the Eskimo languages, where the case concerned is called the **relative** case.[26] The following example is from Yup'ik Eskimo (Reed et al. 1977: 83). An explanation for the complex gloss on the possessed noun is given below in connection with (63) and (64).

(59) *Angute-m   nera-a   neqa*
      man-REL   eat-3SG.3SG   fish
      'The man is eating the fish.'

(60) *Angute-m   qimugta-i*
      man-REL   dog-3PL.ABS.3SG.ERG
      'the man's dogs'

In a number of languages the pronominal affixes that mark the person and number of the possessor are the same as those used for subject function or the same as those used for A function. An example of an ergative-genitive series of bound pronouns in Konjo was given above (Table 5.1). An ergative-genitive series is also found in the Mayan languages and in Abaza. To appreciate what is going on here it is interesting to look at languages that use bound forms for both the possessor and possessed. The first example is from Abaza (Northwest Caucasian), a language which has extensive cross-referencing of pronominal elements on both the verb and the noun. The example is taken from a paper by W. Sidney Allen, who was perhaps the first to draw attention to parallels in the expression of A and possessor (Allen 1964: 340). In Abaza there is an ergative-absolutive distinction in third person bound pronouns.

(61)   *D-l-pa-b*
        3SG.MASC.ABS-3SG.FEM.ERG-son-is
        'He is her son.'

(62)   *D-l-šə-d*
        3SG.MASC.ABS-3SG.FEM.ERG-kill-PAST
        'She killed him.'

In (61) the prefix *d-* acts as a class marker to the noun, and in relation to *-l-*, which marks the possessor, it represents the possessed.

In Yup'ik Eskimo, where the relative case marks both A function and possessor function as illustrated in (59) and (60) above, 'our (dual) boats (dual)' is expressed thus,

(63)   *angya-g-puk*
        boat-3DU.ABS-1DU.ERG
        'our boats'

The bound forms used are the same as for a transitive verb with a first person dual A and third person dual P (Reed et al. 1977: 140).

(64)   *Ceńirciiqa-g-puk*
        visit.FUT-3DU.ABS-1DU.ERG
        'We shall visit them.'

It appears from these examples that the possessive schema is transitive with the possessor encoded as A and the possessed as P. This is obvious where there is a bound form corresponding to the possessed noun, but it may be that possession is conceived of as transitive also in other languages where a subject or an ergative bound form is used to encode the possessor. As we observed in describing nominalisation, the genitive case is often used to encode a complement of a nominalised verb, most often the subject. See sections 4.3.1 and 4.5.1.

A large number of languages have possessive affixes for first, second and third person. In many of these the possessive affix cross-references the possessor. An example from Turkish was given in section 1.1 namely *adam-ın ev-i* 'man-GEN house-3SG.POSS (the man's house)'. Here of course there is a genitive, but in many languages the cross-referencing is the sole means of marking possession.

5.5 Partitive

In eastern Europe it is common to find that partly affected patients are put in the **partitive** case as in Hungarian (Moravcsik 1978: 261).

(65)   *Olvasta   a   könyvet*
         read.3SG   the   book.ACC
         'He read the book.'

(66)   *Olvasott   a   könyvböl*
         read.3SG   the   book.PARTITIVE
         'He read some of the book.'

In Estonian and Finnish the partitive is used for the patient if it represents part of a whole or an indefinite quantity, or if the action is incomplete, or if the polarity of the clause is negative. In Polish and Russian similar conditions determine the choice of genitive as opposed to accusative (Moravcsik 1978: 265, 269; see also Plank (ed.) 1984).

5.6 Local cases

The term **local** in this context refers to 'place'. Local cases express notions of location ('at'), destination ('to'), source ('from') and path ('through'). In languages with inflectional case systems usually at least two different cases are employed to make local distinctions, though not necessarily two exclusively local cases. Indo-European languages originally used two local cases, locative and ablative, with the accusative expressing destination and path. In Turkish there is a locative and an ablative, with destination expressed via the dative. An allative case expressing destination is found in a number of languages including Uralic and Australian languages. A separate case for path is not so common but such a case is found in a few Australian languages (Blake 1987: 40), and is part of the local case system in some Northeast Caucasian languages including Avar (Table 5.4).

Where languages have large case systems it is always through the elaboration of the local cases. Large case systems are characteristic of the Finno-Ugric branch of the Uralic family and of the Northeast Caucasian languages. They arise from a combination of markers for relative orientation ('above', 'beside', etc.) with markers for location, destination, source and path. One dialect of Tabassaran (Northeast Caucasian) is reported to have fifty-three cases (Comrie 1981: 209). In Avar (also

Table 5.4 *Avar local cases*

	locative (location)	allative (destination)	ablative (source)	perlative (path)
on (top of)	-da	-d-e	-da-ssa	-da-ssa-n
at	-q	-q-e	-q-a	-q-a-n
under	-λ̇'	-λ̇'-e	-λ̇'-a	-λ̇'-a-n
in, among	-λ̇	-λ̇-e	-λ̇-a	-λ̇-a-n
in a hollow object	-∅	-∅-e	-∅-ssa	-∅-ssa-n

Northeast Caucasian) there are twenty-seven cases, including twenty local cases deriving from a combination of four 'cases' and five orientation markers. The combinations of orientation markers and 'case' markers are morphologically agglutinative and semantically transparent. (See Table 5.4, which is based on Ebeling 1966.) In a language like this one could simply recognise a layer of orientation markers plus a layer of 'case' markers. If one analyses a further outermost layer of forms as case markers rather than as clitic particles, the system is even larger (Hjelmslev 1937: 2–25).

In Avar, as in other Northeast Caucasian languages, the locative (usually called 'essive' in sources on Caucasian languages) is literally unmarked and the perlative is doubly marked, consisting of the ablative *-a* plus *-n*. This distribution of marking in Northeast Caucasian languages fits Hjelmslev's notions of markedness and perhaps played a part in shaping them (see Table 2.11).

The method of labelling local cases builds on the model of the Latin *ablātīvus* 'ablative' which is made up of the preposition *ab* 'from' plus a stem *lātivus* the root of which is *lāt*. This root supplies the perfect participle of *ferō* 'I bear'. Other labels are formed by varying the preposition or by combining prepositions with the stem *essīvus* from *esse* 'to be' (cf. Mel'čuk 1986: 72–75). Some local case labels are presented in Table 5.5.

More often than not the transparency of large local systems is obscured by some fusion of the orientation marker and what could be called the case marker proper, by innovating forms or by semantic shifts. In Finnish, for instance, there are 15 cases of which nine are local. As a first approximation one can say that there are local cases for location, destination and source, which can appear on their own or appear with interior ('inside') and exterior ('outside') markers. These are displayed in Table 5.6. The proto-forms for the cases are *-na* locative, *-ta* ablative and *-ne* allative. As can be seen the formative for interior is *-s-* and for exterior *-l-*. The *n* of the locative and allative assimilated to the preceding consonant to yield the array in (67), which corresponds to Table 5.6.

Table 5.5 *Labels for local cases*

LATIN ROOT	MEANING	CASE LABEL	MEANING
ad	'to'	allative	to(wards) (the exterior of)
in	'into'	illative	into
ab	'from'	ablative	from (the exterior of)
e(x)	'out of'	elative	from (the inside of)
super	'above'	superlative	to the top of
trans	'through'	translative	through
per	'through'	perlative	through, along
		essive	at (cf. locative)
in	'in'	inessive	in(side)
ad	'to'	adessive	at
super	'above'	superessive	above
sub	'under'	subessive	below

Table 5.6 *Finnish local cases*

		LOCATION	SOURCE	DESTINATION
Ø		*-na* essive	*-tta* partitive	*-ksi* translative
INTERIOR		*-ssa* inessive 'in'	*-sta* elative 'from(inside)'	*-(h)Vn, -sVVn* illative 'into'
EXTERIOR		*-lla* adessive 'at'	*-lta* ablative 'from(outside)'	*-lle* allative 'to(wards)'

(67) *-na*   *-ta*   *-ne*
      -ssa (< -*sna) *-sta* *-sse (< -*sne)*
      -lla (< -*lna) *-lta* *-lle (< -*lne)*

A comparison of (67) with Table 5.6 reveals that *-ksi* and *-(h)Vn /-sVVn* have been substituted for the forms expected on comparative-historical grounds. Semantically the system is not as transparent as one would gauge from combining the labels for the rows and columns in Table 5.6. The *-tta* form has a partitive function, the translative *-ksi* is used to mark the category into which something has been changed (*You'll turn into a pumpkin, Translate it into English*), and the allative *-lle* has dative functions.

If one were to take the orientation marker in any of the truly agglutinative systems like Avar to be a stem-forming suffix, then naturally the very large case systems would be greatly reduced. This would leave languages like Finnish, where fusion has partly obscured the transparent agglutinative system, as having the largest case systems.

5.7   Other cases

A variety of languages including Basque, Zoque (Mexican), Ossete (Indo-Iranian), Archi (Northeast Caucasian) and Finnish have a **comitative** case expressing accompaniment. It is also found in Tamil, Telugu and a majority of Dravidian languages, where it is known as **sociative**.

An **instrumental** case encodes the instrument with which an action is carried out as in *She wiped the screen with a cloth.* It is found in the Indo-European family (e.g. Sanskrit), Uralic (e.g. Komi-Permyak), Altaic (e.g. Nanai), Dravidian (e.g. Tamil), Basque, Tonkawa (Uto-Aztecan), Tarascan, Australian and elsewhere. It is sometimes used to encode the agent of the passive in an accusative language (e.g. Russian). In a number of ergative languages the ergative case covers instrumental as well as A function (e.g. Avar, Tibetan and the majority of Pama-Nyungan languages).

In the Uralic language a case called **abessive** (Latin *ab-esse* 'to be absent') or **privative** (Latin *prīvāre* 'to deprive') is found. It means 'lacking', 'not having'. In Finnish, for instance, *rahta-tta* is (money-AB) 'moneyless'. This case is also found in Australia where it is matched by a 'having' case called the **concomitant** or **proprietive**. These two categories tend to show up in many Australian languages in lexicalised formations. In Kalkatungu, for instance, *putu-yan* (stomach-PROP) means 'pregnant'. In light of this and other evidence the 'having' and 'lacking' suffixes have been taken to be derivational. On the other hand they exhibit concord in languages with case concord which suggests they are inflectional and should be considered cases (Blake 1987: 87f; Dench and Evans 1988: 7–13).

The labels **aversive** (lit. turning from), **evitative** (avoiding) and **causal** have been used for a case category common in Australian languages. It indicates what is to be feared or avoided, as in Kalkatungu: *Yanyi-ngungu rumpi* (ghost-AVERSIVE fear) 'S/he is afraid of ghosts' or the cause of a state or activity, again from Kalkatungu: *palpir-tungu uli-nyin* (poison-AVERSIVE die-PART) 'dying from poison'.

The only other case not mentioned up to this point that occurs with any frequency is the **comparative** ('than'), which occurs, for instance, in some Dravidian and some Northeast Caucasian languages. There are certainly more than a dozen or so other case labels to be found in the literature, quite apart from systematic local labels of the type illustrated in Table 5.5. Not all of these are described in detail and some may turn out on closer inspection to be variants of some of the labels presented here. We shall not pursue the matter.

5.8 Inflectional case hierarchy

Morphological case systems range from two members to a dozen or so. However, if one takes all the combinations of orientation markers and case markers proper in some Finno-Ugric and Northeast Caucasian languages as cases, then the figure runs to forty or so (see section 5.6). The question addressed here is whether morphological (inflectional) case systems grow and decay in a certain order. In attempting to answer this question I shall consider first case marking on independent nominals and ignore bound pronouns and word order. However, bound pronouns and word order are relevant to morphological case in that they represent alternative ways of encoding grammatical relations that lie at the top end of the relational hierarchy and therefore preclude the possibility of what otherwise might be implicational relationships. One might consider that a peripheral case like ablative is not likely to be found in an accusative language unless a core case like accusative is also found, but this will not hold in a language where the object is represented pronominally in the verb or only by position after the verb. Similarly one might propose that a language will not have a comitative case (which is only moderately common across languages) unless it has a genitive (which would appear to be more common), but a possessor in many languages is represented by a bound pronoun standing, where necessary, in cross-reference with a noun as in Warndarang (Northern Australian) (Heath 1980).

Comparing cases across languages is problematic from the methodological point of view. If we compare non-isomorphic case systems, then strictly no case in one system will correspond with any case in the other system. As remarked previously, the dative in Ancient Greek, for instance, does not correspond closely with the dative of Latin. Greek lacked the ablative of Latin and the source function ('from') of the Latin ablative was expressed by the genitive, while the locative and instrumental functions of the Latin ablative were expressed by the dative. The Greek dative is a more comprehensive case than the Latin dative. So in comparing cases across languages we need to consider the functions covered by a particular case and we must not accept traditional labels at face value.

If we look at a sample of case systems, ignoring for the moment those languages where some relations are marked exclusively by bound pronouns or word order, we find that indeed they do tend to be built up in a particular order, i.e. a hierarchy emerges.

(68) nom acc/erg gen dat loc abl/inst others

This hierarchy is to be interpreted as follows. If a language has a case listed on the hierarchy, it will usually have at least one case from each position to the left. Thus if a language has a dative case it will have a genitive, an accusative or ergative or both, and a nominative. In a small system of two, three, four or five cases the lowest ranked case will usually have a large range of functions, i.e. it will be a kind of 'elsewhere case'. The hierarchy as it is presented in (68) gives the impression that a language could have a two-case system in which the non-nominative case was accusative or ergative. While it is true that the second case is likely to cover P or A function, it is also likely to cover such a wide range of functions that the label **oblique** would be more appropriate than accusative or ergative.

A number of languages have a two-case system. Chemehuevi, a language of the Numic branch of Uto-Aztecan, has a nominative-oblique system in which nominative marks subject and oblique marks object and possessor. There are also postpositions which attach directly to the stem and perhaps could be said to belong to the case system, but unlike the oblique case marker they cannot figure in concord (Press 1979). A nominative-oblique system plus postpositions is typical of the Uto-Aztecan family (Langacker 1977).

Kabardian (Northwest Caucasian) has a two-case system in which the marked case covers A and possessor function. Two-case systems are also found among the Iranian languages. Yaghnobi has both an accusative construction and an ergative construction, the latter used in tenses based on the past stem. Within the core the marked case is used for a specific direct object in the accusative construction and for A in the ergative construction. Outside the core the marked case is used for possessor, indirect object and object of a preposition (Comrie 1981: 169–70).[27]

In a three-case system there is usually a nominative, an accusative and a genitive/oblique. The Semitic languages have systems like this. Classical Arabic provides an example, though there is accusative-genitive syncretism in the plural. The Nubian languages (Nilo-Saharan) also have a nominative-accusative-genitive system. Modern Greek has a nominative-accusative-genitive system and so has Comanche (Uto-Aztecan) (Robinson and Armagost 1990). Greek also has a vocative, but since the vocative is functionally so different it is not considered a case here (see section 1.2.3).

As the hierarchy in (68) stands, it would appear that a three-case system could contain nominative, accusative and ergative. Accusative and ergative cannot be separated on the hierarchy, but as far as I know there are no languages that have both a case covering A and a case covering P unless a fourth case is present.

A number of languages have the following four-case system:

(69)   nom   acc   gen   dat/obl

The last case often has a variety of functions and is variously named. Languages with this system include Ancient Greek (which also had a vocative), a number of Germanic languages including German, Icelandic and Old English (where there was also a vestigial instrumental), Yaqui and several Nilo-Saharan languages including Fur, Nuer and languages of the Didinga-Murle group where the accusative rather than the nominative is unmarked.

The next case to be distinguished from the elsewhere case is the dative. In Latin, for instance, we have the following system of five cases (plus a vocative) (see also Table 1.2):

(70)   nom   acc   gen   dat   abl/obl

The lowest case in Latin is called the ablative, but the Latin ablative represents a syncretism of an earlier ablative, instrumental and locative (still vestigially distinguishable in classical Latin). The label is somewhat arbitrary. Old and Middle High German had a similar system with an 'instrumental' where Latin had an 'ablative'. The O.H.G. and M.H.G. instrumental expressed locative and ablative functions as well as instrumental.

The only other case that can be placed on the hierarchy with any confidence is the locative. Systems of six or more cases almost always have a locative. In a number of Slavonic languages including Polish, Czech, Slovak and Serbo-Croatian the following system is found:

(71)   nom   acc   gen   dat   loc   inst

The next cases for consideration are the ablative and the instrumental. It does not seem that they can be distinguished hierarchically. Both are quite common, and there are languages with an instrumental but no ablative (like the Slavonic languages where source is normally expressed by a preposition governing the genitive) and there are languages like the Altaic languages where there is an ablative but no instrumental. The case system in Turkish is as follows. The instrumental function is expressed by a postposition.

(72)   nom   acc   gen   dat   loc   abl

Some Altaic languages have both an instrumental and an ablative as does classical Armenian which reflects the system of proto-Indo-European minus the vocative:

(73)   nom   acc   gen   dat   loc   ab   inst

It is doubtful whether the hierarchy can be developed much further. Outside the cases discussed up to this point the most common would appear to be the comitative ('accompanying'), the purposive, the allative ('to'), the perlative ('through') and the comparative ('than'). Tamil, for instance has the seven cases listed in (73) plus the comitative (called sociative in Dravidian linguistics):

(74)   nom   acc   gen   dat   loc   abl   inst   com

Two other Dravidian languages, Toda (Sakthivel 1976: 435–48) and Irula (Perialwar 1976: 495–519) have a purposive as well (plus a vocative):

(75)   nom   acc   gen   dat   loc   abl   inst   com   purp

Dravidian languages mostly have largish case systems. Kodaga (Balakrishnan 1976: 421–34) and Kasaba (Chidambaranathan 1976: 467–80) also have a comparative ('than') case.

The Pama-Nyungan languages of Australia mostly have case systems with eight to ten members. There is normally a common case for A and for instrumental function, most often referred to as the ergative, and there is frequently an allative and often an evitative (indicating what is to be avoided). Some Pama-Nyungan languages lack a genitive, the possessor function being expressed via the dative (Blake 1977, 1987).

In illustrating the hierarchy I have so far avoided languages which encode grammatical relations solely by word order or by bound pronouns, since the use of these alternative mechanisms can mean there are gaps in the morphological case hierarchy. However, the use of word order as the sole means of distinguishing subject and object is practically confined to subject-verb-object (SVO) prepositional languages like French, Cambodian and Thai. The only real competitor for morphological case is the use of bound pronouns. Bound pronouns may be used for subject, object, indirect object and possessor, and in some ergative languages for the absolutive and ergative relations. Naturally there will be gaps where bound pronouns are used instead of morphological case. In Nanai (Tungusic), for instance, there are seven cases but no genitive, the possessor relation being expressed by a cross-referencing bound pronoun (Nichols 1983):

(76)   nom   acc   -   dat   loc   abl   inst   all

Northern Australian languages have cross-referencing for subject and object and some have no core case marking. In Warndarang, for instance, the case inventory is as follows (Heath 1980: 26–8):

(77)   nom loc abl inst all purp

The missing cases are genitive, dative and a second core case, ergative or accusative. All of these gaps can be accounted for by reference to the cross-referencing bound pronouns which encode subject, object and possessor. With the verb for GIVE the object series of bound pronouns encodes the recipient. There is also a verbal prefix *ma-* to indicate that the object series is encoding a beneficiary. In this way the functions that would be associated with a dative are covered.

If morphological case systems are built up on hierarchical lines and if most of the gaps in the hierarchy can be attributed to the use of bound pronouns, then morphological cases and systems of bound pronouns between them define a hierarchy of functions or relations. It seems languages place more importance on having some morpho-syntactic means of expressing relations such as subject and object than on having some morpho-syntactic means of expressing relations such as locative or instrumental. Lower ranked relations like these are often expressed via prepositions or postpositions. Adpositions, although forming closed classes of some dozens or perhaps some scores of members, are mostly lexical rather than grammatical.

There are instances where a number of functions are expressed by a single case. As mentioned above, it is not uncommon in Australian languages to find a genitive-dative case and in Kannada there is syncretism of the ablative/instrumental distinction even though there is a comitative which one would expect to be ranked lower on the grounds of its sparser distribution across languages. In Tarascan (Chibchan) there is also a comitative even though there is no dative or ablative. In this language there is no indirect object; the recipient and beneficiary are expressed in the accusative. The locative covers not only location, but the other local notions such as 'from' and 'to' (Suarez 1983: 87):

(78)   nom acc gen loc inst com

The fact that syncretisms occur and gaps, mostly attributable to an alternative grammatical device, precludes the possibility of establishing implicational relationships between cases, but the syncretisms and gaps do not render the hierarchy vacuous. Case systems tend to be built up in a certain sequence 'with overwhelmingly greater than chance frequency', to borrow a phrase from Greenberg (1963).[28]

On the point of one case expressing more than one function, it is interesting to note an asymmetry between the treatment of ablative and allative. An ablative is much more widely distributed than an allative. The *to*-function is frequently expressed by another case such as the accusative (Latin and some other Indo-European), the dative (Turkish and other Altaic) or the locative (Yidiny).[29] Of course instances like these where a case expresses more than one function or role raise the question of how these cases are labelled. It seems that it is widely accepted practice to label on the basis of the higher function on the hierarchy. Where a particular case expresses, say, A function and instrumental function, it is usually labelled ergative. This practice will of course create apparent gaps in the hierarchy at the point where the lower function occurs.

6
Life cycle of case systems

6.1 Origin

It is generally recognised that in the historical development of language grammatical forms develop from lexical forms and bound forms from free forms. There are two common lexical sources for case markers, one verbal and the other nominal, of which the verbal is probably the more fruitful. Adverbial particles also provide a source. The sequence of development is from noun, verb or adverb to preposition or postposition, and from postposition to suffix.[1]

In many areas case marking is of long ancestry as witnessed by formal complexity (suppletive variants and fusion) and semantic complexity. This is true of case marking in Indo-European languages, for instance, and in such a situation the prospects for determining the origin of particular case markers are not too promising. On the other hand there are some languages, including the Indo-Iranian branch of Indo-European, where the development of 'new' case markers is attested, and there are many languages in which we can plausibly reconstruct the origin of postpositions and phrase-final postposition-like case markers.

6.1.1. *Verb to case marker*

The key to understanding the verbal origin of adpositions lies in the notion of an argument implied by a predicate. A predicate like COME is a two-place predicate implying a comer and a destination. A predicate like LEAVE is a two-place predicate implying a leaver and a source. A predicate like FLY is a one-place predicate implying a flyer, but there will be a need for languages to express 'X flies to Y' or 'X flies from Y'. One way to do this is to use pairs of predicates. To express 'fly to' the predicates FLY and COME can be used; to express 'fly from' the predicates FLY and LEAVE can be used. Here are examples from Thai:

(1)   a. *Thân   cà   bin   maa   krungthêep*
           he   will   fly   come   Bangkok
           'He will fly to Bangkok.'

b. *Thân   cà   bin   càak   krungthêep*
he   will   fly   leave   Bangkok
'He will fly from Bangkok.'

These constructions are usually described as serial verb constructions, but note that the second verb cannot be modified independently of the first for tense, mood, aspect or polarity (in Thai these modifications are via free forms like *cà* in (1a) and (1b)). The second verb is non-finite. It cannot take an expressed subject; its missing subject must be interpreted as being that of the first verb. As is obvious from the translations, the second verb is functionally equivalent to a preposition. A preposition is rather like a non-finite verb. Consider the translation of (1a), for instance. The preposition *to* is a two-place predicate. One argument has the role of destination (Bangkok); the other argument is not expressed and must be interpreted as being coreferential with S.

Now consider the word *hây*. It can occur as the sole lexical verb in the clause, where it has the meaning 'give' (2a), or it can be used following another verb, where it has either the meaning 'give' or 'on behalf of' (2b) (Kullavanijaya 1974: 51, 85).

(2)   a. *Phɔ̂ɔ   hây   ngən   Pùk*
father give   money   Pook
'Father gives money [to] Pook.'

b. *Mɛ̂ɛ   yép   sŷa   hây   Pùk*
mother   sew   garment   give   Pook
'Mother sews the garment [and] gives [it to] Pook.'
'Mother sews the garment on behalf of Pook.'

In (2b) *hây* cannot be modified for tense, mood, aspect or polarity. It could be analysed as a non-finite verb or as a derived preposition. Kullavanijaya suggests that it is a non-finite verb when it means 'give' and a derived preposition when it means 'on behalf of'.

The reanalysis of a verb as an adposition is clearer in a language where verbs have bound forms, but adpositions do not. In Ewe, a language of the Kwa branch of the Niger-Congo family, the form *ná* can appear as a verb meaning 'give' (3a) or as a preposition meaning 'for' (benefactive or purposive) (3b). In (3a) *ná* bears person/number marking for the subject; no such marking is possible in (3b) (Heine et al. 1991: 1).

(3)   a. *me-ná   ga   kofí*
1SG-give   money   Kofi
'I gave Kofi money.'

b. *me-wɔ   dɔ´   vévíé   ná   dodókpɔ́   lá*
 1SG-do   work   hard   give   exam   DEF
 'I worked hard for the exam.'

The morphological difference between *ná* in (3a) and *ná* in (3b) matches the difference in meaning and confirms that while the first *ná* is a verb the second is a preposition.

   The development of serial verbs into adpositions is a widespread phenomenon. It is particularly common in the languages of West Africa, New Guinea, Southeast Asia and Oceania. There are also similar developments in a wide variety of languages involving verb forms morphologically marked as non-finite. In English, for instance, there are examples of prepositions deriving from the present participle such as *regarding, following* and *concerning.* Similarly in German where *betreffend* 'concerning' derives from a present participle. *Betreffend* is a postposition since the originating participle is clause-final, German subordinate clauses being verb-final.[2] Similar developments have occurred in the Dravidian languages where the postposition *pārttu* 'towards', which governs the accusative, derives from the participle *pārttu* 'looking at' (Steever 1987: 736), and also in Sanskrit where the postposition *sahita* 'with' derives from a past participle of a verb meaning 'join' (Andersen 1979: 26).

   Not surprisingly a survey of the development of adpositions reveals clear tendencies. The semantic roles that are in frequent demand are the local notions of location, source and destination plus a few others such as instrument, purpose, beneficiary and accompaniment. A verb meaning 'come' provides an obvious source for an adposition meaning 'to' (compare (1a) above); a verb meaning 'leave' is a likely source for an adposition meaning 'from' (compare (1b) above), and a verb meaning 'give' is a regular source for an adposition meaning 'for' (see (2) and (3) above). There are also examples of adpositions with a purely grammatical function deriving from verbs. The most widely quoted example involves *bǎ* in Mandarin Chinese. Mandarin is basically an SVO language with no adposition or affix to mark the object. However, there is a construction in which the notional object is preceded by *bǎ* and the *bǎ*-phrase precedes the verb (Li and Thompson 1981: 464).

(4)   *Tā   bǎ   fàntīng   shōushi-gānjing   le*
         3SG   dining.room   tidy-clean   PERF
         'S/he tidied up the dining room.'

bǎ derives from a verb meaning 'take hold of' or 'grasp' and the construction in (4) derives from a construction of the form *X take Y and (X) verb (Y).* The original verb *bǎ* has lost its literal sense of 'take hold of', but though it is generally described as an object-marking preposition, it is significant that it is confined to definite or generic patients and cannot generally be used with verbs such as *ài* 'to love' and *xiǎng* 'to miss (someone)'. A similar restriction appears with the object-marking preposition *kè* in the West African language Gā. This preposition also derives from a verb meaning 'take' (Lord 1982: 286-8).

Verbs meaning 'take' often come to mark instruments. A construction that is literally 'X taking axe chopped wood' becomes reinterpreted as 'X with axe chopped wood'.

Here are some examples of recurrent types of development of verbs to adpositions. They are grouped according to the function of the resulting adposition:[3]

(5)   object
Yatye *awá* 'take', Yoruba *gbà* 'get', Mandarin *bǎ* 'take hold of'

            dative/benefactive
Yoruba *fún* 'give', Mandarin *gěi* 'give', Ewe *ná* 'give', Thai *hâi* 'give'

            allative
Nupe *lō* 'go', Mandarin *dào* 'arrive', Ewe *ḍé* 'reach'

            comitative
Tamil *koṇṭu* (< **kol* 'take'), Mandarin *gēn* 'follow'

            instrumental
Mandarin *yòng* 'use', *ná* 'take', Ewe *tsɔ́* 'take'

            locative
Mandarin *zài* 'be at', Ewe *lé* 'be at'

            ablative
Mandarin *cóng* 'follow', Ewe *tśo* 'come from'

            perlative
Ewe *tó* 'pass by'

6.1.2 Noun to case marker

Adpositions and case affixes of nominal origin are common in the expression of the local case relations. As mentioned in section 1.3.3 languages often specify relative orientation by using a relator noun such as *top* in *It stands on top of the cupboard. Top* is the head of a noun phrase that has a prepositional phrase (*of the cupboard*) as a post-head modifier. The essential predication is between *it, stand* and *cupboard*. Although *top* is syntactically the head of the phrase *top of the cupboard* it is semantically subordinate in that its function is to specify more precisely the relationship of *cupboard* to *stand*. (*On* is not too important either here, since *stand* expects a locative complement.) Not surprisingly relator nouns like *top* become adpositions and sometimes affixes (as noted in section 1.3.3 one could interpret *on-top-of* as a compound preposition).

This kind of development is common in the Dravidian languages. In Kannada there are forms like *horage* as in (6) (Madtha 1976: 143):

(6)   *Klāsina   horage   hōgu*
         class.GEN   outside   go
         'Get out of the class!'

Forms like *horage*, sometimes referred to as secondary case markers, are postpositions. The form *hora* derives from a noun meaning 'exterior'. It betrays its nominal origin in governing a complement in the genitive, the main adnominal case (compare Hindi-Urdu example given as (11d) in chapter 1).

This kind of development is also common in Uralic languages. In Finnish *kohta* 'place' in the adessive *kohdalla* 'at the place' is used with a genitive dependent as in *talo-n kohdalla* (house-GEN place-AD) 'at the house'. Here *kohdalla* functions as a postposition.

In the Finnic language Karelian, the comitative is marked by *-ke* as in *velle-ŋ-ke* 'with the brother' where *-ke* derives from **kerða-lla* 'at a turn, at time of' used with genitive attributes. Compare Finnish *koira-n keralla* (dog-GEN with) 'with the dog'. The genitive *-n* is reflected as *-ŋ* in *velleŋke* (Anttila 1972: 149). In developments like this the original head (**kerðalla* in this instance) eventually becomes an affix and the original dependent a stem. In another Finnic language, Komi-Permiak, there are five cases where the first formative is *-vv-*: *-vva* superlative 'to the top of', *-vviś* sublative 'down from', *-vvyn* superessive 'on', *-vvəʒ* supertermi-native 'up to' and *-vvət* perlative 'via'. The formative can clearly be related to the noun *vyv* 'top' (Austerlitz 1980: 237).[4]

The Hungarian case suffix *-bel/-ba* 'into' derives from *bél* 'innards, guts' in its allative case form: *vilag-bel-e* (world-insides-to) yields modern Hungarian *világba* '(in)to the world' where *-be/-ba* is the illative case marker.

In Persian a noun root *rādi* meaning 'reason' or 'goal' gave rise to a postposition *rādi* 'by reason of, concerning'. It reduced to *rā* and came to indicate cause, purpose or reference ('as for ...') and then later to mark indirect and direct objects. In modern Persian it is used with indirect objects and specific direct objects (Windfuhr 1987: 534, 541f).

Where nouns develop into prepositions, postpositions and case suffixes, the development is almost always to a local form, which may later develop more abstract or grammatical functions. Here are some examples grouped under local labels. The most common source would appear to be body parts (cf. Heine et al.).

(7)   inside, into

Swahili *ndani* (< *da* 'guts'), Mixtec *ini* 'heart', *čīhi* 'stomach' (also 'under'), Cakchiquel -*pan* 'stomach', Kpelle -*lá* 'mouth'

to

Kpelle -*túe* 'front', Mixtec *nuu* 'face' (also develops other local functions)

in front of

Swahili *mbele* (from a root meaning'breasts'), Hausa *gàban* < *gàbā* 'front', Jacaltec *sat* 'face'

on top of, above, on

Hausa *kân* < *kai* 'head', Tamil *mēl* 'sky', Kpelle -*mâ* 'surface', Jacaltec *wi'* < *wi'e* 'head'

near

Kpelle -*kɔlɛ* 'vicinity'

behind, at the back of

Kpelle -*polu* 'back', Hindi *pīche* 'rear', Ewe *megbé* 'back', Gujerati *puṭhe* 'back'

below

Tamil *nēḍe* 'ground', Swahili *chini* (< *ci* 'ground')

from

Kpelle -*yée* 'hand'

6.1.3 *Adverbial particle to case marker*

Some adpositions have their immediate origin in adverbs or particles. In the Indo-European languages there appear to have been free forms which developed into prepositions on the one hand and components of compound verbs on the other. In Latin, there are forms like *per* 'through', *in* 'in', *trans* 'across' and *ē/ex* 'out of' which show up as prepositions and as the first member of compound verbs. Compare *Ambula per aedes* (walk.IMP through house.ACC) 'Walk through the house!' where *per* is a preposition governing the accusative and *Perambula aedes* where *perambulare* is a transitive verb governing the accusative.[5]

In Sahaptin (Penutian) there are two ergative suffixes. Rigsby calls one (-*in*) 'obviative' (it is used when O is third person) and the other (-*nɨm*) 'inverse' (it is used when A is third person and O first or second person (Rigsby 1974)). Rude argues that *-nɨm* is derived from a particle meaning 'hither' (1988). Both the putative source and the derived function are illustrated in the following example where the hypothesised particle is reflected as a verb suffix and a noun suffix (Jacobs 1931: 126).

(8)   *Áw=naš   xwɨsaat-nɨm   i-twána-m-aš*
        now=1SG   old.man-ERG   3SG-follow-hither-IMPF
        'Now the old man is following me.'

In the closely related Nez Perce there is an ergative marker *-nim* cognate with the Sahaptin form. Faced with an ergative and a 'hither' form of similar shape, one would not be inclined to see them as related. In fact one would probably expect an ergative to have an origin in a 'from' form rather than a 'to' or 'hither' form, but the Sahaptin evidence is highly suggestive. It makes obvious sense to use a 'hither' form to mark action directed towards the speech act participants (cf. the discussion in section 5.2.6). Rude suggests the inverse ergative has widened its scope to become a general ergative in Nez Perce. He also suggests that the accusative suffix in Sahaptin (*-na* or *-nan*) and Nez Perce (*-ne*) derives from a particle meaning 'to', 'toward' or 'thither'.

6.2   Developments within case systems

When a verb or noun becomes an adposition, it does not necessarily lose its lexical character, though it becomes a member of a relatively small closed class of a score or two of members. When a postposition becomes a case suffix, two significant changes occur. First of all it is liable to develop variant forms according to the phonological properties of its host, and secondly it becomes a member of a much smaller set of forms, usually no more than ten or so. Since all noun phrases, no matter what semantic role they bear in relation to their governor, must be marked by one member of a small set, it is inevitable that at least some case suffixes will cover a broad semantic range. We will discuss the phonological factors first, then the semantic ones.

6.2.1   Phonological factors

It is a general principle of language that grammatical forms are less prominent than the lexical forms they relate. As nouns and verbs develop into adpositions, they become unstressed and pronounced as if they were an unstressed syllable of a neighbouring word. The neighbouring word will be either the nominal that is the head of the phrase governed by the adposition or simply the nearest word in the phrase. In a consistent modifier-head language like Turkish a postposition will always be adjacent to the noun that is head of the noun phrase it governs. But adpositions and the heads of noun phrases are not always adjacent. In English, for instance, the preposition is not necessarily adjacent to the head of the noun phrase. Postpositions are likely to become suffixes and develop variant forms according to the phonological shape of the stem to which they attach. In this way paradigms develop. The Pama-Nyungan languages provide a convenient example. The ergative tends to be realised as *-lu* following vowel stems of more than two syllables and *-Tu* following a consonant-final stem. *T* stands for a stop which assimilates in point of articulation to the final consonant. An original *l* has hardened to a stop and then assimilated to the point of articulation of the final consonant of the stem. Vowel stems of two syllables take the variant *-ngku*. According to an hypothesis originally advanced by Hale disyllabic vowel stems at one stage of their history had a final velar nasal. The *l* of the ergative hardened to a stop and assimilated to the velar nasal in point of articulation. Subsequently the velar nasal was lost in word-final position so that a word like **marang* 'hand' with an ergative**marang-ku* became *mara* with an ergative *mara-ngku*. The proto-Pama-Nyungan locative is reconstructed as **-la*. It developed a parallel series of variants (Hale 1976). Some examples of these are shown in Table 6.1 from Djaru (Tsunoda 1981). The dative is also included. Here an original **-ku* has developed a weakened variant *-wu* after vowels.

Once paradigms develop there is scope for exchange of forms between paradigms. Distinctions made in one paradigm may be levelled by analogy with another (see section 6.3 below) or an important functional distinction made in one paradigm may be copied in another (see (9) below).

The model of adpositions developing into affixes leaves one manifestation of inflectional case unexplained, namely case concord. One way concord could come about is through the discontinuous expression of the content normally expressed through a noun phrase in a language like English. As illustrated earlier in the text with examples from Latin and Warlpiri (see (8), (9) and (10) in chapter 4) it is common in some languages to represent an English phrase like *that tall woman* by two or even three separate phrases. Naturally each of these phrases will require its own marking. We could consider that any such matching in marking constitutes a system of concord, but it may be that all such phrases are sisters, each governed by the same head, usually the verb. If the possibility of discontinuous representation was lost and the marking of the erstwhile phrases retained, then the result would be multiword phrases with concord.

Affixes are always liable to fall prey to the reductive phonological processes of assimilation, loss, vowel centring to schwa, and fusion. The effect of such changes is to reduce the differentiation between cases. In some Pama-Nyungan languages vowel reduction to shwa or vowel loss has obliterated the distinction between the

Table 6.1 *Djaru case markers*

	disyllabic vowel stems 'water'	longer vowel stems 'food'	consonant stems 'man'
nom	*ngapa*	*mangarri*	*mawun*
erg/inst	*ngapa-ngku*	*mangarri-lu*	*mawun-tu*
loc	*ngapa-ngka*	*mangarri-la*	*mawun-ta*
dat	*ngapa-wu*	*mangarri-wu*	*mawun-ku*

ergative and the locative. As we shall see below, reductive phonological changes can all but destroy a morphological case system. Languages do not normally take prophylactic measures to restrain the eroding effects of phonological change on a case system, they simply employ an alternative means such as using word order to distinguish subject and object or using prepositions or postpositions. However, occasionally a language takes therapeutic measures to repair the damage done by phonological change. In Latin there were syncretisms resulting from reductive phonological processes at different periods of its history. The reconstructed accusative plural is -*ns*. However, in early Latin *n* dropped out before *s* in final syllables and the preceding vowel lengthened.

(9)   1st declension   *dominā-ns*   >   *dominās*   'mistresses'
       2nd   "   *domino-ns*   >   *dominōs*   'masters'
       3rd   "   *consul-ns̩*   >   *consulēs*   'consuls'
       4th   "   *manu-ns*   >   *manūs*   'hands'
       5th   "   *diē-ns*   >   *diēs*   'days'

This produced nominative-accusative syncretism in the third consonantal declension and in the fourth and fifth declensions (see Table 1.2). In the second declension a form -*oi* (later *ī)* was introduced from the demonstrative paradigm, which restored the nominative-accusative distinction. The form *ī* was then adopted in the first declension where the sequence *aī* reduced to a diphthong (*ae* in the orthography).

6.2.2   Non-phonological factors

An inflectional case system is small. It typically contains half a dozen or so members and rarely more than a dozen. The whole point of having a case system, or any morphological system for that matter, is to provide brief signals for broad categories that will be sufficient for communication most of the time. Where a case system does not provide a sufficiently explicit indication of the semantic role of a dependent, then the secondary system of adpositions or relator nouns can be employed, or, in rarer instances, a more elaborate paraphrase can be used.

The small case system with its broad categories is sufficient most of the time because of the redundancy inherent in lexical choices. A predicate implies arguments, so all a case system is required to do with complements, at least from the functional point of view, is to distinguish arguments (recall the discussion in section 5.2.6). With adjuncts the role will often be determinable from the choice of noun. Suppose we have a sentence in which the lexical items are MAN, DOG, HIT and STICK. There is hardly any need for case marking to express the propositional content. In the absence of an indication to the contrary one naturally assumes that MAN will be agent, DOG patient and STICK instrument.

The notion that case categories are broad and that they are able to function as broad categories because of a certain amount of redundancy arising from lexical choice is fundamental to understanding how a case system evolves. A schematic outline of some of the major developments is given in Figure 6.1. When nouns, verbs or adverbial particles develop into adpositions and when postpositions develop further into suffixes they are usually semantically homogeneous with a concrete meaning, typically a local meaning. There is evidence that adpositions and case suffixes extend to cover more abstract meanings and to mark syntactic categories (shown by the horizontal arrows to the left in Figure 6.1). When a case system withers away (see section 6.3 below), the marking remains on the bound pronouns, which mark the purely syntactic functions.

What is not shown in Figure 6.1 is the tendency for cases to merge or syncretise. The reverse of this, namely a case splitting into two, is rare but an example from Pitta-Pitta is given at the end of this section.[6]

	nom	acc erg	gen	dat	semantic
marking of bound pronoun	♦	♦ ↑	♦ ↑	♦ ↑	
suffix on nominal		♦ ⇐	♦ ⇐	♦ ⇐	♦ ↑ post
adposition		♦ ⇐	♦ ⇐	♦ ⇐	prep ↑ ↑
open lexical class					verb noun adverb

Figure 6.1 Development of adpositions, suffixes and bound pronouns

It is generally agreed that semantic cases, especially local cases, can expand their territory and come to cover syntactic relations such as direct object, thereby becoming grammatical cases, but hard evidence is difficult to come by (Lehmann 1982: 111). The development is to be expected on the grounds that the expression of abstract categories in general derives from the extension of morphemes or combinations of morphemes with a concrete meaning. To take one lexical example from thousands, the word *education* derives from the Latin *ē-duc-ātiō* (out-lead-NM), literally a physical leading out.

With adpositions it is easier to find documented examples of the development of a local marker to the marker of a syntactic relation. This kind of development is captured by the lower row of left-pointing arrows in Figure 6.1.

The Latin preposition *ad* 'to' is reflected in Spanish as *a*. It still retains its local meaning (10), but it has come to mark the indirect object (11) and the direct object, the latter where the object is animate and specific (12).

(10)   *Juan   vuelve   a   su   hotel*
        Juan   return.3SG   to   his   hotel
        'Juan returns to his hotel.'

(11)   *Le   expliqué   el   caso   a   mi   hermano*
        3SG.IO   explain.PAST.3SG   the   case   to   my   brother
        'He explained the matter to my brother.'

(12)   *Vi   a   mi   hermano*
        saw.3SG   my   brother
        'I saw my brother.'

In Rumanian the Latin preposition *per* 'through' is reflected as *pe* and it too has come to be used as a direct object marker.

The Latin preposition *dē* 'from' is reflected as a function form in Romance including *di* in Italian and *de* in Spanish. These forms mark adnominal dependents and the complements of certain verbs low on the transitivity scale. The following examples are Spanish:

(13)   a. *la casa de la señora Garcia*
           'Mrs Garcia's house'
        b. *corrida de toros*
           'bullfight'
        c. *asustarse de la luz*
           'to be afraid of the light'

       d. *cambiar de vestidos*
       'to change clothes'

English *of* and *off* reflect Old English *of* 'from'. The Old English word with its unstressed pronunciation [əv] has developed into a grammatical marker while the same word with its full pronunciation has been retained in its local function. Modern English *of* is rather like Spanish *de* and Italian *di* in that it has become the default marker for the complement of nouns and adjectives (*student of linguistics, full of emotion*).

When we turn to morphological case systems, we are dealing with systems of marking that are of some antiquity and it is naturally more difficult to find clear examples of semantic cases developing into grammatical cases. Certainly there is no shortage of languages where a grammatical case expresses a purely syntactic relation plus a semantic role that lies outside this relation. In various Indo-European case languages the accusative expresses destination as well as direct (and sometimes secondary) object. In Latin, for instance, one can say *Mīsī legātōs Rōman* (sent.I legates.ACC Rome.ACC) where *legātōs* is the direct object and *Rōman* a complement expressing destination. In many ergative languages the ergative case covers a non-core function. In Pama-Nyungan languages the ergative usually covers instrumental function as well as A (see section 3.2.1); in Sumerian the ergative also expressed location. A dative will often express destination as well as indirect object and a genitive sometimes expresses a local function as in Ancient Greek where it expresses source.

Examples where there is some comparative-historical evidence that a local case assumed a syntactic function include the development of *-e/-a* in Turkish from an allative to a dative-allative, the analogous development of *-man* in Quechua (Lehmann 1982: 109), and the assuming of genitive function by the Pama-Nyungan locative in Pitta-Pitta (see below).

Where a passive develops in a language with a morphological case system one of the non-core cases will be chosen to express the demoted subject. Passives provide a class of clear examples of cases assuming a new syntactic relation. The demoted subject is expressed in the genitive in Ancient Greek, the instrumental in Russian, Czech and several of the Dravidian languages, and the ablative in Latin and Armenian.

In all of these examples of local or other concrete forms extending their range to cover syntactic relations, the redundancy that arises from lexical choices plays a part. Destinations can often be distinguished from roles such as patient subsumed under direct object by the fact that they will normally only occur with verbs of motion; instruments can be distinguished from roles such as agent subsumed under the ergative relation on the grounds that instruments are almost always inanimate and agents animate, and so on. Lexical redundancy also plays a part in other mergers. In some languages there is a locative-allative case and one suspects there has been a merger. In Hittite there is positive evidence of such a merger. In Late Hittite the '*to*' case (called allative in this text but directive in some sources) merged with the dative-locative, which resulted from an earlier merger of the dative and the locative (Luraghi 1987). An allative-locative merger is possible because destination will normally occur only with verbs of motion.

With some mergers it can be said that the cases in question had some overlap to start with in the sense that there are extra-linguistic situations that can be interpreted as belonging to one case or the other. Take ablative and instrumental, for instance. Besides situations in which there is a clear source (*She walked all the way from the station*) and situations where there is an obvious instrument (*She swatted the fly with a rolled up newspaper*), there are situations which could be interpreted as ablative or instrumental, mainly with reference to a resultant state. Suppose a natural spring provides irrigation for a garden. One could speak of the garden being watered from a spring (source) or by a spring (means, instrument or perhaps agent). Here are some other possibilities, but it should be noted that they are not meant to illustrate the interchangeability of the English prepositions *from* and *by*.

(14)   *battered by/from the gale*
         wounded by/from shrapnel
         smoothed by/from rubbing
         warped by/from the heat

Ablative-instrumental syncretism occurred in a number of Indo-European languages including Hittite.

As noted in section 6.2.1, Pama-Nyungan languages usually reflect an ergative *-lu* and a locative *-la*. In most of these languages the ergative covers A and instrumental relations, but in some Pama-Nyungan languages the locative case markers have come to express instrumental as well as locative leaving the -*lu* to express just A. In English the preposition *by*, formerly a purely local form (*He stood by the window*) came to acquire a sense of means or instrument. The *Oxford English Dictionary* suggests that it acquired its instrumental sense via expressions such as *She read by candlelight* where the *by*-phrase, originally a locative (Where did she read?), was reinterpreted as instrumental (How did she read it?). It is not hard to find situations that allow a locative or instrumental interpretation and which could facilitate a locative or instrumental form adopting both functions. Here are some examples:

(15)   *wash the cloth in/with water*
             cook meat on/in/with fire
             carry wood on/with shoulder
             come on/by horse
             go along/by means of the back road
             see someone in/by means of the firelight
             mix flour in/with water

A merger of instrumental and locative also occurred in Middle Indo-Aryan, but there the cases merged under the instrumental forms. In Latin there was a syncretism of the Indo-European instrumental and ablative and then the syncretism of these two with the locative (the latter merger not quite complete as we saw in section 2.2.2). The forms of the Latin ablative reflect markers of the three syncretised cases. The *-ō* of the second declension singular is from an Indo-European ablative, the *-īs* of the second declension plural (borrowed into the first declension also) is of instrumental provenience and the *-e* of the third declension singular of the consonant stems reflects an Indo-European locative (Palmer 1954: 241ff).[7]

Of a slightly different kind is the merger of the genitive and dative under the dative form in a number of modern German dialects. As mentioned in section 5.3, a dative can be used to signal possession. In some languages all possessive datives are predicative; in others an attributive use develops which overlaps with the genitive. In Pennsylvania German the dative has become the only way of expressing possession so that there is effectively a genitive-dative case. Note that the construction in the following example involves a possessive adjective cross-referencing the possessor (Burridge 1990: 41).

(16)   *Des*   *is*   *em*   *Gaul*   *sei(n)*   *Schwans*
          this   is   the.DAT   horse.DAT   his   tail
          'This is the horse's tail.'

As mentioned earlier it is possible for a case to split, though this would appear not to be too common. In the Pama-Nyungan languages there is usually a locative case which is represented by *-la* with vowel-final stems of more than two syllables, by *-ngka* with disyllabic vowel stems, and by *-Ta* with consonant-final stems (compare section 6.2.1 above). In Pitta-Pitta there are no consonant stems so not surprisingly there is no *-Ta*. The case markers *-ngka* and *-la* appear, the former as *-nga* (a sound change of *ngk* to *-ng* is independently attested). However, each marks a different case. The marker *-nga* signals the genitive/purposive and *-la* the evitative (what is to be avoided). The locative is marked by *-ina*, an apparent innovation. What appears to have happened is that two allomorphs of a locative have come to mark two separate cases. The locative in some Australian languages covers purposive and evitative functions as well as location. It is likely that at some earlier stage in the history of Pitta-Pitta the locative covered this range of functions and an association came to be made between particular allomorphs and particular functions. The evitative is semantically similar to the ablative. The ablative simply refers to motion away from, but the evitative has the sense of keeping away from an entity or moving away from an entity because it is a source of danger and the like. If someone simply walked away from a fire, this would be expressed in the ablative (*maka-inya*). If, however, they moved away to avoid the heat or smoke, this would be expressed in the evitative (*maka-la*). There are some instances of the evitative being added to the ablative (*maka-inya-la*). Perhaps this usage is responsible for the association of -*la* and evitative. If at some earlier stage the locative expressing avoidance was added to the ablative expressing motion away from, the -*la* allomorph would have been used because the ablative-marked form would have been a vowel-final stem of more than two syllables.

6.3   Loss of case marking

As we have seen in the previous section cases may merge and in this way a case system will be reduced unless new members are recruited. And as we saw in section 6.2.1 phonological change, which tends to be reductive especially in unstressed syllables, may obliterate case distinctions. The case system of Classical Latin was severely eroded by phonological change (the reader should consult Table 1.2 in reading this section). Word-final -*m*, which was the characteristic marker of the accusative singular, must have been reduced, probably to nasalisation. It is occasionally omitted in inscriptions, and word-final syllables in -*m* are elided before vowels in verse: *dōnum exitiāle* 'doomed gift' is pronounced as if it were *dōnexitiāle*. In Vulgar Latin in the first three centuries of the Christian era the distinction between short *a* and long *ā* was lost in unstressed syllables (hence the ablative was no longer distinguished from the nominative and accusative in the first declension singular) and *i* merged with *ē* (as *e*) and *u* merged with *ō* (as *o*). The merging of *u* and *ō*, together with the loss of word-final -*m*, meant that in the second declension singular there was a common form for accusative, dative and ablative.

As these reductive phonological changes began to accumulate and severely reduce the number of distinctions, a number of other changes took place. The two small declensions merged with larger ones, the fourth with the second and the fifth with the first. The neuter gender was eliminated with neuters that declined like *bellum* 'war' taking on the nominative in -*s*, thus *caelus* 'sky' for earlier *caelum*, *fātus* 'fate' for earlier *fātum*. Some neuter plurals in -*a* were reinterpreted as feminine singulars of the first declension, e.g. *folium* 'a leaf' had a plural *folia* which was taken to be a feminine singular and is reflected in Italian *la foglia*, Spanish *la hoja*, French *la feuille*, etc.

As the case distinctions began to be reduced, the use of prepositions increased until the situation found in the modern Romance languages emerged where grammatical relations outside the core are expressed only via prepositions. The use of reflexes of *dē* 'from' came to mark adnominal noun phrases and reflexes of *ad* 'to' came to mark indirect objects as well as destination, these innovations replacing the genitive and dative respectively. Compare the following sentence from the Vulgate (Luke XV.15) and its Italian (17b) and Spanish (17c) translation (in the Latin of the Vulgate all the morphological distinctions of Classical Latin are retained). The literal translation of the Italian is 'He put himself to service of one of the inhabitants of that region' and of the Spanish 'He put himself to serve to a citizen of that land'.

(17)　　　a. *Adhaesit*　　*ūnī*　　　*cīvium*　　　*regiōnis*
　　　　　　　adhere.PERF.3SG　one.DAT　citizen.PL.GEN　region.GEN
　　　　　　　illius
　　　　　　　that.GEN
　　　　　　　'He attached himself to one of the citizens of that region.'
　　　　　b. *Si mise a servizio di uno degli habitanti di quella regione*
　　　　　c. *Se puso a servir a un ciudadano de aquella tierra*

By the time the Romance languages began to emerge in the early Middle Ages no noun displayed more than two distinctions, nominative and oblique. Table 6.2 gives representative forms of the first, second and third declensions. In the upper part of the paradigm forms from western Romance are shown where *-s* was retained. In the lower part of the table Italian forms are shown representing eastern Romance where *-s* was not retained. Rumanian was more conservative than Italian in retaining to the present day the neuter gender and developing a direct-oblique case system, i.e. one where the direct or nominative covers core functions and the other case covers the functions formerly expressed by the genitive and dative. (See note 27 in chapter 5.)

The history of English provides another example of a case system withering away. In Old English there were four cases (nominative, accusative, genitive and dative) plus a vestigial instrumental. Representative nouns from the more numerous paradigms are shown in Table 6.3. *Stān* 'stone' represents a masculine noun, *scip* 'ship' a neuter and *talu* 'tale' a feminine. *Nama* represents the *-an* declension which contained masculine and feminine nouns and the odd neuter. *Nama* is masculine. The cases in Old English are only weakly differentiated, with more differentiation in the demonstrative than in the noun. For this reason the demonstrative 'that' has been included in the table (compare the German case forms in Table 4.1).

Table 6.2 *Early Romance noun declensions*

	1 'moon'	2 'year'	3 'dog'
	Western Romance		
sg. nom.	*luna*	*annos*	*canes*
obl.	*luna*	*anno*	*cane*
pl. nom.	*lunas*	*anno*	*canes*
obl.	*lunas*	*annos*	*canes*
	Italy		
sg. nom.	*luna*	*anno*	*cane*
obl.	*luna*	*anno*	*cane*
pl. nom.	*lune*	*anni*	*cani*
obl.	*lune*	*anno*	*cani*

Table 6.3 *Old English case inflection*

	'stone'		'ship'	
	singular			
nom	*se*	*stān*	*thæt*	*scip*
acc	*thone*	*stān*	*thæt*	*scip*
gen	*thæs*	*stānes*	*thæs*	*scipes*
dat	*thæm*	*stāne*	*thæm*	*scipe*
	plural			
nom	*thā*	*stānas*	*thā*	*scipu*
acc	*thā*	*stānas*	*thā*	*scipu*
gen	*thāra*	*stāna*	*thāra*	*scipa*
dat	*thæm*	*stānum*	*thæm*	*scipum*
	'tale'		'name'	
	singular			
nom	*sēo*	*talu*	*se*	*nama*
acc	*thā*	*tale*	*thone*	*naman*
gen	*thǣre*	*tale*	*thæs*	*naman*
dat	*thǣre*	*tale*	*thæm*	*naman*
	plural			
nom	*thā*	*tala*	*thā*	*naman*
acc	*thā*	*tala*	*thā*	*naman*
gen	*thāra*	*tala*	*thāra*	*namena*
dat	*thæm*	*talum*	*thæm*	*namum*

The Old English case paradigms are strikingly similar to those of German, whether old or modern, but while German has lost only the instrumental from Old High German to modern German, English lost almost the entire system between the late tenth and thirteenth century. With nouns only the genitive remained distinct from the nominative. With pronouns the genitive was reinterpreted as a possessive adjective and a nominative-oblique distinction remained, the oblique reflecting a merger of the accusative and dative.

Two phonological changes destroyed the system. One was the reduction of unstressed vowels to schwa which involved the loss of a number of distinctions. The other was the loss of word-final *n* in inflections which affected not only the *-an* paradigm but all datives in *-m*, since *n* had been substituted for *m*. Virtually the only forms to survive these changes were those ending in *-s*, the genitive singular of nouns in the general masculine and neuter classes and the nominative-accusative plural of nouns in the general masculine class. Both these forms were extended to all paradigms so that by the end of the Middle English period the system was as in Modern English:

(18)   nom sg   *the stone, ship, tale, name*
         gen sg   *the stones, shippes, tales, names*
         plural   *the stones, shippes, tales, names*

The nominative forms of the demonstrative with initial *s* (*se, seo*) adopted the *th* of the rest of the paradigm. The loss of inflection entailed the loss of grammatical gender and *thæt*, formerly the nominative-accusative singular demonstrative with neuters, remained as a singular demonstrative for all genders while *the*, which reflects the rest of the demonstrative paradigm, weakened semantically to become a definite article.

The near elimination of case in English and Romance makes an interesting comparison. In both areas the use of prepositions increased as the case system was eroded so that all adverbal relations outside the core eventually had to be expressed via prepositions. Here is an Old English version of the verse from Luke given as (17) above and Wyclif's fourteenth-century translation.

(19)   a. *He   folgode   an-um   burg-sitt-end-um   menn*
            he   followed   one-DAT   town-dwell-ing-DAT   man.DAT
            thaes   rices
            that.GEN   land.GEN
         b. *He clevede* [= attached himself] *to oon of the citizeins of that contré*

Table 6.4 *Latin and Old English pronouns*

| | Latin | | Old English | |
	1	2	1	2
nom	*ego*	*tū*	*ic*	*thū*
acc	*mē*	*tē*	*mē*	*thē*
gen	*meī*	*tuī*	*mīn*	*thīn*
dat	*mihi*	*tibi*	*mē*	*thē*
abl	*mē*	*tē*		

Table 6.5 *French and Italian singular pronouns*

| | French | | | | Italian | | | |
| | 1 | 2 | 3 | | 1 | 2 | 3 | |
			m	f			m	f
subj.	je	tu	il	elle	**io**	**tu**	**lui**	**lei**
obj.	me	te	le	la	mi	ti	lo	la
ind.obj.	me	te	lui	lui	mi	ti	gli	le
oblique	**moi**	**toi**	**lui**	**elle**	**me**	**te**	**lui**	**lei**

In both areas SVO word order emerged and served as the normal means of distinguishing A from P.[8]

In both areas case distinctions were retained more on pronouns than nouns. To start with, Latin and Old English made stronger case distinctions in pronouns than nouns in the sense that the marking consisted in some instances of a change to the stem (rather than a suffix) including suppletion. Consider, for instance, the first and second person singular pronouns given in Table 6.4. In English a three-way distinction was retained *i/me/min* etc., but the genitive forms even in Old English, were reinterpreted as stems and came to be used as possessive adjectives (*my*, *thy*) and possessive pronouns (*mine*, *thine*).[9] In Romance there is always a distinction between direct and indirect object forms at least in the third person clitics. The singular pronouns of French and Italian are given in Table 6.5. Free pronouns are in bold. French has clitic pronouns for subject, object and indirect object plus a series of free, stressable pronouns which can be used in isolation (*moi*), with prepositions (*avec moi* 'with me'), predicatively (*L'état c'est moi* 'The state, it is me') or when stress is required (*Moi, je le vois* 'I see it'). In Italian, which is more representative of Romance, there are no subject clitics, the subject being represented inflectionally in the verb.

It is generally true that case distinctions are retained more on pronouns, especially clitic pronouns, than on nouns, hence the arrows in Figure 6.1 indicating that the final resting place of case marking is on bound pronouns where 'bound' includes clitics and inflection.

It is common for nouns in oblique cases to be reinterpreted as adverbs, particularly adverbs of place, time and manner. In Latin, for instance, there are adverbs of degree such as *multum* 'much' and *quantum* 'how much' which are accusative case forms in origin that have been reanalysed as adverbs; similarly there are adverbs that derive from ablative case forms such as *prīmō* 'in the first place' and *quārē* 'why' which is a fossilised ablative phrase *quā rē* 'by what matter'. When a case system disappears these fossilised case markers may remain. English *why* is from OE *hwȳ* the instrumental of the interrogative root (cf. *hwā* 'who', *hwæt* 'what'). Even in Old English the instrumental was vestigial, but this lexicalised formation has survived. Examples of the Old English genitive survive in adverbs like *besides* and *sideways* as well as in *once*, *twice*, *thrice* and *since* where the voiceless sibilant [s] is spelled differently from the voiced [z].[10]

6.4 Derived functions of case marking

Forms used to mark case may come to mark other functions. It sometimes happens, for instance, that case is marked on verbs, that the case function is reinterpreted, and that the marking remains and signals the new function. It is also possible for inflectional case to be lost and for the marking to remain only for one or more derived functions.

Local expressions normally cover the domain of time as well as space, so not surprisingly local case marking often comes to mark tense or aspect with verbs. Archaic English expressions like *The times, they are a-changing* illustrate a local preposition (OE/ME *an/on* 'on') used with the present participle to indicate ongoing activity. In French the expression *venir de* 'to come from' refers to time as in *Je viens de manger* (I come from eat.INF) 'I've just eaten', similarly in Pitta-Pitta *Tatyi-ka-inya nganytya* (eat-NM-ABL I) 'I've just eaten' where the ablative corresponds to the French preposition *de*.

Perhaps the neatest example of the transference of case marking to verbs is to be found in Kala Lagau Ya, a Pama-Nyungan language of the Western Torres Strait. Practically the whole system of cases and their markers have been transferred to the domain of time and they show up as part of the system of tense/aspect markers on the verb. There is one problem of identification. In Kala Lagau Ya -*n* appears as an ergative marker with nouns and as an accusative marker with pronouns. Table 6.6 displays the identifications. Given this data one can easily 'explain' the correspondences albeit in a post hoc way. In fact one could justify a transference of either ergative or accusative to completive, since both are associated with high semantic transitivity, one of the correlates of which is perfective aspect (see section 5.2.6). Examples (20) and (21) illustrate -*pa* the dative with nouns and incompletive with verbs respectively (Kennedy 1984):

Table 6.6 *Kala Lagau Ya case and tense/aspect matchings*

marker	case	tense/aspect
-*n*	ergative	completive
	accusative	
-*pa*	dative/allative	incompletive
-*pu*	comitative	habitual
-*ngu*	ablative	yesterday past
-*nu*	locative	immediate past

(20)   *Nuy   ay-pa   amal-pa*
        he   food-DAT   mother-DAT
        'He [went] for food for mother.'

(21)   *Ngoeba   uzar-am-pa*
        1DU.INC   go-DU-INCOMPLETIVE
        'We two will go (are endeavouring to go).'

A dative indicates activity directed towards a goal, so it is appropriate for an aspect that marks 'incomplete actions in the present, including present continuous actions [and] ... actions in the past where the speaker wishes to emphasise purposiveness or goal orientation' (Kennedy 1984: 160).

The infinitives of some languages derive from the reinterpretation of case-marked verbs. The infinitives in Indo-European languages arose in this way. In Vedic Sanskrit, for instance, a verb could take the accusative *dātu-m* 'giving', dative *bhuj-é* 'enjoying', genitive-ablative *nidhāto-s* 'putting down' or locative *neṣáṇ-i* 'leading'. In a sentence such as *Vaṣṭi ārábham* (desire.3SG begin.ACC) 'He wants to begin, he wants a beginning' the accusative is identifiable as such. In classical Sanskrit, however, the accusative-marked form was the only one to survive. It extended its scope to cover the functions previously marked by the others, so that in a sentence like *Avasthātu-m, sthānañtara-m cintaya* (stay-INF place.other-ACC think.IMP) 'Think of another place to stay' the -*m* on the verb is hardly to be identified with the accusative, but rather as a marker of a category of non-finite verb, the category that came to be called the infinitive (Burrow 1955: 364–6).

In Indo-European the infinitive normally remains a non-finite, subordinate form, but in Australian languages such forms come to be used as independent finite verbs. Most examples involve dative-marked forms which come to be used as purposive forms. The following examples are from Kalkatungu. In (22) there is a dative marked noun. In (23) there is a verb plus nominalising suffix -*nytya*- plus dative (-*aya*). This verb is non-finite, but since Kalkatungu is a syntactically ergative language, it is the absolute relation (SP) that remains unexpressed. In (24) a verb marked by *-nytyaaya* is used as an independent finite verb.

(22) *Yurru   ingka-nha   natha-aya*
      man.NOM   go-PAST   nurse-DAT
      'The man went for the nurse.'

(23) *Yurru   ingka-nha   natha-ngku   nanyi-nytya-aya*
      man.NOM   go-PAST   nurse-ERG   see-NM-DAT
      'The man went so the nurse could have a look at him.'

(24) *Natha-ngku   yurru   nanyi-nytyaaya*
      nurse-ERG   man.NOM   see-PURP
      'The nurse is going to have a look at the man.'

The use of an originally subordinate verb form as a main verb probably arises from the ellipsis of semantically weak governing verbs with meanings like 'go' (cf. the aspectual-like force of *go* in English *I'm going to wash*).

As mentioned at the beginning of the section, case marking that has acquired a new function may remain even though inflectional case is lost. The infinitive in Latin, for instance, reflects a formation consisting of a verb root plus derivational suffix *-s-* plus locative *i*, e.g. **deike-s-i > *dikese > dikere* i.e. *dicere* 'to speak'. In Latin *-re* is analysable as the marker of the infinitive and it is this *-re* that survives in Italian infinitive forms like *dire*.

In some languages there is formal identity of case markers and switch reference markers. This identity can be seen in the Muskogean, Yuman and Uto-Aztecan languages (Jacobsen 1983: 151) as well as in Australian languages (Austin 1981b). The following examples are from the Yuman language Diegueño (Langdon 1970: 150–4). In (25) *-(v)c* marks the subject; in (26) it marks the fact that the unexpressed subject is the same as the subject of its sister clause and is glossed SS (same subject).

(25) *Sin^y-c   ʔəcwəyu-w-m   ʔəyip-s*
      woman-NOM   3SG.sing-DS   1SG & 3SG.hear-ASSERT
      'I heard the woman sing.'

(26) *ʔamp   n^{y}a-ta ʔam-c   ʔəwu-w-s*
      1SG.walk   when-1SG.be.around-SS   1SG & 3SG.saw-ASSERT
      'As I was walking, I saw him.'

The suffix -(*v*)*m* marks direction away from the point of reference and toward the object as in *ʔəwa-vəm* 'away to the house' as well as instrumental and accompaniment. It is also used to indicate that a verb has a different subject from that of a sister clause. This is illustrated in (25) where it is glossed D(ifferent) S(ubject). There is general agreement that same-subject and different-subject markers derive from case marking forms.

Austin has shown that in Australia locative case markers have developed into markers for different subject in one large area and into markers for same subject in another large area. Allative markers have also developed into different-subject markers. Austin has also demonstrated that the development of same-subject and different-subject markers covers a continuous area involving languages that are not all closely related. This suggests that the development is subject to diffusion (Austin 1981b: 329–32).

NOTES

1 Overview

1 The symbol *ɪ* indicates a high, back, unrounded vowel.

2 Lewis 1967 refers to this case as the absolute case.

3 It also has postpositions that govern the genitive with singular pronouns but the nominative with other nominals. Such a postposition is *gibi* 'like': *kim-in gibi* (who-GEN like) 'like whom', but *bu adam gibi* (this man.NOM like) 'like this man'.

4 The singular base can be inflected for plural and/or for the person and number of the possessor: *adam-lar-ɪm-la* (man-PL-1SG.POSS-LOC) 'with my men'. If one takes both of these types of inflection into account, there are 84 word forms. However, since the case system remains separate from the number system and the possessor system, i.e. there is no fusion of the case marking and any other marking, one can say there is a case paradigm of six members rather than a paradigm of 84 members.

5 In Turkish there is a syllable-final devoicing of stops. Compare *kitaba* 'to the book' and *kitapta* 'on the book'.

6 I use **concord** to refer to case/number/gender matching between nouns and their dependents and **agreement** to refer to person/number matching between the verb and its subject or other complements. This represents majority practice, but some writers do not distinguish between the two terms.

7 A nominal in the vocative can take dependents as in Catullus' poem addressed to Cicero (xlix), which begins *Disertissime Romuli nepotum* (eloquent.most.VOC Romulus.GEN grandson.GEN.PL) 'Oh, most eloquent of the descendants of Romulus' where *disertissime* is a noun in the vocative with a genitive dependent which in turn has a genitive dependent.

8 Mohawk has no case marking, but there is, or was, an address form (Marianne Mithun, personal communication).
In Maori bisyllabic names, but not longer names, used as terms of address are preceded by a preposition *e* which otherwise marks the demoted subject in the passive.

9 These secondary postpositions are nominal in origin, hence the use of the genitive *ke*. Compare English 'in the middle of the night', 'at the bottom of the stairs'. See also section 6.1.

10 With the less-used co-ordinator *kuliko* all co-ordinands take case marking (Jae Jung Song, personal communication).

11 I take a particle to be a free form belonging to a closed set. Most particles have adverbial functions. A particle does not govern a noun; a postposition does.

12 See, for instance, Bresnan and Mchombo 1987. See also section 3.2.2.

13 See note 2 in chapter 5.

14 Other valency-changing derivations are illustrated in section 3.2.1.

15 An alternative is to take expressions such as *on top of* and *in front of* to be complex prepositions.

2 Problems in describing case systems

1 I am using 'complement' for all the phrases that realise arguments including the subject. In one usage of the term the subject is excluded.

2 It is difficult to demonstrate this directly, since place names are not normally modified directly, rather a common noun is used in apposition as in (1). However, there are odd examples of place names being modified by adjectives referring to places, e.g. *Suessae Auruncae* 'at Auruncan Suessa' (Woodcock 1959: 36).

3 The use of pre-theoretical syntactic entities derives originally from Dixon's description of Dyirbal (Dixon 1972: xxii) and they have proved particularly useful in comparing case marking within languages and across languages. Dixon uses S, A and O; others, including Comrie, prefer S, A and P (see, for instance, Comrie 1978). P is more logical in that it bears a relationship to patient that is analogous to that borne by A to agent. It needs to be remembered that P covers the patient of a transitive verb and extends to other roles that are treated the same way grammatically. It follows from this that it does not cover the patient in 'I got hit by a car', since the patient in this construction is not treated the same way as the patient argument of a transitive verb; nor does it cover the patient in constructions where another role is advanced and treated as P while the patient is demoted to an adpositional phrase or peripheral case. See, for instance, (3) in chapter 3 where the role of instrument is treated as P and the patient appears in the dative. For a definition of transitive verb, see the *Guide to terminology*.

4 My preference is to use nominative for the case that is used to encode S irrespective of whether this case covers S + A or S + P or indeed whether it is exclusive to S or covers S + A + P. This case will normally be unmarked and will be the case used in isolation from constructions. I will reserve the term **absolutive** for a grammatical relation that subsumes S and P.

5 Some Pama-Nyungan languages mark case only on the final word of a phrase (phrase-marking languages), others mark case on all nominals (word-marking languages). In some word-marking languages the nominals translating an English noun phrase tend not to cohere. It may be that there are no noun phrases only nominals in parallel. Under this interpretation there would be no concord in the sense of dependent-to-head concord.

6 Where nominals appear in parallel as in (3), it is likely that only one bears the grammatical relation and that the other is an adjunct. In (3) the pronoun would be a likely candidate for direct object since it can be replaced by an object clitic. The construction is described in semantic terms ('patient of a transitive verb') to leave the syntactic interpretation open.

7 For a discussion of the differences between Australianist practice and traditional practice, see Goddard 1982, Blake 1985.

8 Wierzbicka (1983:249ff) denies that there is a partitive case and takes the *-u* to be the genitive case marker used with certain nouns to indicate uncountable 'stuff', i.e. it is a case marker that cumulatively represents another semantic notion.

9 The nominative is the morphologically unmarked case and is referred to as the absolute case in some grammars of Turkish. See also note 2, chapter 1.

10 Compare (11) in chapter 1.

11 The Roman writer Varro took the nominative to be the canonical word form from which the oblique cases could be developed (Robins 1967: 52), though technically this is not always true of Latin (nor of the other Indo-European case languages). For instance, with a stem in -*g*, there will be assimilation of *g* to the voiceless -*s* in the nominative so that the word for 'flock' has nominative *grex* (*/greks/*), genitive *gregis*. However, since there are stems in /-*k*/, there are words like *dūx* (*/du:ks/*) nominative, *dūcis* (*/du:kis/*) genitive. This means that one cannot predict the genitive or any oblique form from the nominative. For this reason dictionaries give the genitive as well as the nominative since the genitive shows the oblique stem.

12 In Latin, many of the verbs that take a peripheral- or indirect-marked complement are deponent verbs; in fact, all the verbs that take the ablative rather than the accusative are deponent: *fungī* 'to busy oneself with, to perform (a duty)', *fruī* 'to enjoy (oneself in)', *ūtī* 'to use', 'to avail oneself of', *potīrī* 'to have possession of' and *vescī* 'to use as food', 'feed upon'. Deponent verbs are described as passive in form but active in meaning. Historically they derive from reflexives and in some of them the sense of a patient coreferent with the subject is still apparent. It is because of this patient that the overt complement has come to be represented peripherally.

Potīrī can also govern the genitive and occasionally the accusative where it tends to mean 'get control over' as opposed to 'be in control of' (de Carvalho 1982: 263ff).

13 See the discussion in section 5.2.6.

14 Examples include:

acc.	*ad bene vīvendum*	'for living well'
gen.	*ars scrībendī*	'the art of writing'
dat.	*pār disserendō*	'equal to arguing'
abl.	*dē bene vīvendō*	'about living well'

15 The dative is not taken to be local in this system even though the dative could be said to encode an abstract destination (compare the systems of Simon (Table 2.8), Martin (Table 2.9) and Jakobson (Table 2.13). In some languages the dative rather than the accusative expresses destination and there is no question that the dative would have to be taken to be [+ local].

3 Modern approaches to case

1 The antipassive in Kalkatungu also has a syntactic function. See (50) (51) in chapter 4.

2 This statement about the marking of the whole and the part is couched in semantic terms to leave open the question of whether both the whole and the part bear the syntactic relation that one might expect on the basis of the role and the marking.

3 Some linguists use the terms subjective case and objective case rather than nominative and accusative. This is not well-motivated terminology when one considers that cases are multifunctional.

4 For the original version of the model see Chomsky 1981. Case theory is described in various sources including Chomsky 1985, van Riemsdijk and Williams 1986, Baker 1988 and Haegeman 1991.

5 An example of structural case assignment in Lexical Functional Grammar was presented in section 2.3.4.

6 The term **predicate** is used in two different but overlapping senses. In traditional grammar the predicate is opposed to the subject and covers the verb, its complements and its

adjuncts, less the subject of course, and less any constituents moved out of the predicate phrase, typically to the front of the sentence. In logic **predicate** is opposed to **argument** where predicate is a term expressing a property of an entity or a relation between entities. The entities are the arguments of the predicate. A predicate can be simple or complex. Where a predicate takes in various complements, as in the traditional predicate versus subject, it is a complex one-place predicate with the subject as its argument.

7 Stowell (1981) proposes a **Case Resistance Principle** to the effect that those word classes that assign case cannot receive it.

8 In a more widely accepted analysis *him* would be taken to have been raised into the higher clause and to be the direct object of the higher clause. See also note 19.

9 Yip, Maling and Jackendoff (1987) present a theory to account for case assignment in accusative and ergative languages. In their theory (Case in tiers) syntactic case is assigned directionally, first the unmarked case, then the marked case (accusative, ergative). In an accusative language the direction of assignment is left-to-right. In an ergative language right-to-left. By this method of assignment the unmarked case is applied to S or A in an accusative language and to S and P in an ergative language. Consider the following examples from West Greenlandic and their English translations.

(i) *Kaali   pisuppoq*
    Karl   walks
    NOM

(ii) *Kaali-p* (ERG) *Hansi   takuaa*
     ERG   NOM   R-to-L
     Karl   sees   Hans
     NOM   ACC   L-to-R

However, this system makes no distinction between syntactic ergativity and morphological ergativity; it makes certain assumptions about word order that do not apply to all ergative languages; it cannot handle pragmatic as opposed to grammatical word order; it cannot handle languages that use ergative and accusative case marking on the basis of lexical content or aspect (see section 5.2.4), and it cannot handle active systems (see section 5.2.3).

10 Sources for Lexical-Functional Grammar include Bresnan (ed.) 1982, Bresnan and Kanerva 1989 and Neidle 1988 which contains a neat outline of the theory.

11 Fillmore treated the effected patient (*She built a sand castle*) as factitive (1968) and later as goal (1971).

12 But see section 3.5.4 on role hierarchies. Some would claim that roles are relevant to the grammaticality of reflexives and passives.

13 See (8) and (10) above where a whole and a part share a role.

14 See discussion in Jackendoff 1972: 34–6; also Somers 1987.

15 The gerundive is a passive-like adjective derived from a verb. It has the sense of 'X is requiring to be Verb-ed'. There are fossilised Latin gerundives in English: *Amanda* 'female requiring to be loved', *memoranda* 'things requiring to be remembered', *agenda* 'things requiring to be done'.

16 For a similar interpretation of analogous pairs of sentences see Dik 1978: 99f.

17 Sources include Perlmutter (ed.) 1983, Perlmutter and Rosen (eds.) 1984 and Blake 1990.

18 In a sentence like *John took himself off to the pictures* the [erg] and [abs] are represented separately.

19 In the sentence *The child seems to hear* the noun phrase *the child* belongs semantically with the verb in the non-finite, dependent clause. We can demonstrate this by substituting an inanimate noun and reflecting on the source of the semantic incongruity: *The stone seems to hear.* We can also compare *It seems that the child/the stone hears.* One way to analyse a sentence like *The child seems to hear* and to relate it to *It seems that the child hears* is to posit an underlying structure *seem [child hear].* The sentence *It seems that the child hears* can be derived directly simply by meeting certain grammatical requirements (adding *it, that* and verb agreement), and the sentence *The child seems to hear* can be derived by raising *the child* to become the subject of *seem.* In the sentence *The doctor expected the child to recover* the logical object of *expect* is the proposition *[child recover],* (compare *The doctor expected that the child would recover*) but the noun phrase *the child* is grammatically the object of *expect,* at least in the most widespread interpretation, though not in the Government and Binding interpretation (see (19) in this chapter). Under this interpretation *the child* is described as having been raised into the higher clause (Postal 1974).

It is common to talk about subject-to-subject raising, but in fact there is never raising to A, only to S. In Relational Grammar raising verbs like *seem* and *appear* are taken as having an initial 2, so the appropriate generalisation is that the target of raising is always a 2. This covers the *seem* type as in (53) and the *expect* type as in (54).

20 The missing subject of the infinitival adjunct is not grammatically controlled. If there is an agent in the governing clause, the missing subject will be interpreted as being coreferential with the agent, but it is possible to construct examples that show that the missing subject is not necessarily coreferent with a particular role or relation in the governing clause:

> *Sand was spread to prevent slipping*
> *It was sanded to prevent slipping*
> *It rained to complete the miserable scene*

The following example was actually uttered with reference to the manuscript of this book,

> *Chapter one was moved across there to look up something*

A few verbs like *promise* are exceptions to the rule that the PATIENT controls the missing subject of an infinitival complement, at least in varieties of English in which one can say *He promised me to mow the lawn.* Here the AGENT appears to control the missing subject, but Starosta, following Jackendoff 1972, takes *promise* to be intransitive. Independent motivation would appear to be weak.

21 In some languages such as Dyirbal, Kalkatungu (and also Tagalog if one accepts an ergative analysis) only the absolutive can be relativised. See (11), (12) and (13) in this chapter.

22 The analysis of Tagalog and a number of other Philippines-type languages is controversial. Tagalog has been described as being syntactically accusative, syntactically ergative and neither. The view that it is syntactically accusative is clearly false, both the other analyses have supporters. I am of the view that Tagalog is syntactically ergative (Blake 1988b, Blake 1990: 149–55).

23 One could take the *'s* to be derivational marking the derivation of a determiner; compare *his dog* and *the man over there's dog.* However, this would mean taking the whole noun phrase as a word.

24 For further examples of various patterns of cross-referencing see sections 5.2.2 and 5.4.

25 Double-object constructions are common across languages. It is interesting to note that verbs for GIVE are practically never marked for what would be, in Relational Grammar terms, an advancement of indirect object to direct object. It would appear that though the double object is a marked construction, it is unmarked or natural for GIVE.

26 For a discussion of the felicity of passives see Wierzbicka 1980: 49–69.

4 Distribution of case marking

1 In Classical Arabic to express 'X is Y' one uses a nominal predicate that shows concord with the subject. However, to express 'X was Y' one uses a transitive verb *kaana*, which takes an accusative complement.

   (i)   *muḥammad-u*   *kabiir-un*
         muḥammad-NOM   old-NOM
         'Mohammed is old.'

   (ii)   *kaana*   *muḥammad-u*   *kabiir-an*
         was   muḥammad-NOM   old-ACC
         'Mohammed was old.'

2 In traditional descriptions of European languages the verb is normally said to agree with the subject, but in languages with cross-referencing pronominal representation in the verb it makes more sense to characterise the verb as requiring certain categories of noun phrase to match the representation on the verb. In Latin, for instance, a verb form like *vēnit* 'S/he has come' is marked as including a third person singular subject. It can be characterised as expecting a third person singular noun phrase in the nominative with which it can be construed. This expectation need not be met, but the so-called agreement can be described in terms of the head (the verb) controlling the dependent (the subject noun phrase).

    The concord between a predicative noun or adjective and a subject would normally be described as concord of the predicative word with the subject, since it typically involves inherent features of the subject being marked on the predicate. In the Latin sentence *Maria acuta* 'Maria is sharp' the inherent properties of *Maria* (feminine singular) show up on the predicative adjective *acuta*.

3 One analysis that would take [*Cicerōnem cōnsulem*] to be a constituent of the higher clause is the 'small clause' analysis of Chomsky's Government and Binding Theory (Haegeman 1991: 50, 112–13). For a description of a raising analysis see note 19 in chapter three. For control of the missing subject of non-finite clauses see section 3.4.5.

4 With pronouns there are genitive forms that are used in objective function but not subjective function. These forms (*mei, tui, nostri* and *vestri*) resolve some ambiguities.

5 For Gooniyandi see McGregor 1990.

6 Pitta-Pitta, which is fairly closely related to Diyari, also has determiners morphologically identical to third person pronouns. See (20) to (25) in chapter 5.

7 Compare the Old English case inflections in Table 6.3.

8 See Cutler, Hawkins and Gilligan 1985. Frachtenberg (1922: 324f, 462f, 570) reported a 'discriminative case' prefix in Coos and Siuslaw, possibly an ergative case marker, and a 'modal or instrumental' prefix in Coos. The case status and the formal status (prefix versus proclitic) is not entirely clear. Both these languages have cases marked by suffix. See also Sherzer 1976: 69f, 261f.

9 Prefixed class/case marking may arise from the use of free form generic nouns preposed

to more specific nouns, a practice not uncommon in Australian languages. The generic noun takes case marking in parallel with the more specific noun. It presumably takes less stress than the specific noun and undergoes phonological attrition and absorption into the specific noun. In some languages there is transparent case marking on the class prefix. The following paradigm is from Mangarayi (Merlan 1982: 57). *Gardugu* is 'woman' and *nga-* is the feminine class marker. The form *nga-* is cognate with the *nga-* of *nganyi-*, the class/case oblique prefix for class 2 (feminine) nouns in Nungali.

nom   *ngarla-gardugu*
acc   *ngarlan-gardugu*
dat   *ngaya-gardugu*
loc   *ngaya-gardugu-yan*
all   *ngaya-gardugu-rlama*
abl   *ngaya-gardugu-wana*

10 An example of number marking preceding case marking in Turkish is given in (1) in chapter 1. A paradigm showing case and number marking in Archi is given in Table 4.3.

11 See Comrie 1980 for a discussion of how this order arose.

12 The suffix *-rla*, glossed as indirect object, indicates that the object enclitic is to be interpreted as encoding an indirect object. There is no overt form, however, for third person singular object.

13 Normally modal case covers the whole of the verb phrase including the verb itself. It is not proposed to discuss the absence of the modal case from the verb in (34), since this would take us too far afield.

14 The expression of multiple case need not be agglutinative. Dench and Evans 1988 give an inventory of 'sequence conditions' and illustrate portmanteau case markers, case haplology (one marker where two identical markers are expected), the use of empty morphs to separate case markers, etc.

15 See Silverstein 1976: 163 for a more elaborate hierarchy of clause types.

16 In a syntactically ergative language it is SP, the absolutive, that remains unexpressed with non-finite verbs. See (23) in chapter 6.
    For a non-finite verb with a subject see (20) in chapter 3 and (46) in this chapter.

17 See section 3.4.5.

18 See note 19 in chapter 3.

19 Possessive adjectives like *his* clearly belong to the class of determiners, but the analysis of *'s*-phrases is controversial. I am taking *'s* to mark the derivation of a determiner from a noun phrase.

20 Another example of the Latin accusative-and-infinitive construction is given in (20) in chapter 3. In connection with an analogous example in English (19) it was pointed out that under a popular analysis the noun phrase that expresses the subject of the infinitive is interpreted as having been raised to become the direct object of the governing verb. See also note 19 in chapter 3.

21 See the discussion of Hopper and Thompson in section 5.2.6.

22 For a discussion of an analysis that takes subordinating conjunctions to be prepositions in English see Huddleston 1984: 338–41, 390.

5 Survey of case marking

1 The examples are from Comrie (1989: 132–6) which contains a useful discussion of the labels 'definite' and 'specific'.

2 As mentioned in section 1.3.1 it is sometimes possible to isolate an apparent case marker in a bound pronoun system. A number of Northern Australian languages are like Rembarnga in having first person singular subject *nga* and first person singular object *ngan*. However, it is not really appropriate to call -*n* an accusative case marker, since it occurs in a system that marks particular grammatical relations. It is better to describe the bound pronoun system in terms of subject forms and object forms. Where a marker can be isolated, as with -*n*, it can be called an object marker. All this of course assumes that the bound pronouns are taken to be clitics. If they are analysed as person/number/relation inflection, it would be quite inappropriate to refer to case marking.

3 For languages of the Amazon basin see Derbyshire and Pullum 1986, 1989, 1990, 1991, and for information on the distribution of ergative languages see Dixon (to appear).

4 The system reported here is not peculiar to Avar. A similar lack of conflation between agent, experiencer and perceiver is found in other Northeast Caucasian languages.

5 Fore has both ergative and accusative marking and therefore falls within the type described in section 5.2.4. It is mentioned here since it provides a clear example of ergative marking determined by the relative position of A and P on the hierarchy. The accusative marking in this language appears as the first formative in the verb induced by a preceding P.

6 See also Table 2.4 'Core case marking in Pama-Nyungan'.

7 See (61) and (62) for Abaza examples.

8 See section 5.4 on the genitive.

9 See (53) for an example.

10 See also the case-marking schema in Pama-Nyungan illustrated in Table 2.4.

11 See (47) below.

12 A language like Thai with SV, AVP word order can be described as accusative, but there is no case.

13 de Carvalho, describing the dative independently of the data from Pitta-Pitta and other languages that use it in the future, characterises it thus, 'Le datif est, en quelque sorte, l'homologue du futur' (de Carvalho 1983: 64).

14 The original source is Wolfart 1973. These examples have been taken from Foley and van Valin 1984: 333ff.

15 This hierarchy is adapted from the findings of DuBois 1987. DuBois links SP/A alignment in grammar with the universal tendency for new information to appear preferentially in S or P function, at least within the core. See also Givón 1976 for various hierarchies of 'topicality' and their significance for agreement patterns.

16 For Dyirbal see Dixon 1972: 249. For general discussion see Durie 1986.

17 Following Silverstein we could give a more conservative version of the hierarchy in which 1 and 2 share the first position. In a few languages 2 outranks 1 but usually in the matter of priority of representation. In many languages one finds that in clitic combinations involving 1 and 2, only one person can be directly represented. Against the few languages in which there is evidence that 2 outranks 1 there are many more affording evidence that 1 outranks 2.

18 In the Australian language Mangarayi the ergative is distinguished only with inanimates. With higher categories there is a nominative-accusative system. For a paradigm of feminine nouns see note 9, chapter 4.

19 For Pintupi see Hansen and Hansen 1978. For Dargwa see Wierzbicka 1981. The other sources for sections (c) and (d) are in Mallinson and Blake 1981: 88–9.

20 Another interpretation of split ergativity not dissimilar to the views presented here can be found in Delancey 1981.

21 For examples see (42) in chapter 4 and (25) and (26) in chapter 6.

22 See also section 3.2.

23 See also Croft 1991: 171.

24 The reader might wonder why (53b) is considered to be an accusative construction with a direct object in the dative rather than an intransitive construction. The grammatical relations can be established from the bound pronouns on the verb. Note too that if *sama-jurs* in (53b) were an indirect object, there would be a problem in accounting for the grammatical relation of *šen*. In Harris's Relational Grammar analysis of (53c) the dative-marked constituent is an initial subject that has been demoted to indirect object pushing the initial indirect object *(šen)* into chômage where it is marked by the benefactive *(šen-tvis)*. The fact that two datives are allowed in (53b) is consistent with *samajurs* being direct object.

25 *Una compagna d'ufficio* is subject by the criteria of (a) control of agreement and (b) case (the distinctively nominative pronoun *lei* can be substituted for *una compagna d'ufficio*). *A Giorgio* has one subject property, namely control of the missing subject of various types of infinitival complement. In a multi-stratal analysis of the type used in Relational Grammar, different participants can be subject in different strata. *Giorgio* would be taken to be the initial stratum subject and the final stratum indirect object. *Una compagna d'ufficio* would be the initial direct object. However, it is not taken to be the final stratum subject despite the fact that it controls the verb agreement and appears in the nominative case. The construction is taken to be impersonal (see Blake 1990: 84 for references). The statement in the text that *una compagna d'ufficio* is the subject is based on the conventional analysis. See the discussion of inversion in section 3.4.3.

26 There is a common case for A and possessor in Kabardian and Ubykh (Northwest Caucasian), Lak (Northeast Caucasian) and Laz (South Caucasian).

27 Rumanian is said to have a two-case system (plus a vocative). One case, which Mallinson calls the nominative-accusative, covers subject and object, and the other, which Mallinson calls genitive-dative covers the non-core functions. There are separate pronoun forms, both clitic and free, for subject, object and indirect object, but free object pronouns are governed by a preposition *pe*, which also governs nouns in object function that are high on the animacy scale (Mallinson 1988).

	noun 'star'	pronoun	clitic pronoun
		first person singular	
subject	*stea*	*eu*	*eu*
object	*stea*	*pe mine*	*mă*
indirect object	*stele*	*mie*	*îmi*

Old French is usually described as having a nominative-oblique case system, but masculine demonstratives show a three-way nominative-accusative-dative distinction (*cil/cel/celui* 'that', *cisti/cest/cestui* 'this').

Clitic pronouns in Old French, as in the Romance languages generally, have three series of forms, one for subject, one for object and one for indirect object; the direct and indirect object forms are distinct only in the third person.

28 Croft (1991: 237) gives a useful list of roles that are subsumed under a single form using a forty-language sample.

29 The source for Yidiny is Dixon 1977, which contains a useful discussion of the classification of cases (124ff).

6 Life cycle of case systems

1 As noted in section 4.3.2 prepositions seem not to develop into prefixes. They can, however, fuse with determiners as in French *au* (=*à le* 'to the'), German *zur* (=*zu der* 'to the.*DAT*').

2 See also section 4.3.2.

3 Sources include Givòn 1975: 93, Norman 1988: 163, Lord 1982, Heine et al. 1991.

4 Compare the local forms discussed in section 5.6, especially Table 5.4.

5 The use of the transitive verb can express a higher degree of transitivity than the intransitive verb plus preposition. *Perambulare aedes* can mean 'inspect the house'.

6 See also the Margany example given in Table 2.7.

7 In early Latin the dative singular of the o-stems was *oi* which developed into -*ō*. The ablative was -*ōd*, but word-final *d* was lost to produce the dative-ablative syncretism shown in Table 1.2. In the singular of the *ā*-stems there was an inherited genitive-ablative syncretism with the form -*s*. However, the genitive -*s* was replaced by the -*i* of the second declension and a new ablative in -*ād* was formed on the model of the second declension singular (Palmer 1954: 233ff).

	first declension			second declension		
gen.	**ās*	*āī*	> *ae*	**oī*	> *ī*	
dat.	**āi*		> *ae*	**ōi*	> *o*	
abl.	**ās*	*ād*	> *ā*	*ōd*	*o*	

8 Although subject-verb-object is normal in transitive clauses, verb-subject is normal in intransitive clauses in some Romance languages (not French) with verbs of motion, location, state and change of state.

9 See section 1.3.4.

10 An interesting example of reinterpretation of case marking as part of the stem is to be found among some central Australian languages. The example is interesting because it involves case marking that is of purely phonological provenance. Among the Pama-Nyungan languages nouns in SP function are generally unmarked (see Table 2.5), but in some languages there is a phonotactic requirement that all words end in a vowel. Some of these languages have augmented consonant-final stems with a syllable -*pa* (alternatively -*ba*, there not being any voiced/voiceless opposition). In the table below, the left-hand column represents a language that allows consonant-final stems and the middle column illustrates the augmentation. Now in some languages the case marker -*pa* is reinterpreted as part of the stem to produce the paradigm shown in the right-hand column of the following table. The root illustrated means 'tongue' (Hale 1973a, Dixon 1980: 209f).

	Luritja	Pitjantjatjara	Warlpiri
SP	*ťarlinʸ*	*ťarlinʸpa*	*ťalanʸpa*
A	*ťarlinʸťʸu*	*ťarlinʸťʸu*	*ťalanʸparlu*
dative	*ťarlinʸku*	*ťarlinʸku*	*ťalanʸpaku*

GUIDE TO TERMINOLOGY

The following is a guide to the terminology used in this text. It covers the terms relevant to case, grammatical relations and some related concepts such as transitivity. In general it does not contain the terms that appear in one section only, nor does it contain labels for semantic roles, which are listed in section 3.4.

Terms in bold within an entry appear in the guide as headwords.

A. The agent argument of a transitive verb plus any other role that is treated in the same way grammatically. See also **S** and **P**. See section 2.2.3.

abessive. This label has been applied to cases such as the Finnish abessive which means 'lacking': *rahta-tta* 'money-less'. It is based on Latin *ab-esse* 'to be away from', i.e. 'to be absent'.

ablative case. The case that expresses the role of source, which is expressed by *from* in English. See also **elative** case.

absolutive. In this book 'absolutive' is used for the **grammatical relation** embracing S and P. In some sources the term 'absolutive' is used for the case that expresses S and P.

accusative case. The case in which the **direct object** is expressed. In some works this case is referred to as the objective case.

accusative language. A language in which morpho-syntactic rules identify **A** with **S** opposing SA (the subject) to **P** (the object).

accusative system. A **system** of **inflection**, **adpositions**, **clitics**, etc. that identifies **S** with **A** opposing SA to **P**.

active language. A language in which the **core** grammar is organised on a basis that could be described roughly as agent versus patient irrespective of transitivity. The agent-like argument of a one-place verb is treated like the **A** of a **transitive verb** and the patient-like argument of a one-place verb is treated like the **P** of a **transitive verb**. The term is from Klimov. Other terms include split-S and split intransitive. See section 5.2.3.

active voice. The active is opposed to the passive in the voice system of the verb. In the active voice **A** is the **subject** of a **transitive verb**. In the passive, which is a derived intransitive, **P** is advanced to become **S**, and **A** is demoted to **adjunct** status.

adessive. A case expressing 'at' or 'near'.

adjunct. A dependent that is not a **complement**, i.e. a dependent not representing an argument and so not implied by the governing **predicate**. An adjunct is always optional as

196

with the prepositional phrase in *He did it with ease*.

adnominal. An adnominal **dependent** is a dependent of a **nominal**.

adposition. Cover term for **preposition** and **postposition**.

advance, advancement (promotion). The term 'advancement' was popularised by Relational Grammar and is now in general use. It refers to the promotion of a participant up the hierarchy of **grammatical relations** by such means as using a derived verb. The passive can be described in terms of the advancement to **subject** of the participant holding the **direct object** relation.

adverbal. An adverbal **dependent** is a dependent of a verb.

adverbial. An adverbial **dependent** is one that has a function frequently expressed by an adverb, e.g. manner, time, location. It can be applied to words, phrases or clauses. Applied to cases it can cover any non-core case or even an 'adverbial' function of a core case such as the adverbial accusative in Latin: *Nūdae lacertōs* (bare.FEM.PL.NOM arms.ACC.PL) 'bare as to the arms'.

affix. Cover term for prefix, suffix and infix.

agreement. The marking of the **person**, number and sometimes gender or class of **arguments** on the verb is usually referred to as agreement. The term implies agreement in person, number and gender or class between the marking on the verb for a particular argument and any noun phrase representing the same argument. This marking is always organised on the basis of **grammatical relations** and it is the **subject** whose properties are most often represented. In some languages the person and number of a possessor in a noun phrase is marked on the **head** noun, which encodes the possessed (section 5.4). Agreement is almost always of a type that has been called cross-referencing. In this type the pronominal marking can represent an argument and a noun phrase representing the subject or possessor or whatever relation is cross-referenced can be omitted. In a few languages such as English there is non-cross-referencing agreement where the noun phrase controlling the agreement cannot be omitted (compare *He runs* with *They run* where the sibilant inflection in *runs* agrees with a third person singular subject that cannot be omitted).

allative. A case expressing 'to'.

analytic case marker. **Adpositions** are analytic in the sense that they are free forms and they are **case markers** in that they serve to mark the relation that their dependent noun bears to the governor of the adposition. In the sentence *He put it in the drawer* the preposition *in* marks the relation between *put* and *drawer*. A **relator noun** can also be an analytic case marker.

analytic language. The perfect example of an analytic language would be one in which each morpheme was a lexeme, i.e. one where there were no bound morphemes. No such language exists, but languages like Chinese and Vietnamese have relatively few bound morphemes.

antipassive. A detransitivised derived verb in an **ergative language**. In the antipassive construction the **A** of the **transitive verb** becomes S and P is expressed as a non-core relation. See also sections 3.2, 4.5 and 5.3.

In Relational Grammar the term 'antipassive' is not confined to ergative languages, but a distinction is made according to the fate of the demoted P. If P is demoted to **indirect object**, this is called direct-to-indirect object retreat. If P is not demoted to indirect object, then it is considered to have been demoted to **chômeur** status and the construction is referred to as antipassive.

argument. See **predicate**.

aversive. This label is sometimes used for a **case** indicating what is to be avoided. Another term that has been used is 'evitative'.

bound pronouns. In this text the term 'bound pronouns' refers to any kind of pronominal representation on the verb whether by forms analysable as clitic pronouns or by inflection. In a few languages bound pronouns are enclitic to the first constituent of the clause.

case. 1. A **system** of marking dependent nouns for the type of relationship they bear to their heads. Originally applied to inflectional systems, but sometimes used of other systems such as systems of **postpositions**.

2. A member of such a **system**, e.g. the dative case in Turkish.

case form. Where a lexeme can bear **case** the word forms expressing the lexeme in the various cases will be case forms. In Latin *manum* is the accusative case form of the lexeme for 'hand' (Table 1.2).

case grammar. Fillmore's 1968 conception of a generative grammar was one in which semantic roles or 'deep cases' were basic. This approach to grammar and similar approaches are referred to collectively as 'case grammar'.

case language. A language with an inflectional case system.

case marker. An **affix** that marks a case. In Turkish *-da* in *Istanbul-da* is the case marker for the a**blative** case.

case relation. This term is sometimes used as an alternative to **grammatical relation**. In this text it is used for the syntactic-semantic relations found in Anderson's Localist Case Grammar (section 3.4.4) and Starosta's Lexicase (section 3.4.5).

case system. The set of cases in a language.

chômeur. In Relational Grammar a **participant** holding a **core** relation may be demoted to chômeur status. In the passive the subject of the active is said to be demoted to hold the chômeur relation where it is realised as a **peripheral adjunct**. See section 3.4.3.

clitic. A form that is treated as a separate element in the syntax, i.e. as a word, but as part of an adjacent word in the phonology, i.e. as an affix. A form that attaches to the following word is a proclitic as in French *J'arrive* 'I arrive', and a form that attaches to a preceding word is an enclitic as in Italian *comprandolo* 'buying it' where *lo* is the enclitic. See section 1.2.5.

comitative. A case expressing with whom an entity is located. Usually used of animates. In the sentence *The dog is with his master* the phrase *his master* would be encoded in the comitative in a language with such a case.

comment. See **topic**.

complement. In this book a complement is taken to be a dependent representing an argument. This means that the finite verb in a language like English is described as having a **subject** as a complement. The **direct object**, **indirect object** and some prepositional phrases are also complements. In the following examples the complements are in bold:

She sent *a cheque to the missionary.*
She sent *the missionary a cheque.*
She put *the money in the bank.*
He was ready *for a try at the title.*
A student of *the classics.*

See also **adjunct**.

compound case marking. Where a case is marked by more than one segment it can be described as having 'compound case marking'. See Tables 2.14 and 5.4 and section 4.4.3.

concord. Where a determiner or an attributive adjective displays marking for categories of the head noun such as **case**, number or gender, it is said to exhibit concord with the head noun (section 1.2.1). There may also be concord between a predicative adjective and a **controlling** nominal (section 4.2). This phenomenon is sometimes referred to as **agreement**.

control, controller. The terms 'control' and 'controller' are useful in two contexts. Where there is **concord** or **agreement** the word that provides the source may be referred to as the controller. In the following examples the controller is in small capitals and the controllee in bold:

This BOOK *is on the table.*
These BOOKS *are on the table.*

The terms 'control' and 'controller' are also used with reference to pronouns and to unexpressed subjects. In the following example the noun in small capitals controls the pronoun in bold and the covert subject represented by [ ].

TOM saw **himself** *in the mirror and* [ ] *began to* [ ] *worry.*

core. The core grammatical relations cover various organisations of **S, A** and **P** including subject, direct object or absolutive and ergative. Where a three-place verb takes two P-like relations (as in English *She gave me the apples*), both these relations are included.

core case. One of the **cases** used to encode the **core** relations: **nominative, ergative, accusative**. See also **absolutive**.

cross-referencing, cross-referencing agreement. See **agreement**.

cumulation, cumulative exponence. Where two or more grammatical categories have fused representation throughout the language, the categories can be said to have cumulative exponence (Matthews 1974/1991). In Latin number marking and case marking can never be separated (Table 1.2).

dative case. The case that encodes the **indirect object**.

declension. Declension is inflection for case, or case and number. Sometimes the set of word forms expressing case or case and number is described as a declension; more often the term is used to refer to a class of words that inflect in the same or a similar way. Latin nouns that inflect like *manus* in Table 1.2 are said to belong to the fourth declension.

default. The default value or setting is the one that will be in force if no value or setting is specially assigned. The term has been popularised recently in the wake of the widespread use of computers. It is very similar in meaning to 'unmarked' as opposed to **marked**.

definite. An entity that is specific and which the speaker assumes can be identified by the hearer is referred to as definite. In English a common noun may be marked as definite by the use of the definite article (*the*), a demonstrative (*this*, *that*), or a possessive determiner (*my book*).

dependent. See **head**.

dependent marking. See **head marking**.

derivation. Where one lexeme is made up on the basis of another, it is said to be derived from that lexeme. For example, *foolish* is derived from *fool*, and *foolishness* is derived from *foolish*. In this book derivation is used mostly with reference to the forming of a verb with a new **valency**.

detransitivise. To derive an intransitive verb from a **transitive** one.

direct case. In a number of Indo-Aryan languages the unmarked case covers **S**, **A** and **P** and is often referred to as the direct case.

direct-inverse. The terms 'direct' and 'inverse' refer to the hierarchy of **person**. In some languages the speech-act participants (first and second person) are given some kind of priority over third persons or first person may be given priority over second as well. In some languages there are also distinctions within third person between a more topical person (proximate) and a less topical person (obviative). If A is higher than P on the hierarchy, the combination is 'direct'. If A is lower than P on the hierarchy, the combination is 'inverse'. See also **person**.

direct object. The grammatical relation that covers **P** and does not cover **S** or any part of **S**. In this book the recipient or beneficiary object is generally taken to be the direct object in **double object constructions** like *She gave him bread. She bought him a scarf.* This is controversial in English but clearly true of some other languages. See sections 3.2.2 and 3.4.3.

double-object construction. A construction like *She gave the beggar some money* where two noun phrases have pretensions to being considered direct object or where one noun phrase can be identified as **direct object** and where there is a second noun phrase that is marked in the same way. See also **direct object**, **secondary object**.

elative. A case expressing 'out of'.

enclitic. See **clitic**.

ergative. 1. A case encoding **A** but neither **S** nor **P**.

2. A grammatical relation corresponding to **A**. In this text the term '**A**' is applicable to any language, but the term 'ergative relation' is considered appropriate only where there is morphological or syntactic evidence to demarcate **A**.

3. A system of core grammar that identifies **S** and **P** as opposed to **A**. The term 'ergative' can be applied to case marking, cross-referencing agreement or any other system. The term 'ergative syntax' is applied to syntactic rules that identify **S** and **P**, e.g. a requirement that only the **absolutive** relation (**SP**) can be relativised. The term 'ergative' may also be used with reference to a language that has an ergative system.

essive. A case indicating location. The more common term for such a case is **locative**.

evitative. See **aversive**.

extension. See **intension**.

finite, non-finite. In the classical languages a verb that was marked for the person and number of its **subject** and which could take a noun phrase as subject was described as finite. Forms such as the infinitive and the participle took no person/number marking for the subject and normally took no noun phrase as subject (but see (46) in chapter 4). These forms of the verb were described as non-finite. In section 6.1.1 the term non-finite is used of non-initial verbs in serial verb constructions. These verbs cannot take a noun phrase as subject.

function. In a grammatical system each member can be said to have a function. The **dative** case in some languages may be said to have the function of expressing purpose and the function of expressing the demoted object in a derived **antipassive** construction. In this text function is used informally where it is not clear exactly what **grammatical relations** are involved. It may be that on a consideration of more evidence it would be more appropriate to subsume the purpose function and demoted object function under the grammatical relation of **indirect object**.

genitive case. The case that encodes the **adnominal** relation that subsumes the role of possessor.

Gesamtbedeutung. Cases have been described as having a generalised meaning (German *Gesamtbedeutung*) as well as various particular meanings (*Sonderbedeutungen*). Among these particular meanings it is common to be able to find a principal meaning or *Hauptbedeutung*.

given (information). At any point in discourse the speaker will make certain assumptions about what the hearer knows and treat this as 'given' information as opposed to 'new' information. Given information is typically represented in terms of pro-forms, i.e. pronouns, 'pro-verbs' and 'pro-adverbs': *I asked Bill to leave and **he did so** immediately*. The speech-act participants are given by the very act of communication, though they may represent new information in certain predications.

govern. Where the head of a construction determines the presence of a dependent or its presence and form, it is said to govern the dependent. In some languages a transitive verb may be said to govern a direct object in the accusative case.

grammatical cases. Cases that encode a purely syntactic (as opposed to) semantic relation. Also called syntactic cases (see section 2.3.2). The class includes **nominative, accusative, ergative, genitive** and **dative**.

grammatical relations. The morpho-syntactically determined relations borne by **dependents** to their **heads**. They include purely syntactic relations like **subject** and semantic relations such as **locative**.

head. Most constructions can be described in terms of an obligatory member (the head) and an optional member (the dependent). In the phrase *young woman* the word *woman* is the head and *young* the dependent. In this book the verb is taken to be head of the clause and an adposition to be head of an adpositional phrase.

head marking. Marking grammatical relations on the **head** of a construction rather than on the dependent (dependent marking). This almost always involves using **cross-referencing bound pronouns**.

hierarchy. A classification involving ranking into successively subordinate levels, e.g. a person hierarchy: 1st>2nd>3rd.

holistic interpretation. This term is used in linguistics to mean 'wholly affected' in the context of comparing the expression of a role as **P** or as a non-core relation. Compare *He read the book* (holistic) and *He read from the book* (partial).

hyponym. Where the meaning of a morpheme is included in that of another, the first is a hyponym of the second. *Lion* is a hyponym of *animal* and so is *tiger*. *Lion* and *tiger* are co-hyponyms.

illative. A case meaning 'into'.

indirect object. The indirect object is the major grammatical relation for encoding complements outside the core. It will typically encode the non-subject complement of two-place intransitive verbs or the non-core complement of three-place verbs. It is traditionally described as encoding entities that are indirectly affected by the activity or state denoted by the verb. In a language with a case system of four or more members the associated case is the dative. In this book the term 'indirect object' is *not* applied to the recipient or beneficiary object in the **double-object construction**, but this is a traditional usage that has support.

indirect subject. Where a noun phrase with morphological properties of an indirect object (usually the dative case) exhibits syntactic properties characteristic of the subject, it is sometimes referred to as the 'indirect subject'. See section 5.3, especially (52), (53) and (55).

inessive. A case meaning 'inside'.

infinitive. See **finite**.

inflection. A system for marking grammatical categories on a word, categories such as case, number, aspect and tense.

instrumental. A case expressing the means by which an activity is carried out.

intension, extension. The intension or the intensional definition is the set of defining properties, whereas the extension is the set of entities to which a term may refer. The intensional definition of **locative** case may specify that it refers to location, but the case may cover situations that lie outside this definition.

inverse. See **direct-inverse**.

inversion. Typically a predicate that takes an experiencer argument encodes the experiencer as **subject** and the patient as a **direct object**, **indirect object** or **peripheral** relation. Where the patient of such a predicate is encoded as subject, the assignment of roles to grammatical relations is said to be inverted and the predicate is described as an inversion predicate or as exhibiting inversion.

normal:	*The trainer liked the horse's performance.*
inversion:	*The horse's performance pleased the trainer.*

See sections 3.4.3 and 5.3.

isomorphic. Two systems are isomorphic if the distinctions made in one correspond point-for-point with the distinctions in the other. The hierarchy of ranks in an army could be described as being isomorphic with the ranks in a navy. The **case system** of one language could be isomorphic with that of another. The case **paradigm** of one class of nouns could be isomorphic with that of another class, the two paradigms differing only in details of realisation.

local cases. Cases encoding **roles** relating to position (location) or change of position (source, path, destination).

localist. An approach which interprets the marking of grammatical case as being a metaphorical extension of local case marking.

locative case. The case that expresses the role of location.

marked, unmarked. The unmarked member of an opposition is the normal or **default** member. In a two-way opposition of number, singular vs. plural, the unmarked member is the singular. The terms 'marked' and 'unmarked' refer to the fact that the normal member will usually lack any marking. Compare English *book* vs. *books*.

meaning. In this text cases are described as having meanings or **functions**. A meaning is semantic, but a function can be syntactic or semantic. The **dative** in a particular language may be described as having the function of expressing the indirect object and as having a purposive meaning or function, a beneficiary meaning or function, etc.

modifier. See **dependent**.

multiple case. The appearance of more than one case on a noun. See section 4.4.4.

new. See **given**.

nominal. 'Nominal' is a cover term for noun and pronoun. It may also cover other words that have some properties of nouns but not all. In traditional grammar noun and pronoun were considered separate parts of speech. In contemporary theories noun and pronoun are sub-classes of the same category. This category is often referred to as noun and abbreviated N, but readers need to be aware of 'noun' in the traditional sense and 'noun' in the wider sense.

nominalisation. The derivation of a noun, most often from a verb. In English *destruction* is a nominalisation of *destroy*.

nominative case. In Ancient Greek and Latin the nominative or 'naming' case was used for nouns used in isolation and for nouns expressing the **subject** relation. In this work it is used for the case that encodes S. It may encode only S, S plus A (**subject**), S plus P (**absolutive**) or all **core relations**. Some writers use **absolutive** for a case that encodes SP (the **absolutive** relation) and some use **direct** for a case that covers all **core relations**.

non-autonomous case. Mel'čuk's term for a case that does not have any distinctive forms of its own, but which can be recognised by seeing how a function is treated across a number of different **non-isomorphic paradigms**. See section 2.2.2.

non-finite. See **finite**.

object. This term usually refers to the **direct object**. It may be used to refer to both the objects in the **double-object construction**.

objective case. See **accusative case**.

objective genitive. Where there is a noun that has the same lexical meaning as a verb and a **genitive**-marked dependent encodes what would have been the object or any other non-subject complement of the corresponding verb, the genitive is described as an object(ive) genitive. See (14) in chapter 4.

oblique. Originally the term 'oblique' referred to all the non-nominative cases (section 2.1). It may be used for a single multifunctional **case** opposed to the **nominative** (section 5.8) and it is sometimes used for a multifunctional case in a **system** of three or four cases. In recent linguistics it has sometimes been used to refer to all non-core cases. In Relational Grammar a distinction is made between the 'term relations' (**subject**, **direct object** and **indirect object**) and the 'oblique relations' (**semantic relations** such as **locative** and **instrumental**).

obviative. See **person**.

P. The patient **argument** of a **transitive verb** plus any other role that is treated in the same way grammatically.

paradigm. A paradigm is a set of grammatically conditioned forms based on a particular root such as the set of **case forms** of a particular noun.

paradigmatic opposition. A **paradigmatic opposition** can be said to exist between elements in a system, e.g. a tense system or a case system. In Turkish one could say that there is a paradigmatic opposition between case forms like *adam*, *adama*, etc. (see Table 1.1), or between case markers like *-ø*, *-a*, *-da*, etc. or between the number markers *-ø*, *-lar-*.

participant. 'Participant' can be used with reference to the content of a message or with reference to the speech act. 'Speech act participant' is described under **person**. Participant is a cover term for the entities represented by the complements and adjuncts in a construction. Some participants are arguments and others are not. In the sentence *She bought bread at the convenience store* both *she* and *bread* represent arguments and *she, bread* and *convenience store* represent participants, each with its own role.

partitive. A **case** that indicates an entity partly affected.

passive voice. See **active voice**.

peripheral. In this text 'peripheral' is used to cover the non-**core** grammatical relations and the cases that encode them.

perlative. A case expressing 'through', 'across' or 'along'.

person. The participants in a speech event are classified as first person (speaker) and second person (addressee) as opposed to all non-participants, who are collectively known as third person. In some languages a distinction is made between an inclusive first person (including the addressee) and an exclusive first person (excluding the addressee). In some languages a distinction is made within third person between a proximate (more topical) and obviative (less topical) person. See also **direct-inverse** and section 5.2.5.

phrase-marking language. In this book the term 'phrase-marking language' is used to refer to a language in which **case** is marked only once in a phrase as opposed to a **word-marking language** where case is marked on the head of a noun phrase and on the dependents via **concord**.

postposition. A postposition differs from a **preposition** only in that it follows rather than precedes the **nominal** it **governs**. See **preposition**.

predicate. A predicate is a relational term signifying a property of an entity or a relation between entities. The entities are the arguments of the predicate. FLY is a one-place predicate, i.e. a predicate that implies one argument, the entity that flies. BASH is a two-place predicate and GIVE a three-place predicate. The use of capitals is to distinguish abstract predicates from the verbs that express them. In traditional grammar a sentence was divided into **subject** and **predicate**, where the predicate included the verb and its arguments less the subject. In a sentence like *Vikings attack Wessex* the phrase *attack Wessex* realises a predicate with Vikings as its argument. However, it is a complex predicate, which can itself be analysed into a predicate (represented by *attack*) with Wessex as its argument.

predicative. A phrase instantiating a predicate can be decribed as 'predicative'. In *They elected me chairperson* the noun *chairperson* instantiates a predicate, similarly the adjective in *They painted it red*. Both the noun *chairperson* and the adjective *red* can be described as predicative.

preposition. A preposition is a word that is itself a dependent, but which precedes and governs a nominal. In the sentence *She put the sash on him* the preposition *on* is governed by the verb *put* and in turn governs the following pronoun *him*. The preposition serves to mark the relationship of *him* to *put*.

proclitic. See **clitic**.

promotion. See **advance, advancement**.

proximate. See **person**.

relator nouns. Relator nouns are a specialised sub-class of nouns that behave like **adpositions** in relating a **predicate** to a noun phrase. In *He is standing on top of the cupboard* the word *top* could be analysed as a relator noun showing the relationship of *cupboard* to *stand*. See section 1.3.3.

role. The **semantic relation** borne by a **dependent** to its **head**. In *She washed the tablecloth* the subject *she* could be described as having the role of agent and *the tablecloth* as having the role of patient. Other terms used are semantic role, case role, thematic role and theta role. See section 3.4.

S. 1. The single argument of a one-place **predicate**.

2. In the context of word order it refers to **subject** as in the abbreviation SOV referring to subject-object-verb order.

3. In phrase-structure rules S stands for sentence.

secondary object. Where a **direct object** can be identified in a **double-object construction** the other object can be referred to as the secondary object.

semantic cases. Cases that encode purely **semantic relations**. See section 2.3.2.

semantic relation. In this book semantic relation is synonymous with (semantic) **role**.

specific. In linguistics the term 'specific' carries its normal meaning of 'particular'. It is frequently used with reference to the entity encoded as **P**, where 'specific' means a particular token or particular tokens identifiable by the speaker.

split-S, split intransitive. See **active language**.

stem forming case marking. In some languages forms identifiable as **case markers** in one context are used in other contexts to mark the stem to which other case markers are added. See section 4.4.2.

structural case. In some modern theories such as Lexical Functional Grammar (see (12) in chapter 2) and Government and Binding Theory (see section 3.3), some cases, notably **nominative** for **subject** and **accusative** for **direct object**, are assigned on the basis of the position which the relevant nominal holds in clause structure.

subessive. A case meaning 'under' or 'below'.

subject. The **grammatical relation** that covers **S** plus **A**. In various languages it manifests itself in terms of being represented by a series of **clitic** pronouns or **agreement** on the verb, by being in the **nominative** case, or by occupying the initial position in the clause proper.

subjective genitive. Where there is a noun that has the same lexical meaning as a verb and a **genitive**-marked dependent encodes what would have been the subject of the corresponding verb, it is described as a 'subjective genitive'. See (13) in chapter 4.

superessive. A case meaning 'on top of', 'over' or 'above'.

superlative. A case meaning 'to a position on top of or over'.

syncretism. 1. The merging of formerly distinct grammatical categories.

2. The neutralisation of grammatical categories in a particular environment.

Sense 1 is older and is most often used with reference to the merging of formerly distinct inflectional forms.

syntagmatic. Syntagmatic refers to relations between the constituents of a construction. A word can be said to bear syntagmatic relations to the other words in the same construction, but **paradigmatic relations** with other words that can be substituted for it. In *I saw him* there are syntagmatic relations between the three words and paradigmatic relations between each word and all the other words that can be substituted for them. The verb *saw* is in a paradigmatic relation with *heard, watched*, etc., etc.

system. As used in this book **system** is a set of items that can occupy a position in a word, phrase, clause or sentence structure. Normally only one member of the system can occupy the position in question at one time. **Case** is a system. In an **inflectional**-case language, for instance, each noun in a sentence must bear one case from the system.

theme. 1. In the Functional Sentence Perspective analysis of the Prague School the term 'theme' meant approximately **topic**.

2. Gruber introduced the term for the semantic role that others called patient. 'Theme', 'patient' and 'patient/theme' are now competing terms. See under **patient** in the list of roles in section 3.4.

topic, comment. The topic is what is spoken about as opposed to the comment, which is what is said about the topic. The topic is normally **given information** and typically expressed as the **subject**. There can also be a topic that stands outside the clause proper, usually before the clause set off by an intonation break. There are also discourse topics, topics that are established at some point and hold over some subsequent stretch of discourse. Consider the following sentence from an article about the French singer Edith Piaf:

> *The English too, they admired her.*

The English represents the clause external topic; *they*, the subject, represents given information (given by the clause-external topic) and provides the clause-internal topic, and *her*, which is part of the comment, represents the discourse topic of the passage.

transitive verb. A two-place verb with an agent and an affected patient or any other verb that has the same **valency**. In some languages there are alternative valencies (e.g. antipassive and passive). Only the unmarked valency qualifies as transitive. A verb like *put* that requires the expression of three arguments is often referred to as a ditransitive verb.

translative case. A **case** label meaning 'through', but note that the translative case in Finnish refers to the end point of a change of state. See Tables 5.5 and 5.6.

unmarked. See **marked**.

valency (American: **valence**). A specification of the arguments of a predicate and their expression. The specification would include the number of **complements**, their **role**, their **grammatical relation** and details of their expression (**case**, **clitic**, etc.).

vocative. A case used to mark a nominal as an addressee. See section 1.2.3.

word-marking language. In this book the term 'word-marking language' is used to refer to a language in which case is marked on the **head** of a noun phrase and on the **dependents** via **concord**.

GUIDE FOR FURTHER READING

Despite the fact that case plays a prominent part in European languages there are surprisingly few works devoted exclusively to case, particularly works in English. Among the most useful papers on inflectional case are Mel'čuk's 1986 paper *Towards a definition of case* and two papers by Comrie: *On delimiting cases* (1986) and *Form and function in identifying cases* (1991). The latter is in a volume edited by Frans Plank entitled *Paradigms: the economy of inflection*. This volume is largely about case paradigms and provides a concentrated source for a largely neglected area.

For semantic roles or 'deep cases' there is one particularly useful reference, namely Somers' 1987 book *Valency and case in computational linguistics*. Although one could not guess it from the title, most of the book is a clear, concise summary of the case grammar tradition including Fillmore, Dik, J. Anderson, Chafe, etc.

The description of case inevitably involves grammatical relations and the various grammatical mechanisms languages employ to package the propositional content according to the demands of discourse. There are numerous works to choose from in this field including Foley and van Valin 1984, Givón 1984, 1990 and Croft 1991. Ergative systems figure prominently in the recent literature. Comrie's 1978 paper *Ergativity* and Dixon's 1979 paper with the same title provide a good coverage. Dixon is soon to publish a book under the title *Ergativity*, which provides an updated coverage of manifestations of ergative phenomena in numerous languages.

For those who read Spanish Ana Agud's *Historia y teoría de los casos* (1980) is a comprehensive account of how case has been dealt with over the last two and a half thousand years. Volume one (*Casos y preposiciones*) of Rubio (1966) *Introducción a la sintaxis estructural del latín* provides a solid structural analysis of case in Latin. For readers of Italian Calboli's *Linguistica moderna e il latino: i casi* is a useful summary of analyses of the Latin case system.

REFERENCES

Abondolo, D. 1987. Hungarian. In B. Comrie (ed.), 577–92

Agesthialingom, S. & K. Kushalappa Gowda (eds.) 1976. *Dravidian case system.* Annamalainagar: Annamali University

Agud, A. 1980. *Historia y teoría de los casos.* Madrid: Gredos

Allen, W. S. 1964. Transitivity and possession. *Language* 40: 337–43

Andersen, P. K. 1979. Word order typology and prepositions in Old Indic. In B. Brogyanyi (ed.), *Studies in diachronic, synchronic and typological linguistics* 2 vols., vol. II, part 1, 23–34. Amsterdam: John Benjamins

Anderson, J. M. 1971. *The grammar of case: towards a localistic theory.* Cambridge University Press

　1977. *On case grammar.* London: Croom Helm

　1979. *On being without a subject.* Bloomington: Indiana University Linguistics Club

Anderson, S. 1982. Where's morphology? *Linguistic Inquiry* 13: 571–612

Anttila, R. 1972. *An introduction to historical and comparative linguistics.* New York: Macmillan

Artawa, K. 1992. Two transitive constructions in Balinese. *La Trobe Working Papers in Linguistics* 5: 13–30

Austerlitz, R. 1980. Typology and universals on a Eurasian east-west continuum. In G. Brettschneider & C. Lehmann (eds.), *Wege zur Universalienforschung. Sprachwissenschaftliche Beiträge zum 60. Geburtstag von Hansjakob Seiler*, 235–44. Tübingen: Gunter Narr

Austin, P. 1981a. *A grammar of Diyari, South Australia.* Cambridge University Press

　1981b. Switch-reference in Australia. *Language* 57: 309–34

　1981c. Case marking in southern Pilbara languages. *Australian Journal of Linguistics* 1: 211–26

Baker, M. C. 1988. *Incorporation: a theory of grammatical function changing.* Chicago University Press

Balakrishnan, R. 1976. Kodagu case system. In S. Agesthialingom & K. Kushalappa Gowda (eds.), 421–34

Blake, B. J. 1977. *Case marking in Australian languages.* Canberra: Australian Institute of Aboriginal Studies

　1979a. *A Kalkatungu grammar.* Canberra: Pacific Linguistics

　1979b. Pitta-Pitta. In R. M. W. Dixon & B. J. Blake (eds.), 182–242

References

1982. The absolutive: its scope in English and Kalkatungu. In P. J. Hopper & S. A. Thompson (eds.), 71–83

1983. Structure and word order in Kalkatungu: the anatomy of a flat language. *Australian Journal of Linguistics* 3: 143–76

1985. Case markers, case and grammatical relations: an addendum to Goddard. *Australian Journal of Linguistics* 5: 79–84

1987. *Australian Aboriginal grammar.* London: Croom Helm

1988a. Redefining Pama-Nyungan: towards the prehistory of Australian languages. In N. Evans & S. Johnson (eds.), *Aboriginal Linguistics* 1: 1–90. Armidale: University of New England, Department of Linguistics

1988b. Tagalog and the Manila-Mt Isa axis. *La Trobe Working Papers in Linguistics* 1: 77–90

1990. *Relational grammar.* London: Routledge

Bloomfield, L. 1933. *Language.* New York: Holt, Rinehart & Winston

Boas, F. (ed.) 1922. *Handbook of American Indian languages*, part 2. (Bureau of American Ethnology, Bulletin 40). Washington, DC: Smithsonian Institution

Bowe, H. 1990. *Categories, constituents and constituent order in Pitjantjatjara: an Aboriginal language of Australia.* London: Routledge

Branch, M. 1987. Finnish. In B. Comrie (ed.), 593–617

Brecht, R. D. & J. S. Levine (eds.) 1986. *Case in Slavic.* Columbus, OH: Slavica Publishers

Breen, J. G. 1976. Ergative, locative and instrumental inflections in Wangkumara. In R. M. W. Dixon (ed.), 336–9

1981. Margany & Gunya. In R. M. W. Dixon & B. J. Blake (eds.), vol. 2: 274–393

Bresnan, J. (ed.) 1982. *The mental representation of grammatical relations.* Cambridge, MA: MIT Press

Bresnan, J. & J. Kanerva. 1989. Locative inversion in Chichewa: a case study of factorization in grammar. *Linguistic Inquiry* 20: 1–50

Bresnan, J. & S. A. Mchombo. 1987. Topic, pronoun, and agreement in Chichewa. *Language* 63: 741–82

Burridge, K. 1990. Sentence datives and grammaticization and the dative possessive: evidence from Germanic. *La Trobe Working Papers in Linguistics* 3: 29–48

Burrow, T. 1955. *The Sanskrit language.* London: Faber & Faber

Calboli, G. 1972. *Linguistica moderna e il latino: i casi.* Bologna: Riccardo Patron

Cardona, G. 1976a. Pāṇini: A survey of research. In W. Winter (ed.), *Trends in linguistics, State-of-the-Art reports* (6). The Hague: Mouton

1976b. Subject in Sanskrit. In M. K. Verma (ed.), 1–38

Carroll, P. J. 1976. Kunwinjku (Gunwinggu): a language of Western Arnhem Land. Australian National University: master's thesis

Carvalho, P. de. 1980. Réflexions sur les cas: vers une théorie des cas latins. *L'information Grammaticale* 7: 3–11

1982. Cas et personne. Propositions pour une théorie morpho-sémantique des cas latins. *Revue des Études Anciennes* 82: 243–74

1983. Le système des cas latins. In H. Pinkster (ed.), *Latin linguistics and linguistic theory*, 59–71. Amsterdam: John Benjamins

1985. Nominatif et sujet. In C. Touratier (ed.), 55–78

Chafe, W. 1970. *Meaning and the structure of language*. Chicago University Press

Chidambaranathan, V. 1976. Case system of Kasaba. In S. Agesthialingom & K. Kushalappa Gowda (eds.), 467–80

Chomsky, N. 1965. *Aspects of the theory of syntax*. Cambridge, MA: MIT Press

1981. *Lectures on government and binding*. Dordrecht: Foris

1985. *Knowledge of language: its nature, origin and use*. New York: Praeger

Cole, P. & G. Hermon. 1981. Subjecthood and islandhood: evidence from Quechua. *Linguistic Inquiry* 12: 1–30

Coleman, R. 1985. The Indo-European origins and Latin development of the accusative with infinitive construction. In C. Touratier (ed.), 307–44

1987. Latin and the Italic languages. In B. Comrie (ed.), 180–202

1991 (ed.). *New studies in Latin linguistics: selected papers from the 4th international colloquium on Latin linguistics, Cambridge, April 1987*. Amsterdam: John Benjamins

1991a. The assessment of paradigm stability: some Indo-European case studies. In F. Plank (ed.), 197–213

1991b. Latin prepositional syntax in Indo-European perspective. In R. Coleman (ed.), 323–38

Comrie, B. 1976. The syntax of causative constructions: cross-language similarities and divergences. In M. Shibatani (ed.), *The grammar of causative constructions*. [Syntax and Semantics 6], 261–312. New York: Academic Press

1978. Ergativity. In W. P. Lehmann (ed.), *Syntactic typology*, 329–94. Sussex: The Harvester Press

1980. The order of case and possessive suffixes in Uralic languages: an approach to the comparative-historical problem. *Lingua Posnaniensis* 23: 81–6

1981. *The languages of the Soviet Union*. Cambridge University Press

1986. On delimiting cases. In R. D. Brecht & J. S. Levine (eds.), 86–105

1987. Russian. In B. Comrie (ed.), 329–47

1987 (ed.). *The world's major languages*. London: Croom Helm

1989. *Language universals and linguistic typology*. Oxford: Blackwell

1991. Form and function in identifying cases. In F. Plank (ed.), 41–56

Cook, W. 1979. *Case grammar: development of the matrix model*. Washington: Georgetown University Press

Corbett, G. 1987. Serbo-Croat. In B. Comrie (ed.), 391–409

Croft, W. 1991. *Syntactic categories and grammatical relations*. University of Chicago

Crowley, T. 1983. Uradhi. In R. M. W. Dixon & B. J. Blake (eds.), 306–428

Cutler, A., J. A. Hawkins & G. Gilligan. 1985. The suffixing preference: a processing explanation. *Linguistics* 23: 723–58

Delancey, S. 1981. An interpretation of split ergativity and related patterns. *Language* 57: 626–57

1987. Sino-Tibetan languages. In B. Comrie (ed.), 797–810

References

Dench, A. & N. Evans. 1988. Multiple case-marking in Australian languages. *Australian Journal of Linguistics* 8: 1–47

Derbyshire, D. C. & G. K. Pullum (eds.). 1986, 1989, 1990, 1991. *Handbook of Amazonian languages,* vols. 1–4. Berlin: Mouton de Gruyter

Dik, S. 1978. *Functional grammar.* Amsterdam: North Holland

Dixon, R. M. W. 1972. *The Dyirbal language of North Queensland.* Cambridge University Press

    1976 (ed.). *Grammatical categories in Australian languages.* Canberra: Australian Institute of Aboriginal Studies, New Jersey: Humanities Press

    1977. *A grammar of Yidiny.* Cambridge University Press

    1979. Ergativity. *Language* 55: 59–138

    1980. *The languages of Australia.* Cambridge University Press

    1987 (ed.). *Studies in ergativity.* Amsterdam: North Holland

    (to appear) *Ergativity.* Cambridge University Press

Dixon, R. M. W. & B. J. Blake (eds.). 1979, 1981, 1983, 1991. *Handbook of Australian languages,* vols. 1–4. Canberra: ANU and Amsterdam: John Benjamins (vols. 1–3); Melbourne: Oxford University Press (vol. 4)

Du Bois, J. 1987. The discourse basis of ergativity. *Language* 63: 805–55

Durie, M. 1985. *A grammar of Acehnese on the basis of a dialect of North Acehnese.* Dordrecht: Foris

    1986. The grammaticalization of number as a verbal category. *Proceedings of the Twelfth Annual Meeting of the Berkeley Linguistics Society,* 355–70

Ebeling, C. L. 1966. Review of Chikobava and Cercvadze's 'The grammar of literary Avar'. *Studia Caucasica* 2: 58–100

Evans, N. R. D. 1985. Kayardild, the language of the Bentinck Islanders of North West Queensland. Canberra: ANU doctoral dissertation

Filliozat, P-S. 1988. *Grammaire Sanskrite Pâninéenne.* Paris: Picard

Fillmore, C. J. 1968. The case for case. In E. Bach & R. T. Harms (eds.), *Universals in linguistic theory,* 1–88. London: Holt, Rinehart & Winston

    1971. Some problems for case grammar. *Working Papers in Linguistics, Ohio State University* 10: 245–65

Foley, W. A. & R. D. van Valin Jr. 1984. *Functional syntax and universal grammar.* Cambridge University Press

Frachtenberg, L. J. 1922a. Coos. In F. Boas (ed.), 297–429

    1922b. Siuslawan. In F. Boas (ed.), 431–629

Franchetto, B. 1990. Ergativity and nominativity in Kuikúro and other Carib languages. In D. L. Payne (ed.), *Amazonian linguistics: studies in lowland South American languages,* 407–27. Austin: University of Texas Press

Friberg, B. 1991. Ergativity, focus and verb morphology in several south Sulawesi languages. In R. Harlow (ed.), 103–30

Giridhar, P. P. 1987. A case grammar of Kannada. University of Mysore: doctoral dissertation

Givón, T. 1975. Serial verbs and syntactic change: Niger-Congo. In C. Li (ed.), *Word order and word order change*, 47–111. Austin: University of Texas Press

1976. Topic, pronoun and grammatical agreement. In C. Li (ed.), *Subject and topic*, 149–88. New York: Academic Press

1984a. *Syntax: a functional-typological introduction*, vol. 1. Amsterdam: John Benjamins

1984b. Direct object and dative shifting: semantic and pragmatic case. In F. Plank (ed.), 151–82

1990. *Syntax: a functional-typological introduction*, vol. 2. Amsterdam: John Benjamins

Goddard, C. 1982. Case systems and case marking in Australian languages. *Australian Journal of Linguistics* 2: 167–96

Greenberg, J. H. 1963. Some universals of grammar with particular reference to the order of meaningful elements. In J. H. Greenberg (ed.), *Universals of language*, 73–113. Cambridge, MA: MIT Press

Groot, W. de. 1956. Classification of cases and uses of cases. *For Roman Jakobson*, 187–94. The Hague: Mouton

Gruber, J. 1965. Studies in lexical relations. Cambridge, MA: MIT doctoral dissertation [reproduced by Indiana University Linguistics Club, Bloomington, Indiana]

1976. *Lexical structures in syntax and semantics*. Amsterdam: North Holland

Haegeman, L. 1991. *Introduction to government and binding theory*. Oxford: Blackwell

Hale, K. L. 1973a. Deep-surface canonical disparities in relation to analysis and change: an Australian example. In T. A. Sebeok (ed.), *Current trends in linguistics*, vol. 11: *Diachronic, areal and typological linguistics*, 401–58. The Hague: Mouton

1973b. Person marking in Walbiri. In S. R. Anderson & P. Kiparsky (eds.), *A festschrift for Morris Halle*, 308–44. New York: Holt, Rinehart & Winston

1976. On ergative and locative suffixial alternations in Australian languages. In R. M. W. Dixon (ed.), 414–20

1982. Some essential features of Warlpiri verbal clauses. *Work Papers of Summer Institute of Linguistics-Australian Aborigines Branch*. A6: 217–315

Halliday, M. A. K. 1985. *An introduction to functional grammar*. London: Edward Arnold

1967–8. Notes on transitivity and theme in English, Parts 1, 2 and 3. *Journal of Linguistics* 3: 199–244, 4: 189–215

Hansen, K. C. & L. E. Hansen. 1978. *The core of Pintupi grammar*. Alice Springs: Institute for Aboriginal Development

Harlow, R. (ed.). 1991. *VICAL 2. Western Austronesian and contact languages. Papers from the fifth international conference on Austronesian linguistics, Auckland, New Zealand 1991*. Auckland: Linguistic Society of New Zealand

Harris, A. 1981. *Georgian syntax: a study in relational grammar*. Cambridge University Press

1984. Inversion as a rule of universal grammar: Georgian evidence. In D. M. Perlmutter & C. Rosen (eds.), 251–91

1985. *Diachronic syntax*. Orlando: Academic Press [Syntax and Semantics 18]

Harris, M. & N. Vincent (eds.). 1988. *The Romance languages*. Oxford University Press

Heath, J. 1980. *Basic texts in Warndarang: grammar, texts and dictionary*. Canberra:

References

Pacific Linguistics (ANU)

Heine, B., U. Claudi & F. Hünnemeyer. 1991. *Grammaticalization*. Chicago University Press

Hewitt, B. G. 1989. *Abkhaz*. London: Routledge

Hinnebusch, T. J. 1979. Swahili. In T. Shopen (ed.), *Languages and their status*, 209–93. Cambridge, MA: Winthrop

Hjelmslev, L. 1935. *La catégorie des cas: Etude de grammaire générale* I. Copenhagen: Munksgaard [Acta Jutlandica: Aarsskrift for Aarhus Universitet 7.1]

1937. *La catégorie des cas: Etude de grammaire générale* II. Copenhagen: Munksgaard [Acta Jutlandica: Aarsskrift for Aarhus Universitet 9.3]

Hoddinott, W. G. & F. M. Kofod. 1976. Djamindjungan. In R. M. W. Dixon (ed.), 397–401

Hopper, P. J. & S. A. Thompson. 1980. Transitivity in grammar and discourse. *Language* 56: 251–99

1982 (eds.). *Syntax and semantics, vol. 15: studies in transitivity*. New York: Academic Press

Hübschmann, H. 1906. Armenica 7: Kasus-Attraktion im Armenischen. *Indogermanische Forschungen* 19: 478–80

Huddleston, R. 1984. *Introduction to the grammar of English*. Cambridge University Press

Hudson, R. 1992. So-called 'double objects' and grammatical relations. *Language* 68: 251–76

Jackendoff, R. 1972. *Semantic interpretation in generative grammar*. Cambridge, MA: MIT Press

Jacobs, M. 1931. A sketch of Northern Sahaptin grammar. *University of Washington* [Seattle] *Publications in Anthropology* 4: 85–291

Jacobsen, W., Jr. 1983. Typological and genetic notes on switch-reference systems in North American Indian languages. In J. Haiman & P. Munro (eds.), *Switch-reference and universal grammar*, 151–83. Amsterdam: John Benjamins

Jakobson, R. 1936/1971. Beitrag zur allgemeinen Kasuslehre: Gesamtbedeutungen der russischen Kasus. In R. Jakobson *Selected writings II: words and language*, 23–71. The Hague: Mouton

1958/1971. Morphological inquiry into Slavic declension: structure of Russian case forms [text in Russian, summary in English in 1971 version]. In R. Jakobson *Selected writings II: words and language,* 154–83. The Hague: Mouton

Jensen, J. T. 1991. Case in Yapese. In R. Harlow (ed.), 215–30

Juret, A-C. 1926. *Système de la syntaxe latine*. Paris: les Belles lettres

Kaye, A. S. 1987. Arabic. In B. Comrie (ed.), 664–85

Keen, S. L. 1972. A description of the Yukulta language: an Australian Aboriginal language of Northwest Queensland. Monash University (Melbourne): MA Thesis

1983. Yukulta. In R. M. W. Dixon & B. J. Blake (eds.), 190–304

Keenan, E. L. & B. Comrie. 1977. Noun phrase accessibility and universal grammar. *Linguistic Inquiry* 8: 63–99

Kennedy, R. 1984. Semantic roles: the language speaker's categories (in Kala Lagaw Ya). In *Papers in Australian Linguistics 16,* 153–70. Canberra: Pacific Linguistics

Kibrik, A. E. 1979. Canonical ergativity and Daghestan languages. In F. Plank (ed.), 61–77

1991. Organising principles for nominal paradigms in Daghestanian languages: comparative and typological observations. In F. Plank (ed.), 255–74

Kilby, D. 1981. On case markers. *Lingua* 54: 101–33

Klaiman, M. H. 1987. Bengali. In B. Comrie (ed.), 490–513

Klimov, G. A. 1973. *Očerk obščej teorii ergativnosti (Outline of a general theory of ergativity)*. Moscow: Nauka

Kornfilt, J. 1987. Turkish and the Turkic Languages. In B. Comrie (ed.), 619–44

Kullavanijaya, P. 1974. Transitive verbs in Thai. Honolulu: University of Hawaii doctoral dissertation [available from University Microfilms, Ann Arbor, Michigan]

Kuryłowicz, J. 1949. Le problème du classement des cas. *Biuletyn* PTJ 9: 20–43 [Reprinted in *Esquisses linguistiques*, 131–50. Wroclaw-Krakow: Ossolineum. 1960]

1964. *The inflectional categories of Indo-European*. Heidelberg: Carl Winter

Langacker, R. W. 1977. *Studies in Uto-Aztecan grammar*: vol. 1. *An overview of Uto-Aztecan grammar*. Arlington: The Summer Institute of Linguistics and The University of Texas at Arlington

Langdon, M. 1970. *A grammar of Diegueño: the Mesa Grande dialect*. Berkeley: University of California Press

Larsen, T. W. & W. M. Norman. 1979. Correlates of ergativity in Mayan grammar. In F. Plank (ed.), 347–70

Lehmann, C. 1982. *Thoughts on grammaticalization: a programmatic sketch, vol. 1*. (Arbeiten des kölner universalien Projekts 48). Cologne: Institüt für Sprachwissenschaft

1985. Latin case relations in typological perspective. In C. Touratier (ed.), 81–104

Levin, B. 1987. The middle construction and ergativity. In R. M. W. Dixon (ed.), 17–32

Lewis, G. L. 1967. *Turkish grammar*. Oxford: Oxford University Press

Li, C. N. & S. A. Thompson. 1981. *Mandarin Chinese: a functional reference grammar*. Berkeley: University of California Press

n.d. *Wappo*. Typescript

Lindenfeld, J. 1973. *Yaqui syntax*. Berkeley: University of California Press

Longacre, R. E. 1976. *An anatomy of speech notions*. Lisse: Peter de Ridder

Lord, C. 1982. The development of object markers in serial verb languages. In P. J. Hopper & S. A. Thompson (eds.), 277–99

Luraghi, S. 1987. Patterns of case syncretism in Indo-European languages. In A. Ramat et al. (eds.), *Papers from the 7th international conference on historical linguistics*, 355–71. Amsterdam: John Benjamins

1989. The relationship between prepositions and cases within Latin prepositional phrases. In G. Calboli (ed.), *Subordination and other topics in Latin*, 253–71. Amsterdam, Philadelphia: John Benjamins

1991. Paradigm size, possible syncretisms, and the use of adpositions with cases in inflective languages. In F. Plank (ed.), 57–74

Madtha, W. 1976. Case system of Kannada. In S. Agesthialingom & K. Kushalappa Gowda (eds.), 173–54

References

Mallinson, G. & B. J. Blake. 1981. *Language typology: cross-linguistic studies in syntax.* Amsterdam: North-Holland

Mallinson, G. 1987. Rumanian. In B. Comrie (ed.), 303–21

1988. Rumanian. In M. Harris & N. Vincent (eds.), 391–419

Marantz, A. 1984. *On the nature of grammatical relations.* Cambridge, MA: MIT Press

Matthews, P. H. 1974. *Morphology: an introduction to the theory of word-structure.* Cambridge University Press (second edition 1991)

McAlpin, D. W. 1976. Dative subject in Malayalam. In M. K. Verma (ed.), 183–94

McGregor, W. 1990. *A functional grammar of Gooniyandi.* Amsterdam: John Benjamins

McKay, G. R. 1976. Rembarnga. In R. M. W. Dixon (ed.), 494–505

McLendon, S. 1978. Ergativity, case, and transitivity in Eastern Pomo. *IJAL* 44: 1–9

Mel'čuk, I. A. 1986. Toward a definition of case. In R. D. Brecht & J. S. Levine (eds.), 35–85

Merlan, F. 1982. *Mangarayi.* [Lingua Descriptive Series No. 4]. Amsterdam: North Holland

Mithun, M. 1991. Active/agentive case marking and its motivation. *Language* 67: 510–46

Moravcsik, E. A. 1978. On the case marking of objects. In J. H. Greenberg (ed.), *Universals of human language 4: syntax*, 249–89. Stanford University Press

1984. The place of direct objects among the noun phrase constituents of Hungarian. In F. Plank (ed.), 55–85

Neidle, C. 1982. Case agreement in Russian. In J. Bresnan (ed.), 391–426

1988. *The role of case in Russian syntax.* Dordrecht: Kluwer

Nichols, J. 1983. On direct and oblique cases. *Berkeley Linguistics Society* 9: 170–92

1986. Head-marking and dependent-marking grammar. *Language* 62: 56–119

Norman, J. 1988. *Chinese.* Cambridge University Press

O'Grady, W. 1991. *Categories and case: the sentence structure of Koran.* Amsterdam: John Benjamins

Palmer, L. R. 1954. *The Latin language.* London: Faber & Faber

Perialwar, R. 1976. Irula case system. In S. Agesthialingom & K. Kushalappa Gowda (eds.), 495–519

Perlmutter, D. M. 1982. Syntactic representation, syntactic levels, and the notion of subject. In P. Jacobson & G. Pullum (eds.), *The nature of syntactic representation*, 283–340. Dordrecht: Reidel

1983 (ed.). *Studies in relational grammar* 1. Chicago University Press

Perlmutter, D. M. & P. M. Postal. 1983. Some proposed laws of basic clause structure. In D. M. Perlmutter (ed.), 81–128

1984. The 1-advancement exclusiveness law. In D. M. Perlmutter & C. Rosen (eds.), 81–125

Perlmutter, D. M. & C. Rosen (eds.). 1984. *Studies in relational grammar 2.* Chicago University Press

Pinkster, H. 1985. Latin cases and valency grammar: some problems. In C. Touratier (ed.), 163–90

Plank, F. (ed.) 1979. *Ergativity.* London: Academic Press

1984 (ed.). *Objects: towards a theory of grammatical relations*. London: Academic Press

1990. Suffix copying as a mirror-image phenomenon. *European Science Foundation, Programme in Language Typology: Working Paper* 1: 1–11

1991 (ed.). *Paradigms: the economy of inflection*. Berlin: Mouton de Gruyter

Postal, P. M. 1974. *On raising: one rule of English grammar and its theoretical implications*. Cambridge, MA: MIT Press

1977. Antipassive in French. *Proceedings of the Seventh Annual Meeting of the North Eastern Linguistics Society*, 273–313

Press, M. L. 1979. *Chemehuevi: a grammar and lexicon* [University of California Publications in Linguistics 92]. Berkeley and Los Angeles: University of California Press

Ramarao, C. 1976. Markedness in case. In S. Agesthialingom & K. Kushalappa Gowda (eds.), 221–40

Reed, I., O. Miyaoka, S. Jacobsen, P. Afcan & M. Krauss. 1977. *Yup'ik Eskimo grammar*. University of Alaska: Alaska Native Language Center and the Yup'ik Language Workshop

Riemsdijk, H. van. 1983. The case of German adjectives. In F. Heny & B. Richards (eds.), *Linguistic categories: auxiliaries and related puzzles*, vol. 1, 223–52. Dordrecht: Reidel

Riemsdijk, H. van. & E. Williams. 1986. *Introduction to the theory of grammar*. Cambridge, MA: MIT Press

Rigsby, B. 1974. Sahaptin grammar. Typescript

Robins, R. H. 1967. *A short history of linguistics*. London: Longman

Robinson, L. W. & J. Armagost. 1990. *Comanche dictionary and grammar*. Arlington: The Summer Institute of Linguistics and The University of Texas at Arlington

Rosen, C. 1984. The interface between semantic roles and initial grammatical relations. In D. M. Perlmutter & C. Rosen (eds.), 38–80

Rosen, C. & K. Wali. 1988. Twin passives, inversion and multistratalism in Marathi. Cornell University: typescript

Roth, W. E. 1897. *Ethnological studies among the north-west-central Queensland Aborigines*. Brisbane: Government Printer

Rubio, L. 1966. *Introducción a la sintaxis estructural del Latin, vol. I. Casos y Preposiciones*. Barcelona: Ariel

Rude, N. 1985. Studies in Nez Perce grammar and discourse. University of Oregon: doctoral dissertation

1988. On the origin of the Nez Perce ergative NP suffix. [Conference on Grammaticalization, University of Oregon, 12–15 May 1988]

Sakthivel, S. 1976. Toda case system. In S. Agesthialingom & K. Kushalappa Gowda (eds.), 435–48

Saltarelli, M. et al. 1988. *Basque*. London etc.: Croom Helm (Croom Helm Descriptive Grammars)

Schooneveld, C. H. van. 1986. Jakobson's case system and syntax. In R. D. Brecht & J. S.

References

Levine (eds.), 373–85

Scott, G. 1978. *The Fore language of Papua New Guinea*. Canberra: Pacific Linguistics

Seidel, H. 1988. *Kasus: zur Explikation eines sprachwissenschaftlichen Terminus (am Beispiel des Russischen)*. Tübingen: Gunter Narr

Serbat, G. 1981a. *Cas et fonctions*. Paris: Presses Universitaires de France

1981b. Le système des cas est-il systématique? *Revue des Etudes Latines* 59: 298–317

Sherzer, J. 1976. *An areal-typological study of American Indian languages north of Mexico*. Amsterdam: North Holland

Silverstein, M. 1976. Hierarchy of features and ergativity. In R. M. W. Dixon (ed.), 112–71

1981. Case marking and the nature of language. *Australian Journal of Linguistics* 1: 227–44

Sittig, E. 1931. *Das Alter der Anordnung unserer Kasus und der Ursprung ihrer Bezeichnung als 'Fälle'*. Stuttgart: Kohlhammer (Tübinger Beiträge zur Altertumswissenschaft 13)

Smith, W. 1888. *A first Greek course*. London: John Murray

Somers, H. L. 1987. *Valency and case in computational linguistics*. Edinburgh University Press

Starosta, S. 1971. Some lexical redundancy rules for English nouns. *Glossa* 5: 167–201

1985. Relator nouns as a source of case inflections. In R. L. Leed.& V. Z. Acson (eds.), *For Gordon Fairbanks*. [Oceanic Linguistics Special Publications No. 20] 111–33. Honolulu: University of Hawaii Press

1988. *The case for lexicase*. London: Pinter

Steever, S. B. 1987. Tamil and the Dravidian Languages. In B. Comrie (ed.), 725–46

Stokes, B. 1982. A description of Nyigina, a language of the West Kimberley, Western Australia. Canberra: ANU doctoral dissertation

Stowell, T. 1981. The origins of phrase structure. Cambridge, MA: MIT doctoral dissertation

Suarez, J. A. 1983. *The Mesoamerican Indian languages*. Cambridge University Press

Torrego, M. E. 1991. The genitive with verbal nouns in Latin: a functional analysis. In R. Coleman (ed.), 281–93

Touratier, C. 1978. Quelques principes pour l'étude des cas (avec application à l'ablatif latin). *Languages* 50: 98–116

1979. Accusatif et analyse en morphèmes. *Bulletin de la Société de Linguistique de Paris* 74(1):43–92

1985 (ed.). *Syntaxe et Latin: actes du IIeme Congres International de Linguistique Latine, Aix-en-Provence, 28–31 Mars 1983*. Aix-en-Provence: Université de Provence

Tsunoda, T. 1981. *The Djaru language of Kimberley, Western Australia*. Canberra: Pacific Linguistics (ANU)

Tucker, A. N. & M. A. Bryan. 1966. *Linguistic analyses: the non-Bantu languages of North-Eastern Africa*. Oxford University Press

Vennemann, T. 1973. Explanation in syntax. In J. P. Kimball (ed.), *Syntax and semantics*, vol. 2, 1–50. New York: Seminar Press

Verma, M. K. (ed.). 1976. *The notion of subject in South Asian languages*. Madison:

University of Wisconsin, South Asian Studies

Weber, D. J. 1989. *A grammar of Huallaga (Huánuco) Quechua*. Berkeley: University of California Press

Whitney, A. H. 1956. *Finnish*. London: Hodder and Stoughton

Wierzbicka, A. 1980. *The case for surface case*. Ann Arbor: Karoma

    1981. Case marking and human nature. *Australian Journal of Linguistics* 1: 43–80

    1983. The semantics of case marking. *Studies in Language* 7: 247–75

    1988. *The semantics of grammar*. Amsterdam: John Benjamins

Williams, C. J. 1980. *A grammar of Yuwaalaraay*. Canberra: Pacific Linguistics (ANU)

Windfuhr, G. L. 1987. Persian. In B. Comrie (ed.), 523–46

Wolfart, H. C. 1973. *Plains Cree: a grammatical study*. Transactions of the American Philosophical Society 63, part 5. Philadelphia: American Philosophical Society

Woodcock, E. C. 1959. *A new Latin syntax*. London: Methuen

Yallop, C. 1977. *Alyawarra: an Aboriginal language of Central Australia*. Canberra: Australian Institute of Aboriginal Studies

Yip, M., J. Maling & R. Jackendoff. 1987. Case in tiers. *Language* 63: 217–50

AUTHOR INDEX

Author index

LANGUAGE INDEX

Language index

Pama-Nyungan, 13, 25–7, 29, 97, 101–2, 106–7, 114, 118, 127, 140–1, 156, 160, 169, 170, 174–6, 182, 187, 193, 195
Pama-Nyungan, proto, 170
Panoan, 122, 126
Panyjima, 118
Papuan, 101, 122, 123, 165
Pashto, 129
Penutian, 122, 140, 168
Persian, 15, 167
Philippines-type, 190
Pintupi, 141, 193
Pitjanjatjara, 27, 195
Pitta-Pitta, 16, 43, 117, 127, 129, 145, 147, 172, 174, 176–7, 182, 191, 193
Polish, 153, 159
Pomoan, 126
Pomo, Eastern, 127, 128
Punjabi, 129

Quechua, 101, 104, 108, 111, 117, 174

Rembarnga, 121, 123, 130, 143, 193
Romance, 120, 173, 178–9, 180–1, 194–5
Rumanian, 121, 173, 178, 194
Russian, 9, 23–4, 28, 30, 34, 40–2, 46–7, 105, 120, 153, 156, 174

Sahaptin, 168–9
Sanskrit, 52, 65–6, 75, 89, 118, 156, 183
Semitic, 15, 101, 106, 151, 158
Seneca, 126
Serbo-Croatian, 105, 159
Siouan, 126
Siuslaw, 191
Slavonic, xiv, 105, 120, 159
Slovak, 159
Sora, 141
Spanish, 80, 120–1, 173–4, 178, 208
Sulawesi, South, 124
Sumerian, 174
Swahili, 13, 14, 16, 17, 88, 91, 141, 168

Tabassaran, 96–7, 102, 153
Tacanan, 122
Tagalog, 89, 190

Tamil, 106–7, 156, 160, 166, 168
Tarascan, 156, 161
Telugu, 44, 91, 156
Thai, 15, 88, 92, 160, 163–4, 166, 193
Tibetan, 122, 156
Tibeto-Burman, 122, 124
Tiwa, 141
Toda, 160
Tonkawa, 156
Tsimshian, 122
Tungusic, 101, 160
Tupí-Guaraní, 122
Turkana, 140
Turkic, 101
Turkish, 1–3, 10, 13, 15, 28, 30, 88, 91, 101, 106, 114, 120, 140, 153, 159, 161, 169, 174, 186–7, 192, 198, 204

Ubykh, 194
Uradhi, 101
Uralic, 119, 140, 151, 153, 156, 167
Uto-Aztecan, 13, 102, 156, 158, 184

Vietnamese, 15–16, 197

Wakashan, 141
Walmatjari, 141
Wangkumara, 126
Wappo, 91, 140
Warlpiri, 97, 108, 170, 195
Warndarang, 157, 160
Welsh, 61

Yaghnobi, 158
Yalarnnga, 58
Yapese, 9
Yaqui, 102, 159
Yatye, 166
Yidiny, 161, 194
Yoruba, 166
Yukulta, 110, 118
Yuman, 184
Yuwaalaray, 107–8

Zoque, 122, 151, 156

226

SUBJECT INDEX

A, 25–30, 49–56, 132–3, 196
abessive, 156, 196
ablative, 2–7, 20, 39–40, 43–5, 81–4, 154–5, 157–61, 166, 196
absolute, 186–7
absolutive, 26–9, 56–8, 80–4, 136–7, 187, 196
accusative, 1–6, 20, 31, 42, 157–61, 196
accusative and infinitive, 115
accusative language, 26, 119–21, 132–44, 196
active language, 125–6, 196
active voice, 196
adessive, 155, 196
adjunct, 34–5, 43, 187, 190, 196
adnominal, 151, 197
adposition, 9–13, 72, 99–100, 164–9, 172, 178–80, 197
advancement, 67, 83, 86, 141, 197
adverb, 16–17, 25, 168–9
adverbal, 43, 197
adverbial, 197
affix, 196
agent, 69
AGENT, 85–7
agglutinative, 3
agreement, 14, 22, 140–1, 197, *see also* concord
allative, 39–40, 44, 154–5, 166, 197
analytic case marker, 9–13, 197
analytic language, 197
animate object, 121
antipassive, 49–50, 116–17, 188, 197
apposition, 24–5, 28–9, 52
argument, 1, 189, 198
ascriptive, 41–2, 46–7
aversive, 29, 44, 156, 198

benefactive, 145
beneficiary, 70
bound pronoun, 14, 52, 193, *see also* clitic

case, 2, 19, 49, 54–5, 198
   abstract case, 59–60
   adnominal case, 43, 98–9, 151
   compound case, 42, 107–8, 199

core case, 34–5, 44, 51–6, 119–44, 199
   grammatical case, 32–5, 201
   inherent case, 59–63
   multiple case, 103–4, 108–10, 203
   non-autonomous case, 23–5, 28, 203
   peripheral case, 34–5, 44–5, 51
   semantic case, 32–5, 205
   structural case, 47, 59–63, 205
   ungoverned case, 9
   universal case, 63
case feature, 36–47
case form, 2, 19, 21–2, 25–9, 198
case grammar, 48, 64, 67–87, 198
case in tiers, 189
case inflection, 1–7
case language, 1, 198
case marker, 2, 9–13, 163–85, 191–2, 198
   analytic case marker, 9–13
   synthetic case marker, 10
case marking, 94–118
   exceptional case marking, 62
   loss of case marking, 177–81
case relation, 2, 64, 81–7, 198
case resistance, 189
case system, 3, 198
case/number form, 19
casus, 19
causal, 136
chômage, 81, 198
clitic, 12–13, 27, 52–4, 97, 125, 198
coherence, 39
comitative, 156, 160–1, 166, 198
comment, 198, 206
comparative, 156
complement, 34–5, 43, 187, 198–9
concomitant, 156
concord, 4, 7–8, 94–118, 170, 191, 199, *see also* agreement
control 27, 149, 194, 199
core, 119–44, 199, *see also* case, core
CORRESPONDENT, 85–7
cross-referencing, 14, 51–2, 122, 124, 151–2, 191, 199